P9-DCQ-070

CARIBBEAN BACKGROUNDS AND PROSPECTS

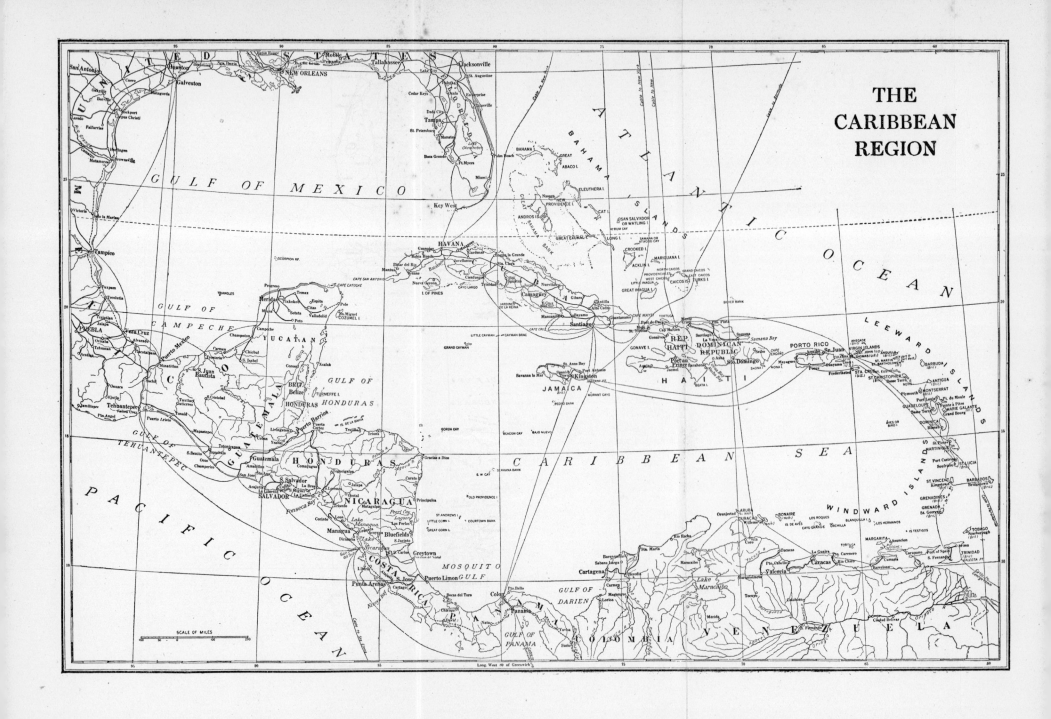

THE
CARIBBEAN
REGION

CARIBBEAN BACKGROUNDS AND PROSPECTS

BY

CHESTER LLOYD JONES

PROFESSOR OF ECONOMICS AND POLITICAL SCIENCE IN THE
UNIVERSITY OF WISCONSIN; AUTHOR OF "CARIBBEAN
INTERESTS OF THE UNITED STATES," ETC.

D. APPLETON AND COMPANY

NEW YORK　　　　　　　　LONDON

1931

TO MY DAUGHTERS
CAROLINE
ELEANOR CHRISTINE
MARY ANN

PREFACE

STUDIES of political developments in the Caribbean region have appeared in large number. Most of them, whether written by residents or nonresidents, emphasize conflicts in international policy and especially developments in the political relations of the various countries with the United States.

This volume is a study of the economic and social factors which have played a part in the life of the communities lying in this same quadrilateral roughly bounded by the Guianas, Panama, Guatemala, and the Bahamas. These factors are influences which appear less frequently in the news but are fundamental to the prosperity of the Caribbean countries.

Attention is given especially to the progress made since 1900, a period of rapid advance from the less favorable conditions of the nineteenth century. In these years problems of public health first received serious attention, transportation services by land and sea greatly increased, the population steadily grew in number, the yield of staple crops showed remarkable advance, foreign trade reached record figures, and foreign investments multiplied many-fold. During this time a fresh stimulus was given to nationalistic movements and the local governments increased in financial strength and political stability.

Economic progress has been steady and spectacular. In little more than a generation the Caribbean territory has reestablished its position as the world's chief source of supply for cane sugar, become the dominant factor in the trade in tropical fruits, taken first place in supplying the export market for petroleum, and risen to second rank among regions supplying the coffee trade. Its enterprises have become an important investment field for foreign capital and its governments have become active borrowers of money with which to finance public improvements. Developments such as these have a far-reaching influence, not only on economic but on political and social conditions.

The printed materials used in the preparation of this volume are largely public documents of the United States and the Caribbean countries. The more important secondary studies drawn upon are cited in the footnotes and bibliography. In a number of cases the facts and opinions presented are the result of residence in the Caribbean region and of interviews with those actively connected with its economic activities. For statistical data and other assistance in securing information on the major industries, I am indebted to the officials of the foreign service of the United States, to the statistical departments of the Caribbean republics, to the Rockefeller Foundation, to the United Fruit Company, and to the oil and sugar producing interests of the region. Dr. J. Fred Rippy of Duke University has read the manuscript and has given many valuable suggestions, but for the opinions expressed the author only is responsible. The preparation of the book has been supported in part by a grant from the University Research Fund.

C. L. J.

CONTENTS

CARIBBEAN BACKGROUNDS
AND PROSPECTS

CHAPTER I

THE CARIBBEAN

AMONG the various regions of the new world probably none carries more continued interest than that surrounding the Caribbean Sea. Off its northern border lies the first land seen by Columbus on his voyage of discovery, and within it is all he ever saw of the new world. In little more than a generation following his death occurred the spectacular spread of Spanish exploration and colonization which brought to Europeans a superficial knowledge of all of the Caribbean region and made it the starting point for expeditions which reached farther north than the site of St. Louis, Missouri, and farther south than that of Santiago, Chile.

In this same short period gold and silver began to find their way back by the Caribbean from Mexico and Peru and to make themselves a doubtful blessing in the mother country, a great stimulus to the commerce of more industrially developed nations, and a potent influence in turning attention from possible development of the Caribbean region itself to the farther territories which offered quicker returns to the adventurous.

Through the waters crossed by the first discoverers soon sailed the Spanish treasure fleets convoyed by warships to protect them from capture by the forces of the countries of northern Europe. On them came to be fought out the long struggle by which these latter sought to break down the

1

Spanish trade monopoly and to secure footholds in the islands and on the coasts for colonies of their own.

For a hundred years Spain had a free hand in the Caribbean. Expeditions by her enemies made scattered attacks on silver fleets, but a century of American history closed without the establishment in the region of a single colony under other than Spanish authority. The following century, 1600 to 1700, brought still greater efforts by three north European nations—the English, the French, and the Dutch—to share in the American trade and to establish colonies in the lands lying across the gateway to the more prized Spanish possessions.

In point of time the English were the first rivals to attempt to occupy lands in the Spanish main. Here was, with the exception of Newfoundland, their first center of economic interest in the new world, and in time they not only took more extensive territories from the nominal original possessor, but to a large degree became the heirs of the other north European claimants. Outposts for preying on Spanish commerce, bases for contraband trade, and lands on which plantations for tropical agriculture could be developed were the prizes sought. These, as the French and Dutch were soon finding in the same period, were easiest to secure and hold in the islands, especially the undefended smaller islands, and on the Guiana coast, regions in which Spain took little interest because of their lack of the precious metals—gold and silver.

Even before the end of the fifteen hundreds, Sir Walter Raleigh had twice led expeditions against Guiana, the first serious attempt by northern Europeans to break down Spanish control in South America. In 1605 the English took possession of Barbados and in the years following seized others of the smaller islands. English colonial activity in the Caribbean was thus contemporaneous with the founding of the first colonies in New England. The middle of

the century had hardly passed when Jamaica fell into English hands (1655). Its capture was, up to that time, the greatest break in the Spanish control of the American tropics.

In the sixteen hundreds France also set up colonial establishments in the Caribbean. They included claims on the Guiana coast and in a dozen of the Antilles from Granada, on the south, to Santo Domingo, on the northwest. These were settlements of varying character. Some were started by unrecognized outcasts like the buccaneers on Tortuga off the northwest coast of what is now Haiti; others were efforts with more direct support of the government intended to exploit the raising of tobacco and sugar, tropical agricultural products which would find a ready sale on the other side of the Atlantic.

The Dutch, likewise having won their independence from Spain, succeeded in establishing control over a portion of the new American territories. The first efforts in Guiana were almost contemporaneous with the settlements there by France. By the middle of the century their possessions had spread into the lesser Antilles and they had seized the small but strategic group of islands of which Curaçao is the most important. These, like the French colonies, were to exploit tropical agriculture. They were to be outposts for the slave trade and bases for attacking Spanish commerce. 1627 saw the Dutch capture of the silver fleet on its way eastward from New Spain, the greatest of their exploits against the former mother country and an incentive for future similar attacks.

Until 1670, Spain refused to recognize that any of these holdings established by other nations gave them legal title. She punished the invasions when she could, but by the end of the century it was evident that her pretense to exclusive control was becoming more and more a fiction. The northern powers held mainland colonies in Guiana, and they

had taken practically all of the smaller Antilles. The English held Jamaica and the Bahamas. French settlements were firmly established in Tortuga and Santo Domingo and at the close of the century, in 1697, Spain was forced to recognize the French claim to the western part of the latter island by the treaty of Ryswick.

Even on the isthmian coasts Spain could no longer make her control unquestioned. Henry Morgan and his buccaneers had landed there in 1671 and captured the treasure which was being held at Puerto Bello for shipment to Seville.[1] English traders and logwood cutters had established themselves in Central America. An attempt had been made, unsuccessful it is true, to establish an English-Scotch colony at Darien.

The long established monopoly of trade and territory had broken down. The "foreigners" were already in control of the islands fringing the eastern Caribbean. They already held one of its larger islands and part of another. Smuggling trade with the colonies was already prosperous for the north Europeans and was becoming more and more general.

The period between 1700 and 1800 was one in which the superficial position of Spain in the Caribbean showed but little change. Four general European wars occurred in the first two-thirds of the century. They were conflicts which on the whole worked to the advantage of England. Fighting occurred in the Caribbean as on other American frontiers, but the Spanish losses of territory there were not of great extent. English claims were strengthened on the Nicaraguan coast and in the region which later became British Honduras. An English fleet with colonial troops from New England captured Havana in August, 1762, but surrendered it again in July of the following year to a new Spanish governor. Judged only from the maps Spain

---

[1] Morgan was later knighted, and made Lieutenant Governor of Jamaica.

seemed almost as strong in the Caribbean at the end of the century as at its beginning.

But the maps reflected only political control. In naval power Spain had steadily lost ground and economically her rôle in trade had become less and less significant. Mastery of the sea had, indeed, long been slipping into other hands. The eighteenth century saw no check in the decline. Efforts were made to strengthen the navy both by increasing the number of vessels and by improving their designs, but the sea forces were never put back into a position to give real protection to the colonies against foreign attack or even to defend the interests of Spanish commerce.

As early as 1713, the English forced acceptance of the famous Asiento by which the right to send a single vessel in the Puerto Bello trade was granted. The privilege was soon abused, for the merchandise to be sold from the ship was steadily replenished by cargoes brought by other craft sailing out of Jamaica. The Dutch soon followed the example of the English, using Curaçao as an *entrepôt* for goods intended for the Spanish colonies as the English had learned to use Jamaica. They soon dominated the trade of Caracas.

As a result of the agreements which Spain had found it necessary to grant and the abuses in commerce which developed both in connection with them and independent of their terms, far the greater part of the trade to the Americas fell into the hands of north Europeans. By 1740, the English alone were said to have as large a share as the Spaniards themselves. "In time every manufacturing nation of Europe, and even the North American colonists, had a part in the Spanish American trade." [2] Just after the end of the century over 19 per cent of all the exports of the recently established United States of America went to the Spanish West Indies, not counting what reached there indirectly by

_____
[2] Albert Galloway Keller, *Colonization* (Boston, 1908), p. 251.

way of other European colonies in which another 39 per cent of the total found its market.[3]

In the last half of the century, Spain liberalized her commercial policy in an attempt to improve her position in the trade of her own colonies. After 1748, merchant vessels were no longer required to sail only when accompanied by naval convoys. In the years following the reëstablishment of Spanish control in Havana the restrictions were further modified, but though trade with the colonies increased, the number of Spanish vessels sailing to the western Atlantic continued low. Often they totaled not more than thirty a year, while the number of ships sharing even in the direct trade of Spain with the colonies reached, in some years, over three hundred.[4]

Thus, though nominal Spanish sovereignty at the close of the seventeen hundreds extended over almost as great an extent of Caribbean territory as at their beginning, the advantages of possession had largely passed to others. Smuggling was profitable and respectable. Illegal trade for many years was of greater value than that carried on under the laws, and legal trade was passing out of Spanish control. Both the foreigners and the colonists profited by the new developments which helped, unfortunately for Spain, to bring about conditions which would shortly break down even the nominal political control which she had been able to maintain.

The nineteenth century in the Caribbean was marked by one disaster after another for the European colonial powers. In its opening years, France lost its highly valued sugar colony, Haiti. The end of the first decade brought revolutionary activity against Spain on the mainland, which, before the first quarter of the century came to an end, left

---

[3] Charles Lyon Chandler, *Inter-American Acquaintances* (Sewanee, Tenn., 1917), p. 23.
[4] Keller, *op. cit.*, p. 251.

her with effective control over only Cuba and Porto Rico, though long after independence was won she continued to refuse to admit the facts and recognize the independence of the new republics. The closing years of the century saw the last remnants of the great American colonial empire of Spain pass out of her possession. Only the British and the Dutch had at the end of the century holdings comparable in extent to those claimed at its beginning.

The Caribbean had come more and more under the control of the local populations. Haiti had proclaimed independence in November, 1803. Later the mainland colonies and the Dominican Republic followed the example. In 1899, steps were being taken to add Cuba to the list of republics and the United States, a new Caribbean power, had come into control of Porto Rico.

From a larger point of view the United States, which from this time on was to play an increasing rôle in its history, had long been a power in the Caribbean. Its interest in the independence of the Latin-American republics had been continuous from the time of their establishment. Possible European encroachments on their territories had at various periods caused anxiety to its statesmen. On a number of occasions it had sought bases in the region to strengthen the position of its navy. Isthmian questions had often claimed its attention, and Cuba, both for economic and strategic reasons, had played an almost continuous part in its foreign policy. But up almost to the close of the century no Caribbean territory had come under the American flag.

From an economic point of view the nineteenth century was on the whole disappointing. In the new republics the old restrictive policies which had held back their development vanished, and they were free to shape their own destinies. The more sanguine of the local leaders and many sympathizers in other countries looked forward to rapid advance in material development and the establishment of stable political conditions. Neither came.

Local capital was unable to undertake extensive exploitation of resources, and the markets for such tropical products as were produced, taken as a whole, did not expand rapidly or yield high profits. Foreign capital did not flow readily into countries in which the personalism characteristic of local politics destroyed the possibility of working under stable conditions.

Disturbances of the public peace discouraged immigration and enterprise and were a drag on social and economic advance. Internal division proved almost as great a handicap to progress as had been the short-sighted policy of Spain.

In the colonial areas also the economic outlook was not bright. The abolition of slavery and the consequent hard times in the sugar industry threw the British colonies into a long decline. The French colonies which were left after the Haitian revolt had an uneventful and, in even the best periods, only a mildly prosperous history. The Dutch possessions for many years were of doubtful value to the home country which found it necessary to contribute grants in aid to the local treasury.

In 1900, an observer, looking back over the more than four hundred years which had elapsed since Europeans had entered the Caribbean region, found much to justify a feeling of pessimism as to its future. One area after another had enjoyed a fitful prosperity and prominence in international trade, but in none had there been established a sound local economy. Commercial policy in the earlier periods had been shaped by the interest of European nations. This had ceased to be the case, but in the colonies the adoption of a more liberal point of view had not brought them prosperity and in the new republics independence had been followed neither by the establishment of stable governments nor prosperous local industries nor steadily expanding foreign trade.

But a close student might already discern factors in the life of the Caribbean which were to strengthen its position, greatly increase its production, and again draw toward it, with a new and greater interest, the attention of the world.

These were not developments which would again make the region a center of international military rivalries, but which would emphasize economic competition. They would not reëstablish the preponderance of the sugar trade, but would augment the number of activities contributing to commerce. The increase in economic yield was to become greater than any that had occurred in any century preceding, greater indeed in many respects than in all the years which had passed, since the period of discovery.

The influences which have shaped recent Caribbean advance have increasingly emphasized new world relationships. Their political phases continue to hold first place in public attention, often to the neglect of the growing importance of economic factors. While political and economic conditions influence each other, it is clear that the material progress of the region in the past thirty years has been more rapid than improvement in the character of the local governments.

The great expansion of international trade has opened new outlets for all the characteristic tropical products. The great increase in population and in industrial activity in the near-by United States has brought into existence unprecedented markets for Caribbean products and has put the United States in better position to supply the broader import demands of its neighbors. Foreign capital has flowed into Caribbean enterprises, chiefly from the United States, and through the creation of greater local taxable resources, has helped to improve the position of the local treasuries, strengthen local credit, make possible better public services, and in general increase the possibility of stable and efficient local governments.

There are few more striking examples of the interdependence, political and economic, which is characteristic of current developments in international relations than that which has come to exist between the United States and the territories around the Caribbean Sea. The development of these economic bonds and the social conditions which promote and limit their growth are the subjects of the following chapters.

Progress has been so rapid and so striking that, not infrequently, enthusiasts both within and outside the Caribbean region overestimate its significance and come to believe that the handicaps and inequalities which have been characteristic of the conditions under which Caribbean communities have struggled in the past have disappeared. These states are now, it is argued, independent politically and economically.

No state, however, is completely one or the other, and the trend of development in the world at large is to make even the strongest powers less so than in times when international relations were a less important factor in public policy and economic exchanges. But the Caribbean states are still subject, in greater degree than other nations termed independent, to handicaps which it is unfair for other states to assume not to exist and which it is unwise for Caribbean communities to refuse to recognize.

Transformation of the life of a region is slow even under the impulse of new forces such as are now changing the outlook of tropical America. It is a process extending not over decades but over generations. Advance is irregular and not unaccompanied by checks and backslidings. Any dispassionate review of the changes which have come since the opening of the present century cannot fail to reveal both unquestionable progress in the political and economic life of the region, and real limitations on what has been accomplished and perhaps upon what may be accomplished.

Like all other nations, the states of the Caribbean are affected by the climatic conditions under which their people live. Temperature, humidity, elevation, and similar factors influence both the character of economic products and the life of the population. Such influences, or the effect of such influences, may be modified by human endeavor. The advance of science has made it possible, for example, to change some of the conditions of life in regions formerly less attractive for human habitation. The staple crops have also been changed. None of the three main agricultural products upon which the American tropics now rely in their foreign trade was native to America. How far such changes may in the future modify the outlook it is impossible to estimate, but it is clear that climatic limitations and the degree to which certain crops are or are not suited to local conditions are still potent influences in shaping local development.

Differences in the populations of the areas of the world affect their civilization. The peoples of the Caribbean have a varied racial inheritance. American, European, and African stocks have contributed to make the inhabitants what they are. Immigration, forced and voluntary, has fundamentally modified the ethnic composition and social organization of every Caribbean community, and migrations still to come may further do so. Sociologists may still differ as to whether the cultural, economic, and political capacities of races are in the long run substantially equivalent, but it is hardly questionable that the complex racial composition of the Caribbean population in our own day is one of the factors influencing the possibility of its current advance.

The political experience of the populations of Caribbean

states does not rest on a long historical development. The aboriginal element had at the discovery of America no political institutions which have survived as distinctive features of the organization of public powers. The Spanish colonists were given no extensive powers of self-government and those from northern European countries were not granted wide political authority. The African immigrants brought with them no political institutions and in the colonial régime had no political rights. In the independent units self-government is in no case much more than three generations old. It is still an experiment carried on under unfavorable conditions, for the prevalent illiteracy and limited economic independence of the greater portion of the common people place serious limitations on the development of public opinion and popular institutions of government.

Finally, the economic foundation of the Caribbean states has, unquestionably, serious limitations, though the development of material resources in the last generation has been unprecedented and has far outrun that in social and political organization. The typical products for export are few in number. Most of them are of a kind which under present conditions tend to outrun demand and therefore are apt to bring irregular returns.

Crops for local consumption are widely cultivated but in many cases recent developments have accentuated dependence on imports of foodstuffs. Local manufacture of articles necessary for more than a low standard of life is poorly developed. Though the foundation of the life of the Caribbean units has been greatly broadened since the colonial era and particularly in the twentieth century, it is still far less securely established than a satisfactory basis for national life requires. On the further diversification of economic activity depends in high degree the achievement of a satisfactory degree of social, economic, and political stability.

Out of the interplay of these various factors the peoples of the Caribbean must work out their destinies. Some of these items can be modified, so far as we can foresee, but slightly. Others are changing rapidly in our own day. As yet the new influences have not brought the local civilizations to positions in all respects comparable to those in the more advanced nations of regions blessed with greater variety of natural resources and with temperate climates. In some of the units such a development may never occur.

In current discussion, conditions in the states of the Caribbean region are too often compared with those in the better developed nations of the world. In social, economic, and political organization these new states suffer in the contrast. A fairer judgment results from measurement against the picture they presented a generation ago. Progress should be reckoned not only from the goal to be reached. It should also be measured from the starting point and from the rate of current advance. The Caribbean states were launched on their course under great disadvantages, some of which they have not even now thrown off and from some of which, at least in part, they may never be free. But the advance they have made in the last generation is assurance that solid progress is possible, and advance is now occurring at a rate far greater than at any previous time.

CHAPTER II

RACIAL FACTORS

Few regions of the world present more interesting population problems than those found in the islands of the Caribbean sea and the adjacent mainland areas. There three racial stocks have come into contact and competition with social, political, and economic consequences which are still after four hundred years in process of development.

In some areas like Venezuela a blending of racial elements has occurred to an unusual degree, in others it is still in process. In others, like Jamaica, the groups different in their origin have to a greater extent remained distinct in spite of their long continued association.

The aboriginal stocks of the island communities have practically disappeared. Insignificant settlements of what are popularly spoken of as Caribs [1] are reported from a number of areas including the Virgin Islands, Porto Rico, the Dominican Republic, and the north coast of Honduras, but unmixed descendants of the stock which Columbus and those who followed him found in possession in the age of discovery are not known to exist and in some cases the characteristics of the inhabitants of the so-called Carib colonies indicate a pure or nearly pure African origin.

The rapidity with which the indigenous population ceased to be an economic factor in the islands is startling. Las Casas declared they numbered in his day six million souls. While this and other early estimates are, it seems, exag-

---

[1] Several tribes of which the Caribs were apparently not the most numerous were found in the islands at the time of their discovery. In popular usage the term Caribs is often used to include all the alleged survivals of the native population of that period.

14

gerated it is clear that contact with Europeans from the beginning resulted in steady depopulation among the islands.

The first of the larger islands to be discovered was Hispaniola or, as it came later to be called, Haiti. Its natives disappeared practically in the first quarter century after the landing of Columbus. Abuses by the Spaniards were notorious from the time of the second voyage of the discoverer. Governor Ovando, who arrived in 1502, soon found the local labor supply deficient and is said to have imported forty thousand natives from the Bahamas. The introduction of sugar cane from the Canaries in 1506 resulted in rapid spread of the sugar industry with increased demand for labor. The Indians, forced into plantation work, continued to die off rapidly. In 1508, their number was estimated at sixty thousand but in 1514 at only fourteen thousand.

Even in Cuba the supply of Indian workers dwindled from practically the time of the conquest, with the result that at least by 1523 Negroes began to be imported for work in the mines and plantations.[2]

Even before the effect of the abuses and heavy labor which the Spaniards forced upon the natives had become generally recognized the first steps were taken looking toward the introduction of Negro slaves. A royal ordinance of September 3, 1500, issued to Ovando, Governor of Hispaniola, authorized the importation of Negroes. It appears that the experiment was at first disappointing, for in 1503 the same governor asked that no more blacks be sent because they escaped and corrupted the natives among whom they lived. Nevertheless, importations continued.

---

[2] Haphazard importations from Haiti probably occurred in the years immediately following the conquest of the island in 1511-12 and Negroes may in fact have been represented in the expedition of conquest itself. See Hubert H. S. Aimes, *A History of Slavery in Cuba, 1511–1868* (New York, 1907), Chap. I.

The slave trade was formally legalized by 1518, and as early as 1522 a slave revolt was reported.

Meanwhile the abuses practiced against the natives came to be reported to the king with increasing insistence, and he gave orders which resulted in delegating to a priest, Bartholomew de las Casas, the duty to draw up a plan which should assure among other things the protection of the freedom of the Indians. Las Casas elaborated a plan for assisting emigration from Spain to the colonies, and at the request of certain colonists in Hispaniola asked that the settlers be allowed to import Negro slaves to replace the Indians who were to be freed. The moral aspects of the grant did not come up for consideration.

This concession only granted the colonists a privilege which Spaniards had enjoyed in their own country for over half a century. Its consequences were far-reaching even in Las Casas' time, and he later declared that had he realized the implications of his plan "not for everything in the world would he have offered it." [3] But even when he saw the results that followed in his lifetime Las Casas could not visualize the far-reaching influence of the introduction of the black race into the new world.

Three streams of black immigration came to be directed across the Atlantic. One to the West Indies started, as has been indicated, in the first years of the sixteenth century. One to Brazil had its beginning at least as early as 1532, when Guinea coast Negroes were imported at the time sugar cane planting was being established in the region near what is now Santos [4] and one started with the arrival of a shipload of Negroes in the harbor of Jamestown, Virginia, in a Dutch ship from the Guinea coast in 1619.

---

[3] Francis Augustus MacNutt, *Bartholomew de las Casas* (New York, 1909), p. 105. See also Sir Arthur Helps, *The Life of Las Casas* (London, 1896).

[4] Roy Nash, *The Conquest of Brazil* (New York, 1926), p. 89, quoting João Ribeiro, *Historia do Brazil* (9 ed., Rio de Janeiro, 1920), p. 70.

In what has since become the United States, the coming of the Negroes stimulated a transformation of the economic life of the southern states, caused the greatest civil conflict in the history of the new world, and gave rise to social problems still far from solution. In Brazil Negro immigration is the basis on which has rested the greatest experiment which the world has ever seen in the fusion of races of highly contrasted characteristics.

For the Caribbean islands the addition of Negroes to the population had consequences even more far-reaching. It raised a group of neglected and unprofitable colonies to the position of the most prized possessions of European nations, by making possible the large-scale production of sugar, an article until then a luxury and since, to an increasing degree, a necessity in the diet of western nations. But the results here also were not only economic.

However desirable the development of the islands, the introduction of Negro slavery was here, as elsewhere, accompanied by the rise of social conditions of the most deplorable sort. In spite of high-sounding laws intended to guarantee the Africans at least a minimum of protection, they were notoriously abused.

In the Spanish colonies conditions were not uniform. Porto Rican slaves were relatively few and well treated, but still, up to the end of the slavery days in the island in 1872, the proportion of the blacks to the whites tended to decline. In Cuba, on the other hand, the relatively good treatment which the blacks had before sugar became a great industry vanished,[5] and writers in the first half of the nineteenth century estimated the average life of a Negro on a sugar plan-

[5] During the sixteenth and seventeenth centuries Spanish policy resulted in the importation into Cuba of only an irregular supply of slaves, insufficient for the economic needs of the island. The number of legally introduced and smuggled slaves increased in the eighteenth century especially after the invention of improved sugar mill machinery. Spain, however, never brought itself to allow "unrestricted" importation of Africans. See Aimes, *op. cit.*, pp. 1-43.

tation at ten years. To keep up the labor supply constant recruitment was necessary. The great prosperity of the French colonies was based on a slavery in which, at least in the more important sugar areas, the blacks were driven so hard that they did not reproduce sufficiently to keep up their numbers.

The British colonies had no better record. In the eighteenth century it is stated that one-fourteenth of the Negro population died annually. Later the decrease was less, but on the whole, except in Barbados, the native Negro population continued to decline except where reënforced by new arrivals.

Negro freedom, when at last it came, brought the economic collapse of the islands and in Haiti, the Dominican Republic, and Cuba, contributed to the elimination of the long-established European control. The rise of beet sugar production also helped to undermine the hold which these communities had on the world markets and accentuate the influence already working for the economic conquest of a large part of the island area by the black race. Racial developments in the last half century, if that period be accepted roughly to comprise the years since the disappearance of slavery from the West Indies, have seen a steady confirmation of the predominance of the black population in most of the Caribbean islands.[6]   Satisfactory

---

[6] Legal slavery disappeared from the West Indies at irregular times and in some cases by the temporary substitution of "apprenticeship" and other regulations which make citing an exact date impossible. The formally accepted dates in a number of communities follow:

British West Indies: law passed August 28, 1833; in effect, August 1, 1834

French West Indies: 1848

Spanish West Indies: Cuba, 1880. (Control was continued by seven years' apprenticeship.)

Haiti: February, 1794, by action of the French National Convention, later retracted. Slavery was, however, not effectively reëstablished.

For the colonies other than Haiti the dates are as given in Henry C. Morris, *The History of Colonization* (New York, 1908). For Haiti, see H. P. Davis, *Black Democracy* (New York, 1929).

figures over a period of years are not available for the smaller scattered islands, but taken as a whole it is clear that their black population has increased while the population of whites has in most cases very considerably decreased. In Haiti the pure white population has been of negligible number and influence since the winning of independence. In what is now the Dominican Republic the proportion of the races in the later eighteenth century appears to have reached an equilibrium not since greatly disturbed though the percentage of white blood in the island has declined. In 1790, the whites were estimated at forty thousand in a total population of about one hundred twenty-five thousand. In the census of 1920, there were reported 894,665 inhabitants of whom 24.9 per cent were listed as white, 49.7 per cent as mixed blood, and 25.4 per cent as blacks. Intermarriage has brought a falling off of the proportion of whites from a third to a fourth.[7]

The figures on the racial composition of the population of Jamaica are more satisfactory than those for the other units. The white population has never been large. The proportion of whites in the small settlements which had been established in the Spanish régime increased shortly after the island passed into British control, but later fell sharply with the development of the sugar industry. In 1843, the white population was estimated at thirty thousand in a total of five hundred thousand, the latter, at least, too high a figure. From 1861 on, the censuses show an increasing colored population—in which are now included East Indian and Chinese elements—but the white population has remained almost stationary. Since 1861 it has never been sixteen thousand and has even shown a tendency to decline in absolute numbers. The percentage of white population

[7] These statements are based on figures given in Sumner Welles, *Naboth's Vineyard: The Dominican Republic, 1844-1924* (New York, 1928), and *Commerce Yearbook, 1929* (Washington, 1929), Vol. II.

has steadily fallen from 3.13 in the census of 1861 to 1.69 in that of 1921.[8] There is now only one white man to sixty-six colored people in the island. White persons are met about as frequently as Negroes are found in Oregon or Michigan.

Two Caribbean units, Porto Rico and Cuba, important in size and population, are exceptions to the marked tendency of the black population to monopolize the island areas. Whether the censuses have classified as white only those who in countries more predominantly white would be so classed has been questioned. In the case of Cuba, at least, well-informed observers are of the opinion that especially in the country districts the term white has been liberally construed. The census figures as they stand show in both cases a large and increasing percentage of white residents.

Black slavery never got a strong foothold in Porto Rico and the numbers of Negroes reported even in the colonial period decreased. The percentage of the population listed as white has grown at every census since the middle of the nineteenth century from 51.5 in 1860 to 73.0 in 1920.[9]

In Cuba, the population in the later years of the eighteenth century showed over 56 per cent white, but thereafter the proportion fell, reaching 41.5 in 1841. Since that time it has risen at every numeration and was reported as 72.8 per cent in 1919.[10] Both Cuba and Porto Rico have,

---

[8] This summary is based on census figures and discussion in *Census of Jamaica and Its Dependencies Taken on the 25th of April, 1921* (Kingston, 1922); Frank Cudnall, *Jamaica in 1928* (London, 1928); W. J. Gardner, *A History of Jamaica* (New York, 1909), p. 504; Morris, *op. cit.*; James M. Phillippo, *Jamaica, Its Past and Present State* (Philadelphia, 1843), pp. 37-38; *Statesman's Yearbook, 1890* (London, 1891), p. 215; *Ibid.*, 1897, p. 228.

[9] Census of Porto Rico taken under the direction of the War Department, U. S. A., Bulletin No. II (Washington, 1900), (Censuses 1860, 1887, and 1899), pp. 7-8; *Statesman's Yearbook, 1920* (London, 1920), p. 637 (figures for 1910); *Commerce Yearbook, 1929*, Vol. I, p. 700 (figures for 1920).

[10] *Census of the Republic of Cuba, 1919* (Havana, n. d.), p. 303.

as reported, percentages of persons of white race in their populations somewhat higher than the south Atlantic and east central states of the United States.

The attitude of those in charge of the local governments toward the Africanization of their populations shows decided variations. In the European colonies, the admitted tendency is accepted as inevitable. Haiti shows no disinclination to consider itself frankly a black republic. Large numbers of whites were killed or fled the island during the War of Independence. In the constitution of 1804, it was provided that all Haitians of whatever color should be known as "blacks," and by constitutional provision white persons were incapable of holding real estate from 1804 until the ratification of the constitution of 1918.

Porto Rico, the Dominican Republic, and Cuba have all regarded the possibility of black domination with apprehension. In overpopulated Porto Rico the question is largely academic. Immigration is negligible and the predominance of race turns on the fertility of the stocks already in the island. In recent years the proportions seem practically stable. So far as statistics indicate, the same condition seems now to exist in the Dominican Republic except that the proportion of the black and white races is reversed.

In the years following its separation from Spain and in the period of "Haitian servitude" which followed soon after, the leaders of the Dominican Republic often sought the establishment of a protectorate by the United States or a European power fearing that Haiti might overwhelm the country politically and through a process of Africanization. Sharp racial discrimination among native Dominicans, however, was then and is now unknown though in certain regions, such as those near the Haitian border and Samaná, Negroes predominate while in others, such as the Cibao, whites are in the ascendant. There is reported to exist a general desire that the black shall disappear before the white and "the stimulation of white immigration has become a general demand." Popular feeling also insists, "that all future immigration into the Republic of members of the coloured race, whether from Haiti or the West Indies except as contract laborers under temporary license to work upon the sugar plantations, be rigidly prohibited.[11]

No success has attended Dominican efforts to increase the influence of the white race through immigration. Opportunities in common plantation labor have not attracted foreigners. The sugar industry has had a satisfactory growth and a number of others have made small beginnings but there is no stream of new arrivals to contribute to the new activities, and the racial division of the population remains not markedly different from what it was in the colonial period. Statistics of immigration and emigration do not exist. At the time of the last census, in 1920, the foreigners living in the country were only some fifty thousand, of whom probably less than two thousand were of western European blood. Almost all of the rest were from other West Indian areas, including a large number of Haitians probably understated at twenty-eight thousand.

The desire of Cuba for European immigrants is unsatisfied but not altogether denied. When times are prosperous a goodly number of immigrants arrive from the Mediterranean countries but a large number are seasonal "swallows" or at least return to their homelands when local conditions turn for the worse. The shrinking in recent years of the stream of desirable immigrants to Cuba from Spain, Italy, and Portugal—it ceased altogether on balance in 1927— has been a cause of keen regret not removed by immigration from eastern Europe and the Orient.[12]

---

11 Welles, *op. cit.*, Vol. II, pp. 909-910.

12 From 1923 to 1927 the Spanish movement showed a serious decline. In the first year the reported excess of Spanish immigrants over emigrants was 77,869. In 1927, Spanish emigrants exceeded immigrants by 3,226. The net immigration gain over emigration as reported for the

Elaborate plans have been made for encouraging immigration and colonization of Latins and other west Europeans in a program to increase the population to ten millions by making the republic more distinctively a "white man's country" through encouragement of manufacturing and stimulation of agricultural development by legislation for agricultural credit and the promotion of small landholdings. This program has not yet had time to prove to what degree it is practical, but even if it does not show the results hoped for, there does not seem to be reason to believe that the population of Cuba is in current years tending to lose the racial proportions which it has had since the beginning of the republic.[13]

The numerical submergence of the white population in most of the West Indies has given rise to numerous attempts to give its cause. Spanish writers, particularly, have argued that the development is of comparatively recent growth and that at least as far as the former Spanish colonies are concerned, it has come to exist as a result of the growth of American economic preponderance in the Caribbean and particularly because of the recent development there of large-scale industry. A review of tendencies over a longer period does not show this contention to be justified.

Porto Rico even in the colonial period had a relatively small black population and continues to do so. What is now the Dominican Republic had a racial composition in the middle of the eighteenth century—when still a colony—

five years 1923-7 was 452,480, of which Spaniards, Italians, and Portuguese constituted 184,648. Cuban authorities believe that this falling off is temporary and due to unprosperous conditions in the sugar industry.

[13] The discussion of Africanization in Cuba turns largely around the immigration which has come from Haiti and to a lesser degree, Jamaica. Seasonal laborers are brought in under license during the cane harvest. The agreements stipulate that they shall, at its end, return to Haiti. Control of their movements by the Cuban authorities is not in all cases strict enough to assure their repatriation.

comparable to that which it now has. It has never been a country of typically large-scale production. Such incomplete statistics as are available seem to show that the Cuban population as early as 1800 was one-third black slaves. By the middle of the century it was reported as having a population half of which was black. It was not then greatly under American influence nor was its industry in large units. The last census reports less than a third in other classifications than white.

Many areas have evidently increased their proportion of black population, but the change came much earlier than is argued and was not due uniformly to the establishment of large-scale production. Haiti in the colonial period had very large estates and became black in population to a remarkable degree. It was not, however, a country of mass production in the modern sense. At the time when independence was won, Negro predominance was accentuated by the killing off and flight of the white inhabitants. Large-scale production such as had developed at the same time disappeared, and a system of small landholdings was built up which still exists.

While large-scale operation on the plantation system did in this case make the community one increasingly of Negro blood, the return to small ownership has confirmed and emphasized that development. Jamaica had formerly a larger precentage of white population than at present, though even now large-scale industry is not characteristic of the island. The smaller islands, though many of them once had a population in fair percentage white, became typically black communities long before modern machinery and production by large units of capital began to enter the Caribbean. Only Cuba and Porto Rico continue to be units primarily white in population and this in spite of the fact that in them large-scale production has progressed farther than in other Caribbean areas.

The spread of the Negro race through the West Indies has more fundamental causes than any recent change in the organization of its economic life. Until the abolition of slavery the Negro's natural increase in numbers was checked by the harsh treatment he received. When freedom was granted, though economic production for the world market was checked and in some cases almost brought to an end, on the whole conditions of life for him improved. Even in so crowded a colony as Jamaica at the present time the effort necessary to win a living on the low standard of life which the West Indian Negro is willing to accept is not great. He has adapted himself easily to the climate which has had for him less marked contrasts with that in which his ancestors lived than has been the case with the white population. His resistance to some diseases—though to others he is an easy victim—has enabled him to multiply in communities where at least until recently sanitary measures were but little observed. But for the high local death rates, which the governments are making good progress in reducing, his race would doubtless before this have increased its numbers even more than it has.

The Negro has prospered also because of his ability to do the heavy unskilled work which local industries demand. His low standard of life has allowed him to live on wages which the European has not been willing to accept. In practically all the West Indian areas he has been able to outwork and underlive his white competitors in common labor lines.

The fecundity of the Negro population under West Indian conditions has been so great that some of the islands have come to rank among the most thickly populated agricultural areas of the world. Jamaica has 203 people to the square mile, Haiti 250, the French West Indies 353; while Barbados on its 166 square miles supports a population the estimated density of which is over 1,000 to the square mile in spite of the fact that the island is almost exclusively agricultural.

Newer developments involving the diversification of industry, the demand for more specialized labor, and sustained, as opposed to seasonal, activity, may change the prospects of the black race. For the immediate future in any case its hold upon the economic life of a large part of the Caribbean is well established and does not seem likely to be shaken.

To many first-time visitors to the West Indies, the ease with which the racial relations between the white and colored population seem to have been adjusted comes as a matter of surprise. Sharp conflicts have occurred in the past, the most striking example of which was in the Haitian revolution against France. That conflict was not only a fight for freedom but a war in which race prejudice played a prominent part. Periods of hard feeling followed the abolition of slavery in practically all the communities but on the whole there are few vestiges of the distrust which then arose.

It is not true, as is often stated, that no race feeling exists. In Jamaica, the most important West Indian unit in which an Anglo-Saxon ruling class lives among a population overwhelmingly black, the relations between the races are friendly, but the attitude adopted by the whites is by no means one that recognizes equality. *The Blackman,* the paper championing the rights of the colored population, is outspoken in its criticism of what it believes to be the position of inferiority in which the economically less favored class is kept.

In the island communities the civilization of which has a Latin background, race feeling not infrequently appears. It reaches its highest level in Haiti. In Cuba, laws have been passed to forbid the formation of political parties on a racial basis because of the danger of a "black party." In the colonial areas, too, the political arrangements are as a rule such, in fact if not in form, as work to keep actual control of public affairs in the hands of the white population and thus create circumstances not wholly acceptable to the majority of the people.

Nevertheless, it is true that race feeling in the West Indies comes to the surface much less frequently than in the United States. To some degree doubtless this is due to the fact that the great mass of the people there are less well educated, less interested in public affairs and less critical as to what the governments may be expected to do to modify the conditions of their simple manner of life. To some degree, too, in the areas where intermarriage of the races has come to be accepted as carrying no stigma, the greater kindliness and tolerance on the part of those who form the ruling class may be due to a recognition that the lines of race are not closely drawn and that distinctions are often only matters of degree.

That persons of Negro or mixed parentage work under decidedly less handicap than in the United States admits of no doubt. In the British West Indies a colored man may take a part in public affairs, for example, with but little limitation because of his race. "There are coloured men who sit side by side with their white brethren on the judicial bench and attain to high rank in Church, Politics, Medicine, Law and Commerce." [14] Such are exceptions but exceptions do exist to a degree unapproached in American communities.

In Cuba not a few Negroes and mulattoes take an active part in public affairs and their acceptance in social circles is by no means exceptional. Probably a very considerable number of those who "pass for white" might be classified otherwise by census takers from the southern states of the United States. Persons of undoubted mixed blood are frequently holders of municipal office and are elected to the legislature. At least two Negroes have become leaders in

[14] Cudnall, op. cit., p. 59.

the political life of the republic and many colored journal-
ists play a not inconsiderable part in shaping public opinion.
In the Dominican Republic, race prejudice appears to be
almost nonexistent in spite of the apparent underlying
preference for the white race.   In Haiti, discrimination runs
against the white man rather than against the Negro.   A
public career for a person of purely Caucasian origin would
be rarely if ever possible.

The population of the chief Caribbean units with the percentage of white persons therein is given in the table on
page 30.[15]

No satisfactory study of racial composition in the mainland population of the Caribbean region is possible.   Official
surveys are available only in scattered and unsatisfactory
form and even where an attempt at racial classification is
made the bases adopted for dividing the various groups are
not uniform.

The outstanding contrast with the island areas is the
relative unimportance of Negro stocks.   Pure-blooded
Negroes are found in most if not all coastal areas and persons with an admixture of African blood are usually present
in greater numbers but the black race is not a preponderant
nor, it appears, a growing factor in any of the republics.
The diffusion of Negro blood appears to be highest in Venezuela, in some parts of which it reaches a considerable
percentage.   It appears to be lowest in Costa Rica.

The racial stocks of the mainland areas are European—in
all but small percentage Spanish—superimposed on the
native Indian population.   The latter in most cases makes
up the larger share of the total.   What the proportion of

---

[15] The figures in this table do not have scientific accuracy. The standards used in the official calculations vary greatly, and in some cases the
results are probably not more reliable than estimates by well-informed
persons. The table has only the merit of presenting the information
available and probably errs by overemphasizing the proportion of the
white population. Unfortunately, too, it is not possible to indicate satisfactorily the percentage of mulattoes among the nonwhite population.

each stock is it is not possible accurately to determine. The variance in the practice followed as to classification is such that a person who would be classified as "white" in one country might be put down in another as of mixed blood. In the latest census of Guatemala, the most populous of the Central American states, there is no separate listing of the small white population. All are classified as "ladinos," a term used to cover mixed bloods, and as Indians.[16] On the other hand Costa Rica reports a population of 80.2 per cent white, the highest percentage in any Caribbean area.

On the basis of the figures as reported, it is clear that the social and economic life of the mainland republics, except in Costa Rica, is heavily dependent on the native Indian stocks though the degree to which that is the case shows a wide variance. Similarly there is a great difference in the extent to which in different areas there has been blending of the races.

In Costa Rica, for example, 80.2 per cent are listed as white, 14 per cent as mestizo, 4 per cent as Negroes and less than 1 per cent as Indians. In Venezuela, where race mixture is found in a high degree, though the number of white persons is small the number of those with a strain of white race is relatively large in the more accessible areas. Guatemala stands at the other extreme. Intermarriage of representatives of white and of Indian stocks has done little to modify the essentially Indian character of the mass of the people, and outside of the towns but few persons are met who carry other than Indian characteristics, although over

---

16 *Censo de la poblacion de la republica levantado el 28 de agosto de 1921,* 4° Censo, Parte 1, p. 131. The Indian population increased more rapidly than the "ladinos" in the twenty-eight and a half years between the censuses of 1893 and 1921. An unpublished study in the files of the direccion general del censo at Guatemala City gives the number of unmixed whites in the country in 1921 as 15,470, or 0.77 per cent of the total. Of these, 14,074 were in the department in which the capital is located. Outside of this department there is only one white person to about 4,500 of mixed or colored race.

White Population in Caribbean Areas

Region	Total Population	Per Cent White
Northern South America		
British Guiana	297,691 [1]	1.11
Colombia	7,967,800 [2]	20.00 [3]
Venezuela	3,116,000 [4]	10.00 [4]
Central America, Panama, and British Honduras		
British Honduras	45,317 [5]	"not over 1,000 whites"
Costa Rica	471,524 [6]	80.20
Guatemala	2,004,900 [7]	0.77
Honduras	700,811 [8]	Not reported
Nicaragua	638,119 [9]	17.00 [9]
Panama	422,522 [10]	11.80
Salvador	1,688,129 [11]	Not reported
The Islands		
Cuba	2,900,000 [12]	72.10
Dominican Republic	984,655 [13]	24.90
Haiti	2,550,000 [14]	Not reported
Jamaica	868,983 [15]	1.69
Porto Rico	1,299,809 [16]	73.00
Trinidad and Tobago	391,705 [17]	"Very small"
Virgin Islands of the United States	26,051 [18]	7.40

[1] The percentage quoted, 1.11, is that of "Europeans." In addition 3.08 per cent are classed as Portuguese. East Indians are 41.97 per cent. Some 9,700 aborigines are not included in the figures. James F. Abel and Norman J. Bond, *Illiteracy in the Several Countries of the World*, U. S. Department of the Interior, Bureau of Education, Bulletin No. 4 (Washington, 1929).

[2] Census, 1928, cited in *Commerce Yearbook, 1929*, Vol. II, p. 171.

[3] Abraham Martinez, *Colombia Yearbook, 1927* (New York, 1928), p. 50.

[4] The percentage figure is as reported in *Venezuela* (Georgetown University School of Foreign Service, Washington, 1921), p. 37, quoting the *Venezuelan Yearbook of 1904*. The population figure is as reported in Census of 1928 cited in *Commerce Yearbook, 1929*, Vol. II, p. 670.

[5] L. W. James, *British Honduras*, Department of Overseas Trade, Information Bulletin No. 158 (London, October, 1923), p. 1.

[6] Department of Vital Statistics of Costa Rica (letter). Figures as of May 11, 1927.

[7] The *Censo de poblacion de la republica levantado el 28 de agosto de 1921, 4°*. Censo, Parte 1 (Guatemala, 1924), p. 139, reports the racial divisions as Ladinos 35.20 per cent, Indians 64.80 per cent. An unpublished study based on the census of 1921 in the Direccion del Censo reports the white population as 15,470 or 0.77 per cent of the population.

[8] *Censo general de poblacion, 1927* (Tegucigalpa, 1927), does not indicate race divisions.

[9] Harold Playter and Andrew J. McConnico, *Nicaragua*, U. S. Department of Commerce, Trade Promotion Series, No. 54 (Washington, 1927), quoting Nicaraguan Census of 1920.

[10] *Statesman's Yearbook, 1929* (London, 1929), p. 1153.

[11] Estimated 1927, *Commerce Yearbook, 1929*, Vol. II, p. 570. The Director General of the Statistical Office of Salvador reports that the racial division is not

a third of the population is reported as of mixed blood.

Again, the Indian stocks themselves show great variations so that conclusions based on a study of such groups as are found in the highlands of Guatemala cannot apply to the populations of interior Venezuela or even of Honduras. The fact is that the Indian populations show so wide a variance in social organization, economic development, and education that it is unsafe to generalize as to the degree to which the groups may develop under the stimulus of modern conditions.

When it is remembered also that the resources of the areas which the groups inhabit are also of decidedly varied character, it is clear that the civilizations which will result as the populations come into greater contact with the rest of the world will have characteristics of much greater dissimilarity than is commonly supposed. Individual countries may develop within themselves contrasts of economic and social organization quite as marked as those found in such nations as the United States. There may be little in common between the highland and lowland sections and between those of scanty and of abundant rainfall, even though the racial composition of the populations living within them may be similar.

Similar contrasts show themselves in the character and influence of the mestizo stocks in different regions, due pos-

---

obtainable but estimates that 80 per cent of the population are "mestizo and white" and 20 per cent Indian.

12 Cuban Census of 1919 quoted by Claudio Capó in *The Island of Porto Rico* (San Juan, 1925), p. 58. It is also pointed out that if the foreign-born whites given as 260,000, be not considered the racial proportion becomes very different.

13 *Commerce Yearbook, 1929*, Vol. II, p. 224, on the basis of the census of 1920.

14 Estimated 1927, *Commerce Yearbook, 1929*, Vol. II, p. 323. The *Statesman's Yearbook, 1929*, p. 983, states that there are some 3,000 white foreign residents not included in population figures.

15 *Commerce Yearbook, 1929*, Vol. II, pp. 679-680. Citing census of 1921 at which time the white population was 14,476. The estimated population for 1928 is 953,768. See also citations in the general discussion of racial divisions in Jamaica.

16 Capó, *op. cit.*, p. 58, on the basis of the census of 1920.

17 Estimated 1928, *Commerce Yearbook, 1928* (Washington, 1928), Vol. II, p. 679. The white population is a very small proportion of the total.

18 By the census of November 1, 1914, quoted in Abel and Bond, *op. cit.*, p. 27.

sibly to the origin of their Spanish ancestors and to the dissimilarities of the native stocks with which they blended. In Costa Rica, for example, the Spanish settlers are reported to come from northwestern Spain, the population of which is noted for its industry and frugality. In other districts, Andalusia is said to have contributed heavily to the Spanish emigration. These variant streams, blending with native stocks as different as the Mayas, and the aboriginal inhabitants of Venezuela, produced mestizo groups far from uniform in character.

In relation to both the Indian and Spanish population the mestizos show great variance in the proportion they make up of the total population. In Costa Rica, they are only 14.4 per cent, in Guatemala, 35.2 per cent, while in Venezuela and Honduras, though statistics are not available, it is accepted that all but a minor fraction of the inhabitants are of mixed blood.[17]

The marked differentiation in racial composition which has developed in the mainland republics makes it impossible to give generalizations which are not subject to exceptions. On the whole, the pure Indian stocks contribute little to economic and cultural advance. In the less accessible sections their production, purchase, and sale of goods other than the things to which they were accustomed at the time of the conquest is negligible. Even where they have come into contact with western European influences they have not shown adaptability to new conditions. The regions in which the racial composition of the population continues distinctly Indian are regularly the least advanced. It is to be remembered, of course, that this condition is one which may not

---

[17] The censuses in a number of cases make no separate classification of persons of mixed blood. An indication of the range in the proportions as reported follows: Costa Rica, 14 per cent; Jamaica, 18; Guatemala, 35.2; Dominican Republic, 49.7; Colombia, 40 per cent mestizos, 30 per cent Negros and mulattoes; Venezuela, 70 per cent. In the islands persons of mixed blood are usually of European and Negro, on the mainland, of European and Indian parentage.

be entirely due to race, for the native American has here as elsewhere been forced to yield the easily exploitable regions to the more enterprising stocks of later arrival.

The mixed-blood population is of widely varying importance in different regions, but on the whole occupies a decidedly better position economically and culturally than does the Indian. The pastoral and agricultural enterprises are largely in their hands, if not in ownership, at least in actual operation. They are an important factor in the trades and in small retail business. In some countries like Guatemala and Honduras, they are well represented in wholesale activities. They are increasingly active in politics, particularly in the smaller units. While general opinion criticizes them as lacking in stability, they are in most of the mainland republics the most important factor in local life, and upon the development of their abilities the fortunes of the republics will, at least in the immediate future, depend. Among them are found an encouraging number of persons of undoubted ability, and this number, with the improvement of opportunity, may reasonably be expected to increase. To the stability in business and public affairs which has developed in countries such as Guatemala, Salvador, and Venezuela, they, as well as their white co-citizens, have contributed.

Outside of Costa Rica and, to a less extent, Colombia, the number of the white inhabitants in the mainland states has been relatively small, but their influence in all the republics has been great. As a rule their intellectual alertness and general culture is greater than their business enterprise and vigor. Politics and the learned professions have been attractive for them, and though they are regularly city dwellers, they are the outstanding owners of the larger estates.

Elsewhere in America the greatest advance has been made in mainland regions in which European stocks have come into the country in large numbers over long periods. The modifications in racial stock which this immigration has brought in Argentina, Uruguay, Chile, and southern Brazil, are notable. If a racial fortification of this sort is essential for the rapid advance of the northern republics, the prospect is not favorable, for at no time since the entry of the Spaniards in the colonial régime has immigration of European stocks been great.

How large the actual entry of foreigners is in current years cannot in most cases be ascertained from the published records. Often the number of arrivals and departures is noted with no indication as to whether permanent residence is contemplated. Even information on arrivals is frequently incomplete and includes, for example, only arrivals by seaports. Naturalization appears to be exceptional.

The greater part of the international population movement in Central America is one among the states of the group and hence adds no distinctly new racial element. In total, it seldom reaches more than a few thousand a year in all of the republics. In some cases—for example Panama in recent years—emigration is greater than immigration. In Guatemala, immigration between 1893 and 1901 is said on balance to have increased the population only by 0.1 per cent [18] and no great change in the population movements has occurred since that time.

The larger mainland republics are in hardly better case. In Venezuela, in the five years, 1923 to 1927, there was a normal average gain by immigration on balance of 2,298 of which part was due to the growth of the oil industry. The figures are incomplete and, so far as they are influenced by the petroleum trade, represent largely transients from Caribbean areas rather than permanent additions.

Colombia also has only an immigration of comparable

---

[18] Statement by the Statistical Department of Guatemala.

amount and character. By a Colombian law passed in 1922, provision was made for granting sixty-two acres of land and other advantages to colonists who by "condition or race would not or ought not to prove disturbing to the public peace." The object was to encourage immigration of European farmer families. Contracts have been made with two companies for settling colonies in zones where the climate and geographical conditions are considered especially favorable. Up to the present, however, "immigration has not been coming in to the degree that Colombia so urgently needs." [19]

A large part of the immigration that does occur to the mainland is of Negro laborers. The overpopulated island areas have for a generation exported some of their surplus to any section of the Caribbean where work offered. Jamaicans, and in less degree Barbadians, have been prominent in such migrations. In fact in many regions "Jamaiquino" is synonymous with "West Indian" labor. These Negroes did a large part of the rough labor in the digging of the Panama Canal. The fruit industry has helped to scatter them among the newer coastal developments, and the recent development of the oil industry in Venezuela has brought in a new contingent. The race of these arrivals is not regularly shown in the statistics, but all but a small percentage are in fact of African blood. Of the noncontinental "foreigners" listed in the population of Honduras, for example, most of the English, French, and Cubans and all of the Haitians and Dominicans are Negroes.

The countries to which these immigrants have gone have not looked on their arrival with unmixed feelings. The competition which they bring to local labor has caused con-

---

[19] Martinez, *op. cit.*, p. 460. For a good discussion of the desire for immigration and the recognized limitations which must be overcome if Colombia is to attract Europeans, see *Mensaje del presidente de la republica de Colombia al congreso national, en las sessiones de 1926* (Bogotá, 1926), p. 115.

cern, as has the effect which an added Negro population will have on the possibility of attracting immigrants of white race. Representatives of the Caribbean republics have joined with most Spanish critics of Caribbean developments in declaring that the Negro migration is the beginning of a general Africanization stimulated by the large-scale production in areas where white labor is not or cannot be employed and encouraged in recent years by the entry of large amounts of foreign, chiefly American, capital.

Up to the present, actual emigration of Negroes from the islands to the mainland has not assumed proportions to justify alarm. A part of the criticism, for example, that is voiced in Costa Rica is based not so much on the disadvantage of the immigration, *per se*, as on the fact that the immigrants are temporary laborers who take or send their earnings to their home communities to which they intend ultimately to return.

It seems clear, nevertheless, that conditions may develop on the continent which will bring greater competition between the West Indian Negro and the native population. As communications improve, as order becomes better established, and the natural resources of the mainland regions come to be opened up, resulting in an increased demand for labor, it is to be expected that the crowded black people of such overpopulated areas as Haiti, Jamaica, and Barbados will flow in greater numbers into regions in which earlier arrivals have already proven their adaptability for the work now available.

Under these circumstances, it is not surprising that the republics have in a number of cases taken measures to discourage Negro immigration. They also have looked with a degree of complacency upon the movement to restrict European immigration into the United States and have felt that, with that door closed, they might at last expect the additions to their populations which they have so long desired. Thus far, these hopes have been disappointed. The immigrant tide to all American countries has remained far below the prewar level in spite of the difficult employment conditions in a number of European countries. No appreciable share of those who do cross the Atlantic enters the Caribbean area in spite of its rapid commercial development and in spite of the improvement in public order, irregular, it is true, but real, which now seems assured.

Though the desire for European immigration is general on the part of the groups controlling the mainland republics, it is not to be concluded that these groups are themselves composed of white persons exclusively, or that there exists among those of European ancestry a racial prejudice which sets them off sharply from those who have aboriginal blood in their veins. The racial relations are here comparable to those in the island areas. Even from colonial times and due in part at least to the distinction then made between "Old Spaniards" and "Creoles," the native-born white population has considered the local population a unit politically and socially. Class distinctions, and sharp ones, do exist but they tend to run on economic and social rather than racial considerations.

Humboldt, in 1803, was of the opinion that if a Creole government should come into existence in Mexico, there would rise a sharp distinction between those of white race and the "castes," but in Mexico and in the states of Latin America as a whole such a development has not occurred. A representative of the British government, writing of conditions as he observed them in Mexico from 1825 to 1827, observed that from the beginning of the revolution "the Creoles were obliged to court the alliance of the mixed classes, and in all their proclamations we find them representing their own cause, and that of the Aborigines, as the same. The distinctions of castes were all swallowed up in the great, vital distinction, of *Americans*, and *Euro-*

peans. . . ." [20]   The tendency thus early observed continues general throughout the mainland countries and is one of the fundamental factors in their social developments.

Review of the information on racial relations allows only the most general conclusions.   The Caribbean region contains a variety of racial elements marked by their contrasts rather than by their similarity.   The meager data at hand make even any statement of the numbers falling in each racial category one lacking definiteness.   This is to be expected in regions in which racial divisions are, in the minds of the people at large, given little emphasis.

Even conclusions as to the portion of the population representing the white race must be made with reservations, for the frequent preference to be considered white cannot be without influence on the census figures.   Estimates of the mestizo and mulatto populations are even less satisfactory since they regularly go no further than to indicate mixed blood.   The bare enumeration of the Indian population also carries little meaning where there is such wide variation in racial inheritance in different areas of the Caribbean.

Generalizations as to the degree to which the various populations are adaptable to more advanced forms of social organization are also difficult because their actual contact with modern conditions has been so limited.   The health conditions locally prevailing, the limited resources at hand, and often the communication facilities have been of such character as to make it impossible to estimate closely the importance of the racial factors.

Looking backward on the four hundred years since the period of the conquest and recognizing that many other factors besides race may have contributed to the result, the following conclusions seem justified:

1.   Advance in civilization for all groups in the popula-

[20] H. G. Ward, *Mexico in 1827* (London, 1828), p. 34.

tion has not been so great in the lowlands as in the high-lands.

2. The white race has been the dominant factor. Those of unmixed European ancestry and those who shared the blood of the European immigrants have been socially, politically, and economically the most active elements in the population.

3. Rough labor has regularly been done by the Negro population in the islands and by the mixed bloods and Indians on the mainland. There is nowhere in the Caribbean region any large group of white ancestry employed in common labor though to this generalization partial exceptions are found in Porto Rico, Cuba, and Costa Rica.

4. Racial composition of the population, except in Cuba, has been but little modified in recent years by the immigration of European stocks and no important flow of European immigration appears to be developing.

5. In the island areas, with the exception of Cuba and Porto Rico, the population is predominantly of Negro blood. Except in these two and possibly in the Dominican Republic the proportion tends to increase. The growth of this population has been steady since the abolition of slavery and tends to reduce the standard of life to the minimum of subsistence. In Porto Rico this low standard of life is found among the white population as well as among the colored. Emigration from the more thickly populated areas to other Caribbean regions has developed to some extent and unless artificial barriers are set up to check it will probably increase as communications improve and local resources are developed.

6. In the mainland areas the population has shown steady increase but except in Salvador and certain parts of Guatemala dense populations are not found and the resources of the country do not place limits on the attainment of a higher standard of life.

7. Up to the present the Negro and Indian populations, though in both cases there are individual exceptions, have not been prominent in economic and political development, though there has been little prejudice against them on account of race. This inaction, however, may have little relation to race. A small group in Haiti, at least predominantly of Negro blood, has shown great political activity and elsewhere individuals of Negro and Indian ancestry have become outstanding leaders. Taken in the large, however, the great mass of the colored population have not developed interest or ability in handling public affairs.

He would be a rash prophet who would attempt to foretell what the social and economic significance of the racial factors which interplay in the Caribbean will be. They are various and unstable and may in the long run again be modified by the introduction of new non-American stocks, though of this there are no early prospects. Until recently this has been an area undynamic socially and economically. The industries have been simple and almost entirely confined to the production of foodstuffs and raw materials. Natural resources have been slow to develop and communication with the outside world has been limited.

Some of the circumstances which have heretofore appeared fundamental in the life of the region are now changing. Health conditions are improving; transportation facilities are being improved; export of local products has grown; education is advancing, though for the masses still only very slowly. These are circumstances which may bring an increase in white immigration or intra-regional migration, especially if the control of sanitary conditions makes it possible for the white race to live and reproduce in larger areas than it now finds favorable. Even if that does not occur, the changed conditions will have a far-reaching influence on the social organization and economic strength of the resident racial stocks.

There seems to be no doubt that the economic advance of the Caribbean will be steady and rapid. It has been so during the generation past and it continues to be so in current years. Social advance may in the long run be equally marked. It has been up to the present much more irregular and slower. Whatever change comes will be greatly influenced by the complex racial composition of the region. The least promising areas are, first, the smaller islands, where the fecundity of the black population and the limited natural resources make any marked advances in civilization difficult, and second, certain of the mainland areas in which peculiarly difficult conditions are present because of inaccessibility, irregular rainfall, and the apparent static social characteristics of the indigenous population. In some of these areas conditions continue to show little change from those of the period of discovery and give little prospect of improvement. Their development, if any important change is to occur in them, will probably come through introduction of foreign stocks or of local stocks from areas in which the population has greater adaptability to modern conditions.

Though the racial groups in these backward areas do not seem likely rapidly to rise in their civilization, the prospect in the greater part of the Caribbean is decidedly more encouraging, particularly in the sections in which European stocks are in preponderance or at least in fairly stable political control. Taken in the large, it is the European stocks and the population which share European blood which has been the leaven working toward advance and it seems probable that this will continue to be true.

The degree to which people of these stocks have been able to assure order has been a fair measure of the extent to which economic development has been possible, and each new increase in economic strength holds up their hands for further advance. In the non-American colonial areas, de facto control by European stocks rather than development of local self-government seems to be an accepted policy. Even Jamaica has now less local self-government than formerly and a step in the same direction has recently been taken in British Guiana. In the republics, on the other hand, popular suffrage without distinction of race in law or fact is still the ideal though in most cases the accomplishment of the standard is still remote.

CHAPTER III

HEALTH PROBLEMS

FOR almost a third of a century there has been going on in the Caribbean a fight for better conditions of public health. The campaigns are not closely followed by public opinion in the United States. The defeats and victories do not bulk large in governmental reports. Upon the outcome of this contest, nevertheless, depends in large measure the future of Caribbean states and the success of all efforts to make them prosperous, orderly members of the family of nations. It is largely a private war supported by philanthropic and business motives but welcomed by all the communities to which its activity extends.

The great plagues of the Caribbean, the conquest of which has been given most attention in our generation, are three: yellow fever, now all but under control, hookworm, the elimination of which is clearly proven possible, and malaria, a disease of which the most that can be said is that decided progress has been made against it in limited areas.

Yellow fever has been characteristically an American disease, though since 1910 it has been recognized as existing on the west coast of Africa. It has not occurred in the Far East and it has never become established in Europe. Its origin is still unknown. The Aztec histories do not indicate that it existed before the discovery of America and the early explorers did not meet it. The first reported epidemic was in Yucatan in 1648, a century and a half after the voyage of Columbus. Thence it spread to the West Indies, to the mainland bordering the Caribbean, and finally to all tropic America.

The United States has not been immune. The disease secured a foothold in the south whence during the hot summer months epidemics spread to the north. In 1793 it broke out in Philadelphia, and in a month and a half carried off almost a tenth of the population. It visited Baltimore, New York, Boston, and the cities of the Mississippi Valley. An epidemic in Memphis which carried off 5,150 people in 1878 spread to other southern areas as far as Virginia. In the first seventy-five years of the past century it was present somewhere in the United States in every year but two. In the north the epidemics "mysteriously" died down with the first frost, but in the south where frosts did not occur there was no such relief. In the Caribbean and Gulf regions it always kept a foothold, especially in such towns as Havana and Vera Cruz.[1]

The cause of the disease was unknown and the widest range of theories was propounded. Elaborate fumigation requirements were enforced which it is now known were futile. Some thought it a filth disease but the worst epidemics sometimes occurred in the cleanest areas of the cities. In fact, the nineteenth century closed with no substantial progress, though a Cuban doctor of British descent, Carlos Finlay, had for twenty years contended that yellow fever was carried by mosquitoes, a belief which later proved true.

Early in 1900, Major Walter Reed was sent to Havana to study the problem. He established a camp on the outskirts of the city where a program was carried out with the help of able collaborators such as Carroll, Lazear, and Agramonte. The results of the work were definitive. The carrier of the disease was found to be the mosquito of the *Stegomyia fasciata* variety, though some others, at least on the west coast of Africa, are now believed to share the guilt. Further research developed other facts important in plan-

---

[1] F. F. Russell, "War on Disease," *Sigma Xi Quarterly*, Vol. XIII, No. 1 (March, 1925), pp. 11-32.

ning a campaign for eradication of the plague. Among these were the discovery that the mosquito becomes capable of transmitting the disease about twelve days after it has bitten a person with yellow fever who is in the first three days of his illness.[2] This period of incubation was determined by Dr. Henry R. Carter of the United States Public Health Service.

But the next step in the war was to try to destroy the disease by getting rid of its carrier. This was a work for a public health officer and fell to General William C. Gorgas, then Health Officer of Havana, and himself immune as he had had yellow fever. He screened all yellow fever cases to stop the spread of infection to new mosquitoes and by fumigation killed the insects in the houses where cases were reported. The control of the carriers was made easier by the fact that the *Stegomyia* is not a traveler but generally passes its life in a single house. Within three months the fight was completely successful. Not a case existed in Havana where the fever had been endemic for a century and a half.

In 1904, Gorgas went to Panama where the French had failed in their work on the Canal, partly due to the ravages of yellow fever and malaria, and where the American activities were just beginning. This was a bigger job. Success in it was helped by further research which proved that the male *Stegomyia* is guiltless, it lives on fruits, but the female before she lays her eggs "must have a meal of blood." She feeds in daytime, preferably at dusk. The eggs are laid in standing water. Attention came to be concentrated on preventing the development of the insects in the larval stage. Water supply was improved, by eliminating household storage of water, and a campaign was carried out to destroy all chance lodgments of water in such places as barrels, flowerpots, or discarded tin cans. A campaign of this sort

[2] *Ibid.,* p. 20.

is slow and expensive, and before it could be accomplished there was not a little criticism of the new work Gorgas was attempting, but by May, 1905, success was assured.

On the opening of the Panama Canal, a still wider fight against the disease was undertaken since ships from still infected areas, particularly the west coast of South America, brought the possibility of the importation of fresh epidemics in spite of any local precautions that might be taken. If the disease were present, too, it might be carried on ships to the Far East.

A Committee of the International Health Board undertook a campaign reaching southward to Peru and Brazil. Guayaquil was a seedbed for the disease. It had had yellow fever for fifty years, and so dreaded was it that steamships brought mail to its hundred thousand inhabitants only twice a month.

This city was the next point of attack. If it were cleared it was believed that the west coast epidemics would die out. The Guayaquil campaign started in November, 1918, and by June the next year the disease had been eradicated. Then a secondary epidemic broke out in Peru, but was overcome in 1922. The west coast was clear of the plague. Meanwhile an effort led by Gorgas was being made to conquer the coast of the entire Caribbean. In Central America, greater use was made of small fish which have an appetite for the mosquito larvæ, a practice first tried out in a large way in Ecuador. Mexico, affected only in the low hot lands, had cleaned up the Vera Cruz region shortly after the work of Gorgas in Havana, but the disease came back during the revolution and the work had to be redone. By 1925, Central America and Mexico had been added to the area in which no cases were reported.

Brazil also promptly after the demonstration at Havana had undertaken to stamp out the disease in its southern states, and by 1923 partially had stamped it out also in the

northern parts. Occasional cases continued to be reported
in the interior where it was believed it would burn itself out.
But, perhaps due to troop movements from the interior,
yellow fever appeared again in the coast ports and even
in Rio de Janeiro, but was soon under control. The only
area in America in which in 1930 an active campaign continued was northern Brazil.[3] There the Rockefeller Foundation and the Brazilian government are coöperating for
its complete eradication.

The success of the fight against yellow fever in America
is now only a question of time. Progress against it has been
made steadily since 1900. The only outstanding strong-
hold of the disease is now on the West African coast to which
the war is at present being extended. How long it has been
there no one knows. Contact of this region with the Caribbean dates from the sixteenth century, and it is possible that
the slave ships carried it back and forth; indeed, so far as
we now know, it may have originally been an African disease
which, transferred to new areas, broke out with renewed
virulence. Though distant areas may continue to threaten
the world with new epidemics for some time, yellow fever,
providing it is given attention, need no longer be a menace
to the world and its ultimate elimination is clearly within
the range of possibility.[4]

Yellow fever has no human carriers. It runs a short
course. If the patient recovers he is immune for life. Of
neither of the other great plagues of the Caribbean can these
statements be made.

---

[3] An account of the work in this region in 1928 is given in *The Rockefeller Foundation Annual Report, 1928* (New York, 1929), pp. 32-38.

[4] The literature on the fight against yellow fever is extensive. Reports
on the advance made in recent years are found in: *The Rockefeller Foundation Annual Reports* (61 Broadway, New York); George E. Vincent,
The Rockefeller Foundation, A Review for 1928 (New York, 1929);
Hideyo Noguchi, "Yellow Fever Research, 1918-24: A Summary," *Journal
of Tropical Medicine and Hygiene*, May 15, 1925, pp. 1-9; W. C. Gorgas,
H. R. Carter, and T. C. Lyster, "Yellow Fever: Its Distribution and Control in 1920," *Southern Medical Journal*, December, 1920, pp. 873-880;

Hookworm is one of the world's most widespread diseases. Those afflicted may suffer from it for years, and reinfection may occur repeatedly. Great numbers of people, practically the entire populations of large areas, may be affected. It causes a progressive anemia, digestive and nervous afflictions, underdevelopment, and loss of initiative. Doubtless the "laziness" attributed to many of the peoples of lowland tropical areas is due in part to this disease.

The larvæ find their way into the human blood through the skin, generally in the foot, and ultimately lodge, preferably in the intestines where the adult form develops to about half an inch in length. The female lays about 9,000 eggs per day which, passing out of the intestines, begin again the life circle. The hookworm does not multiply in the human body. Its forces are increased only by new infections.

The disease is common in most tropical and subtropical areas, and, in warmer weather in favorable localities in temperate zones. In the areas of greatest prevalence the people are regularly of low average standard of life. They are usually or frequently barefoot. Generally the household sanitary equipment is deficient or lacking. These are conditions which favor the passing of the hookworm larvæ into the body of the human host.

The scourge was first identified in November, 1899, by Bailey K. Ashford of the Medical Corps of the United States Army, then stationed in Porto Rico. A widespread campaign was started against it by a government commission in 1904. Probably in no other country has the disease ever been so general or resulted in so many fatalities as in

H. R. Muller and C. Byron Blaisdell, "Studies of the Yellow Fever Epidemic in Salvador, C. A., in 1924," *Journal of Tropical Medicine and Hygiene,* August 1, 1925. M. E. Connor has a series of articles on yellow fever in the *American Journal of Tropical Medicine,* including a general discussion, "Suggestions for Developing a Campaign to Control Yellow Fever," Vol. IV, No. 13 (May, 1924), pp. 277-306. An interesting popular review is "On the Trail of the Yellow Fever Germ," anonymous, *American Review of Reviews,* April, 1920.

this island shortly before and after its occupation by the United States. Of the agricultural population, numbering about 800,000, 90 per cent were heavily infected. Of the same class in 1918, a similar percentage, or almost 1,000,000 people, continued affected.[5]

Later investigation in certain other Caribbean areas showed the population there infected in from 43.9 to 83.6 per cent of the total. In the hot tropical lands of Colombia 84.1 per cent were affected.[6]

The greatest difficulty in combating the disease does not lie in its cure nor control of infection, but in overcoming the prejudices of the population, usually largely illiterate, which suffers from it. In Porto Rico, rich and poor alike were formerly strongly convinced that the cause was poor food, inadequate housing, and the tropical climate, all of which are, of course, important factors influencing local life. In fact, so strong was the local belief that these elements and not disease were responsible for the anemic condition of the population, that at first the preventive campaign had to be limited in order to demonstrate by cures of individuals that the popular assumption was unfounded.

The remedy adopted in early years was a few doses of thymol which affected not a complete but a partial cure. At the same time an educational campaign was carried on to teach the people the necessity of wearing shoes and of building latrines to prevent reinfection. In seven years, two-thirds of the people of the island were treated. Some two hundred twenty-four of the principal planters of the

---

[5] Bailey K. Ashford, "The War on the Hookworm," *Chemistry in Medicine* (New York, 1928), pp. 639-664; Rolla B. Hill, "The Amount and Distribution of Hookworm Infestation in Porto Rico," *Porto Rico Health Review*, Vol. II, No. 3 (September, 1926); Rolla B. Hill, "Public Health Progress in Porto Rico," *American Journal of Tropical Medicine*, Vol. V, No. 3 (May, 1925), pp. 211-217. See also a series of articles in the *American Journal of Hygiene*, Vols. III-VI, and Jorge A. Cerón, "Lucha contra la anemia tropical en Colombia," *Revista agricola* (Bogotá, September, 1919).

[6] Ashford, *op. cit.*, pp. 647-648.

island testified that in the same time the laborers' efficiency increased by 67 per cent. The case was proven. Since 1915, thymol as the curative agent has been displaced by other drugs—chenopodium and carbon tetrachloride.

In the other areas to which anti-hookworm campaigns have since been extended, the ignorance and carelessness of the local population have continued to be a handicap, but the work can now emphasize the necessity of general preventive measures as well as individual treatment.

Since the demonstration in Porto Rico, the Rockefeller Foundation has become the most active agency in extending the anti-hookworn campaign to other Caribbean regions. Experience in the southern United States led by 1915 to extension to British and Dutch Guiana, Granada, Santa Lucia, Saint Vincent, Trinidad, Costa Rica, Guatemala, Nicaragua, and Panama.

By 1928, the fact that people can be freed of hookworm and kept free from reinfection had been so well demonstrated that the private agencies which had been leading the campaign came to feel that they could turn over its prosecution in large degree to the local authorities. In some countries the Rockefeller Foundation continues to give aid in money or in expert advice. These still include all the republics of the mainland Caribbean littoral, Porto Rico, and Jamaica.

This, the second battle against Caribbean disease, is not yet near its end, as is that against yellow fever, but the control of the hookworm plague is possible and awaits only necessary funds, and the completion of an educational campaign which shall convince the people affected of the necessity of self-protection against repeated infection.

The greatest of the campaigns against Caribbean disease is neither of those already described but that against malaria. Yellow fever is a terrible scourge bringing panic to any community affected, but though the death rate is high it affects, after all, restricted communities and the mortality totals at the worst have been relatively low. Hookworm is seldom fatal in communities where the population is fairly well nourished. It is destructive of vigor and initiative but not necessarily the cause of widespread death. Malaria is more insidious and deadly. It probably causes more morbidity than any other single disease. It is believed that more than a hundred million people throughout the world suffer from it every year. It saps the energy of hundreds of people for every one it kills and keeps low year after year the vitality and economic efficiency of the population of large areas. As high as 90 per cent of the sickness in fruit company camps in the Caribbean countries, for example, is due to malaria. Authorities believe that on the coastal plain the whole labor population resident for one or more years has had or now has malarial infection.[7]

Like yellow fever, it is a mosquito-borne disease, but while the *Stegomyia* is practically the only bearer of yellow fever, there are some twenty varieties of the anopheline mosquito to fight, of such widely varying habits that expedients effective against one are complete failures with others. A mosquito once infected can transmit the disease over a period of three months. The yellow fever mosquito is in large degree confined to areas around human habitations. Some of those that carry malaria are wilder and may spread their infection far from the places where they have bitten their first victims.

There is no immunity conferred by the malady and human beings may serve as its carriers up to three years,

---

[7] The discussions of malaria chiefly relied upon in the following paragraphs are: C. C. Bass, "The Battle against Malaria," *Chemistry in Medicine*, pp. 602-611; various articles in *Proceedings of the International Conference on Health Problems in Tropical America Held at Kingston, Jamaica, B. W. I., July 22 to August 1, 1924* (Boston, 1924); *United Fruit Company Medical Department Annual Reports* (Boston); B. E. Washburn, *Report of the Co-operative Public Health Work in Jamaica during 1927* (Kingston, 1928).

spreading it through the communities in which they live, though not themselves acute sufferers. Malaria is a world-wide affliction in tropical and subtropical regions and one which must be studied and fought according to the special conditions obtaining in each locality. Since the World War it has invaded new regions to cause great suffering and loss of efficiency in the working populations of Russia, Poland, and the Balkans.

Formerly, however, this plague, like yellow fever, was of much wider range than at present. It affected the temperate countries generally as well as the tropics. It prevailed in Great Britain and the Continent in times of our grandfathers and was a scourge to the people of the United States from the Great Lakes to the southern border. It was the greatest single cause of death in the southern states at the time of the Civil War. As economic development has progressed, clearing and draining the land for agricultural and other purposes have taken place and the breeding places of mosquitoes have been eliminated. In the last fifty years the area where it is endemic in temperate North America has shrunk by two-thirds without any action by public health authorities.

Conditions much less favorable for fighting the disease are found in the American tropics. The low coastal plains of the Caribbean are especially good ground for mosquito breeding. Rainfall is abundant and the temperature throughout the year is warm. One variety of mosquito which must be fought is reported to have a flight range of two miles or more.

Under such conditions it is theoretically possible to exterminate the disease by exterminating the mosquitoes. Any effective general campaign, however, is impossible by means now known because of its tremendous expense. Neither private organizations nor governments have yet attempted such a task.

But advance in control of malaria has often been demonstrated to be possible within limited areas. Though the source of the disease was not then understood, the fruit companies operating on the Atlantic coast of Central America found that after their town sites had been effectively drained and modern water supplies established malaria greatly diminished. Later, the guilt of the mosquito having been established, a more spectacular example of what can be done was given in the sanitation of the Canal Zone in which malaria and yellow fever together had done much to defeat French efforts to dig the canal.[8]

But what can be done by a great government with ample funds in a restricted area like the Canal Zone cannot be done by the weaker governments of the Caribbean, which have to deal not only with great areas of malaria territory but with a wide variety of conditions which may demand different offensive measures. In fact, even at present, technicians are not agreed as to the best methods of procedure in such regions. Some maintain that malaria tends to disappear automatically as the economic and social standards of the community rise, others that drainage should be the main reliance. Still other opinions are that the mosquito carriers in all breeding districts must be fought, that only those near human habitations are dangerous, that larvæ-eating fish, Paris green, and oil are the best preventives, and finally that the chief reliance should be dosage of those afflicted with quinine.

In spite of varying counsel definite advance is being made. In addition to the United States Public Health Service, two private organizations have coöperated in the work. One is philanthropic, the Rockefeller Foundation, and one, the United Fruit Company, is commercial.

---

[8] In the period 1881-9 it is estimated that at least 16,000 employees died from all causes in a total force averaging not over 10,121 for the period. Col. Weston P. Chamberlain, Chief Officer of the Health Department of the Panama Canal, quoted in New York *Times*, July 5, 1929.

The practice in the Caribbean at present is illustrated by the campaign followed by the latter since the beginning of 1926. For a short radius around habitations the mosquito-breeding places are destroyed where it can be done by draining, destruction of rubbish, and keeping the grass cut. Where draining is not possible they are sprinkled with a mixture of one hundred parts of road dust and one of Paris green which poisons the larvæ, or coated with a film of crude oil, which suffocates them. Drag-line ditches are used to drain extensive swampy areas where other drainage is impracticable. An effort is being made to have the houses screened.

Such measures, to yield results, must have hearty co-operation of the inhabitants whose prejudices still often handicap any effort of this sort for their protection. Houses are whitewashed on the inside to eliminate the dark corners which are favorite daytime resting-places of mosquitoes, and mosquitoes in and near dwellings are destroyed by insecticide sprays. Laborers' camps are inspected daily to catch the disease at its beginning. All fever cases are at once given quinine and if they do not yield to treatment are sent to hospitals.

Human carriers, who may be reservoirs for reinfecting the communities in which they live, are given special treatment by quinine and a new drug, "plasmochin." The use of this remedy is now being extended and many authorities believe it promises the greatest advance in the treatment of the disease since the discovery of quinine.[9]

Time, money, and education and at least the latter two in abundance are necessary for general success of the anti-malarial campaign, but the results already obtained show that with these available the outlook is encouraging. The

---

[9] The detail of these campaigns is described in *United Fruit Company Medical Department Annual Reports, 1927 and 1928.* An excellent study of the disease and its prevention and cure is that by W. E. Deeks and R. C. Connor, *Malaria* (United Fruit Company, Boston, 1930).

gain in divisions in which control is best developed is notable.
In one Cuban area a survey showed 55.9 per cent of the total
population to be infected in May, 1926, while in 1927 the
proportion was only 24.2 per cent, and in 1928, 8.78 per
cent. In another, in 1925, 518 out of every thousand employees were sent to hospitals for malarial treatment, but
in 1928 only 53. In an operation in Honduras, where health
conditions were peculiarly trying, hospital patients fell from
182 per thousand laborers employed, in 1925, to 113 in
1928, and in a similar district in Guatemala, from 325
to 134.

The fight against the diseases that have held back
development in the Caribbean is being won. Like the
"Anaconda policy" of the north in the Civil War and the
"encirclement" program in the struggle in the World War,
the campaigns are gradually narrowing the field of operations and making ultimate surrender sure. Yellow fever has
been driven from the United States, and in spite of its re-
appearance in Brazil its retreat from all America is only a
matter of time. The elimination of hookworm will be slower
because it involves a widespread educational program for
the training of millions of ignorant people in their sanitary
habits but it is surely coming.

Conquest of malaria is a still longer and more expensive
task, and depends upon still further advance in medicine,
popular education, and the availability of large amounts
of money. The gains already made are earnest of what can
be done—and will be done.

Though some of the advantages which follow driving
disease from the Caribbean are self-evident, its full significance is not generally realized. The public health officers
and the philanthropic organizations which have been most
active have felt the great humanitarian motives of lessening
human suffering and needless sacrifice of human life. They
have realized the need of protecting the people of their

own and neighboring countries from epidemics, the severity
of which, once they get out of hand, may be even the greater
because of the success with which for years they have been
held in check. The doctors and sanitary engineers have been
urged forward also by their enthusiasm to advance the scope
of human knowledge. Perhaps all these men and agencies
have realized in addition the larger consequences which may
follow the success of the work they have in hand. Certainly
the public at large does not.

Even the developmental enterprises in local industries,
such as the production of coffee, oil, and fruit, sometimes
think of the fight against disease as one which, in addition
to the benefits already cited, is important chiefly because
it increases the amount of work a man can do in a day and
the effective number of days' work which the average
employee can be counted on to give their activities. For
example, the health campaign in one Cuban area contributed to raise the number of tons of cane cut per day by
the average workman from .961 in 1924 to 1.393 in
1928.[10] In other regions for which records are available,
the hospital cases have been cut to half their former fre-
quency.[11] But the economic consequences are not thus
limited. They reach far beyond the effect upon the
"working day" to establish a broad basis for social and
political advance. An increase in industrial output per
man and in his ability to stay on the job helps bring a
better family income, greater buying power, a higher standard of life, and increased stability of population. With
these go increase in savings, growth of national wealth, and
therefore of possible public income, public education, and

---

[10] *United Fruit Company Medical Department Annual Report, 1928*
(Boston, 1929), p. 103.

[11] *Ibid.*, p. 104. The number of cases of malaria admitted to the hospitals of the Canal Zone was 821 per thousand employees in 1906. It was 14
per thousand in 1928. Col. Weston P. Chamberlain, quoted in New York
Times, July 5, 1929.

public improvements. Local industry and trade are stimulated and import and export trade increased.

The gradual establishment of better social conditions has political consequences. Give a man something he may lose and he becomes a defender of public order. The success of the health campaign in the Caribbean may be the first step in the establishment of a beneficent circle of developments which will lift the region from the backward, dependent, and disturbed conditions under which it has lived ever since its larger units established their independence, yes, ever since the beginning of its history. It may thus be the first step in creating an order of affairs which will make easier the solution of both their local problems and those which have complicated their international relations.

CHAPTER IV

EDUCATION

EDUCATION for everybody is an ideal with the people of all the American republics. Accomplishment falls short of desire in even the most advanced of new world areas. Not one approaches the standard of literacy reached in the better-favored nations of Europe, especially those on the shores of the North and Baltic Seas.

Compared with the less than one per cent illiteracy reported from Norway, Sweden, Denmark, England, and Wales, the 5.1 per cent in Canada and the 6 per cent in the United States make an unfavorable showing. These, the more educationally advanced of new world countries, are dominated by people of European stock and have profited both from their own devotion to education and, through immigration, from that of European nations.

In turn, their showing is favorable as compared to that of other American states and especially to that of the Caribbean republics. The educational advantages enjoyed in the two regions are one of the indices of the degrees of their general cultural development, one of the measures of what the various communities can hope for in current years socially, economically, and politically through popular cooperation in government.

Programs for domestic development of all sorts are practical very largely to the extent that the local population is able to respond to the opportunities offered and its ability to respond depends primarily on the level of popular education. Without that background the best laid plans will fail or be of slow fruition. Development of local resources under private initiative lags if popular education is low except where what is needed is only rough labor. Cultural advance of all sorts is limited. The discharge of the full responsibilities of members of the family of nations by states whose populations are economically weak is difficult or impossible.

The efforts which the Caribbean countries have made to improve the educational equipment of their peoples have often seemed to meet insurmountable difficulties. Without a variety of economic and social activities, public income and facilities for education have been severely restricted. Without a body of well-educated citizens, the creation of a more diversified social and economic organization has been beyond their powers. But limitations of this sort have to be met by most programs for social betterment. They thrust themselves more clearly to attention in connection with education because they there affect not a class, but the entire population and particularly the rising generation. They can be overcome only step by step as sacrifice for education makes possible economic development and as the latter makes a better school system obtainable.

Opinion in the United States is not more committed to the ideal of popular education than is that in the countries southward. The experience of the northern republic in fact has contributed greatly to confirm the conviction of the leaders of thought in the Caribbean states that adequate development of natural resources demands an opening of the doors of opportunity by a widespread and varied educational program.

To most first-time visitors to the southern republics, the degree to which those who have acquired property have appreciated the value of education for their children comes as a surprise.

Both the church and the state during the colonial period were active in providing institutions of higher education of the sort then familiar in the mother country. Many people in the United States still do not appreciate the fact that the first universities were established not in their country but in the Spanish colonies, and that the first two were founded in Mexico and Lima in 1551, only a little over a half century after the conquest and long before even the settlement of the British colonies to the northward. By the early eighteenth century San Marcos, as the University at Lima was known, had almost two thousand students in attendance. Before the end of the colonial period there were some twelve universities in Spanish America in addition to many *colegios*, usually under church control, offering less-advanced instruction.

Interest in higher education has continued a very real factor in the lives of those portions of the population which have won their way to a European standard of life. They have very generally given their children the best that the country can afford, frequently in institutions supported in whole or in part by other than public funds. This training is often supplemented by study in the leading foreign universities. Visitors to the capitals of the middle American states are always impressed not only by the social qualities of the upper classes but by the cosmopolitan character of their educational background.

Impressions of this sort are no mirror of the condition of education in the country as a whole, in which in the average case neither the program followed nor resources available have been adequate to create satisfactory conditions. Two general criticisms seem justified. Popular branches of study have been those leading to the practice of law, medicine, and diplomacy. Though a change in attitude has appeared in recent years, it is still true that engineering, agriculture, teaching, and all vocational activities involving an approach to manual labor have not met with favor as generally as in more industrialized nations.

Prejudice of this sort has in fact been characteristic of education in all Latin countries. The result is the creation of small groups of undoubted culture and accomplishment but ones whose education as a rule lacks organic connection with the daily life of the community. Students are prepared for "white collar jobs," which are few, rather than for the practical activities of new and undeveloped countries in which opportunities are more numerous.

Secondly, the educational facilities do not reach the common people effectively. To a degree, this condition is a consequence of the first, for, since education for the greater number of children must be a means rather than an end, there is no strong impulse to follow an elementary program which will not directly help the student who cannot take a long professional course. In the main, however, education does not reach the common people because the facilities for acquiring even training of the sort planned are inadequate and in many cases in rural communities totally lacking. As a result, in both the colonial areas and the independent republics, the percentage of illiteracy throughout the population as a whole is very high and in some areas shows even at present little or no tendency to decrease.[1]

Though educational statistics are inadequate and allow a satisfactory comparison of neither the advance over a period in the different areas nor comparisons between different areas nor an explicit statement of the conditions which actually exist in any one of them, the accompanying table sets out, so far as it can be done with the information available, what current educational conditions are.[2]

---

[1] A good summary of the conditions of primary education by countries emphasizing the legal course of study more than actual conditions is George W. A. Luckey, *Outline of Education Systems and School Conditions in Latin America* (Washington, 1923).

[2] No adequate data are available for French and Dutch Guiana, the Dutch West Indies, the French West Indies, Honduras, and Haiti. "Experience has shown that in order to have a low rate of illiteracy a country must keep approximately one-fifth of its population in attend-

ILLITERACY IN CARIBBEAN AREAS

Region	Percentage	Base	Year
The Islands			
Cuba	27.0 [1]	Total population	1919
Dominican Republic ..	70.0 [2]	13 years of age, and over, unable to read	1920
Haiti	"75.0 to 98.0" [3]		
Jamaica	47.84 [4]	Total population	1921
Leeward Islands	50.94 [5]	Total population	1921
Porto Rico	48.0 [6]	Persons over 10 years of age	1930
Virgin Islands of the United States	24.9 [7]	Persons over 10 years of age	1917
Central America and Panama			
Costa Rica	23.6 [8]	Total population	1927
	32.2	Population over 9 years	1927
Guatemala	86.82 [9]	Population over 7 years cannot read and write	1921
Honduras	74.0 [10]	Total population	1926
Nicaragua	72.2 [8]	Total population	1920
Salvador	55.0 [8]	Army recruits and marriages	1926
Panama	70.0 [8]	Total population	1920
North Coast of South America			
British Guiana	52.1 [11]	5 years of age and over (unable to write)	1921
Colombia	67.53 [12]	Total population	1918
Venezuela	72.1 [13]	All ages, cannot read and write	1926

[1] Footnote to table on page 63.

ance at educational institutions of some kind." About 12 per cent of the population is enrolled in Honduras and Panama, about 5 per cent in Salvador and Haiti. In British Honduras, Barbados, Bermuda, the Bahamas, the Windward Islands and Cayman from one-seventh to one-fifth are *enrolled.* The attendance in the French West Indies is about one-tenth. James F. Abel and Norman J. Bond, *Illiteracy in the Several Countries of the World,* U. S. Department of the Interior, Bureau of Education, Bulletin No. 4 (Washington, 1929), p. 50.

The statistics quoted in the table are not closely comparable. The standards of measurement lack uniformity as is also in many cases true of the application of the standards announced. The figures are therefore to be taken not as a scientifically accurate compilation, but as one which attempts only to give the best indication of general conditions which is possible with the available information.

The statistics from which this table is made up do not rest on a uniform basis and their accuracy in some cases is subject to question, but they probably err by stating the case too liberally. They amply demonstrate the great handicap under which the people of the region as a whole work. Intelligent opinion on public affairs cannot be created, and trained industrial workers for the development of local resources cannot come into existence while these conditions continue.

Even assuming that the proportions indicated are able to read and write, the picture is far more favorable than the

---

1 This percentage has been questioned. Charles E. Chapman, in his *History of the Cuban Republic* (New York, 1927), p. 592, declares education has gone backward in the republican era and that "Cuba is now fifty-three per cent illiterate. . . ." The *Commerce Yearbook, 1929* (Washington, 1929), Vol. II, states that in 1919, 38.4 per cent of the population over 10 years of age was unable to read.

2 Persons well informed concerning conditions in the Dominican Republic state that no accurate statistics are available. The above citation is as given for persons 13 years of age and over in Abel and Bond, *op. cit.*, p. 36, on the basis of the census of July 6, 1920.

3 No satisfactory statistics available. In 1927-8, 107,551 pupils were enrolled in the schools. This is about one-twenty-third of the population, *Commerce Yearbook, 1929*, Vol. II, p. 323. Under the American occupation the number enrolled has greatly increased. Those enrolled in government schools in 1895 were 44,542 and the number was about the same in 1913. The percentage of illiterates is variously estimated. See for discussion, Raymond Leslie Buell, *The American Occupation of Haiti*, Foreign Policy Association Information Service, Vol. V, Nos. 19-20, pp. 330-331.

4 The *Annual General Report of Jamaica*, together with the departmental reports for 1921 (Kingston, 1922), quoted by Abel and Bond, *op. cit.*, p. 32. Elementary education is denominational but with support from public funds. In 1927, the enrollment was 125,739, the attendance 76,990 in a population estimated in 1928 to be 953,768. This is about one thirteenth of the total population. In Florida, with about an equal population, those in attendance at school were three and a third times as many. See Frank Cudnall, *Jamaica in 1928* (London, 1928), p. 101, and *Commerce Yearbook, 1929*, Vol. II, p. 680.

5 Abel and Bond, *op. cit.*, p. 32, quoting Frederick Henry Watkins, *Handbook of the Leeward Islands* (London, 1924).

6 Census of 1930 "about 48 per cent." *Commerce Yearbook, 1930* (Washington, 1930), Vol. I, p. 663. "It is thought that the census of 1930 will show a reduction" of illiteracy "to nearly 30 per cent." *Twenty-ninth Annual Report of the Governor of Porto Rico, Honorable Horace M. Towner* (San Juan, 1929), p. 63. This and similar local estimates it appears were too sanguine.

7 Abel and Bond, *op. cit.*, p. 27.

8 *Alfabetismo y analfabetismo en Costa Rica segun el censo general de poblacion de 11 de mayo de 1927* (San José, 1928), p. 21.

9 *Censo de la poblacion de la republica levantado el 28 de agosto de 1921, 4° Censo*, Parte 1 (Guatemala, 1924), p. 67.

10 *Censo general de poblacion, 1927* (Tegucigalpa, 1927), p. 118. The census was taken December 26, 1926.

11 Abel and Bond, *op. cit.*, p. 36, quoting census of April 24, 1921.

12 Census of Colombia, 1918, quoted by Abraham Martinez, *Colombia Yearbook, 1927* (New York, 1928), p. 49. This includes all those who are not classed as able to read and write.

13 Estimated by Abel and Bond, *op. cit.*, p. 36, on basis of statistics for six states only, about one-fifth of the total population; about 55,000 Indians not included.

reality for, while in more developed countries literacy is normally an indication of a fairly constant use of the printed page, in the average Caribbean state this is not the case. Visitors to cities like Havana, Kingston, or San José are impressed by the popular demand for newspapers and the lighter sorts of magazines. It seems to indicate an activity in following current affairs at least as great as in northern countries. This appearance is deceptive. The circulation of periodicals in the rural districts is often as surprisingly small as it is unexpectedly great in the cities and towns.[3]

A number of causes contribute to the low educational standards. On the mainland, in Haiti, the Dominican Republic, and during part of its history, in Cuba, the disturbance of public order by civil dissensions has limited the advance which has been possible. The building up of public support has been difficult not only because of the disturbance of the peace but because the slender resources which would otherwise have been available have been diverted to military expenditures. In many cases irregularity of sessions has prevented the development of an *esprit de corps* among the teachers and pupils. Parents have felt that efforts to educate their children are of doubtful value when the living conditions are so unstable.

Elsewhere than in the regions mentioned the maintenance of public order has been better, but the funds available from public or private sources have in no case been adequate to maintain a satisfactory system of common schools. This has particularly been the case in some of the densely populated colonial areas, where general education, if seriously undertaken on more than a rudimentary basis, would overwhelm budgets already frequently unbalanced.

---

[3] See on this subject a discussion by José Guerrero, director of the National Census Office of Costa Rica in *Alfabetismo y analfabetismo en Costa Rica segun el censo general de poblacion de 11 de mayo de 1927.*

The low public income available has limited what could be done even where the percentage of the budget devoted to education has been relatively high. Buildings at public cost have often been unobtainable. Classes have been held in the homes of the teachers or in other private buildings, or even in the open. School equipment has often been of the most primitive sort, and supervision of educational activities by the central authorities has been defective.[4]

Recruitment of the teaching force has been done under serious handicaps. Political influences have controlled appointments in some cases. In others all normal school instruction has been abandoned for terms of years. It has been found necessary to accept as teachers those whose only preparation has been in the schools to which they return to teach. Salaries have been inadequate and irregular. In other districts the state has not considered primary education as one of its functions, or it has been content with making contributions to municipal schools or delegating its educational functions to subsidized groups of religious or lay character, with a loss of authority to control the curriculum. Private schools, where they have existed, have often been of much better grade than those publicly supported, and, by giving good facilities to those able to pay for them, have drawn the attention and support of the more influential away from public education and emphasized the tendency toward cultural rather than vocational training.

In the larger Caribbean units—though the same handi-

---

[4] For a description of unfortunate conditions of this sort in Colombia, see *Mensaje del presidente de la republica de Colombia al congreso nacional en las sesiones de 1926* (Bogotá, 1926), pp. 127-132. The conditions in Haiti before the American occupation were perhaps the least satisfactory. They are thus described by Buell, *op. cit.*, p. 330:

Teachers were usually political appointees, some of whom were even illiterate. The government owned few school buildings, but instead rented houses from favorites, which was a source of graft. Teachers were paid low salaries—in some cases less than five dollars per month; and frequently these salaries were in arrears. In 1906 rural schools had to close because of inadequate appropriations for rent; and even in the case of city schools the government appropriated only 1.20 *gourdes* (about 30 cents) monthly per school for school materials, including books.

cap appears elsewhere to a greater degree than might be assumed—the lack of communication facilities has been and continues to be a serious handicap. As a matter of fact, in considerable portions of Colombia and Venezuela and even in sections of some of the Central American states, public activities continue to be confined almost exclusively to weak policing and tax-gathering organizations, and systematic attempts to furnish education simply do not exist and cannot come into being except as the governments, through increase of income and the gradual improvement of their economic strength, become able truly to incorporate the territory nominally controlled. When all the disadvantages under which the educational authorities have worked are kept in mind the reported degree of illiteracy is lower than might be expected.

It would be unfair, however, to leave the discussion of what has been accomplished without pointing out the differences which exist between the advanced and backward areas.

Fair improvement has been made in Porto Rico in the years since the island came into American possession. The per capita expenditure has steadily risen, and in current years runs over eighteen dollars per student per year. The teachers are in all but small percentage Porto Ricans among whom an excellent spirit of coöperation has been developed. Vocational education has made good progress, and illiteracy has fallen from 83 per cent at annexation. It was about 48 per cent at the census of 1930.

Costa Rica has long claimed first place in educational matters among Caribbean countries and continues to show highly satisfactory advance. The fact that the republic has an exceptional percentage of persons of European blood among its inhabitants, the character of the land—which, though in sections decidedly broken, nevertheless as a whole permits communication more easily than in many other areas—the relatively small extent of the more densely in-

habited sections, and the enthusiasm which its leaders of
public affairs have shown in their support of educational
projects have all contributed to give the republic the unique
position which it holds.

Appropriations for educational and allied purposes have
steadily increased except for two serious setbacks in 1908
and 1918. In 1892, the budget provided for public instruction 463,838 colones.[5] The actual expenditures in
1928 were 6,299,000 colones. In the same period schools
almost doubled, reaching 428 in 1927, the number of
teachers was increased from 477 to 1,451, and the school
registration from 16,815 to 42,031. In the 1928 budget,
public education took 17 per cent or a greater proportion
than any other item except the public debt.

Even in a small country like this there continues to be
a wide variation in education in different districts. In the
less accessible rural areas illiterates rise to as much as 73.9
per cent of the population, but in the capital the census
records only 12.1 per cent. Coeducation now exists in primary, secondary, normal, and professional schools with the
result, unusual in Latin America, that illiteracy is found
among women to only a slightly greater degree than
among men.

The success of the educational program in "banishing"
illiteracy is reflected in the succeeding censuses. In 1864
there were reported 89 illiterates in every hundred inhabitants, in 1892, 68.59 per cent, but in 1927 only 23.6
per cent. The remarkable improvement made is an encouraging illustration of what may be done under Caribbean
conditions.

---

[5] The colon has been stabilized since March, 1924, at 4 colones to one
dollar, United States gold. A table of budget items, 1892–1927, is given in
*Alfabetismo y analfabetismo en Costa Rica segun el censo general de
poblacion de 11 de mayo de 1927*, p. 19, from which the figures in the discussion are taken. The expenditures for 1928 are as given in *Commerce
Yearbook, 1929*, Vol. II, p. 186.

It is safe to say that so far as the United States is concerned the greatest interest in educational advance in the Caribbean has been in developments in Cuba. In the colonial régime, direction of education had been intrusted to the captain-general assisted by a council of twelve persons serving ex officio. The result was a minimum of interest in the supervision of education of all grades. School equipment at the end of the revolution was practically nonexistent outside the cities. Teachers were few and ill-prepared. In sum, no real system of public education had been developed up to the end of the revolution. "About all there was of real education was what might be obtained in private schools." [6]

American responsibility for the policies adopted in the early years of the republic was direct and the expenditures under the administration of General Wood reflected opinion in the United States as to the importance of good school facilities. The school law of the republic was drafted by an American acting as superintendent of schools and recast by another American. Educational facilities were rapidly established, perhaps too rapidly at first, and on them almost a fourth of the revenues were expended. Cuban teachers were recruited and normal training provided both in institutions in the United States and in Cuba. Manual training, civics, and kindergarten classes were emphasized. Barracks were turned into schoolhouses. The importance of better education for the common people was accepted by all classes. The Secretary of Public Instruction declared: "When Cuba was hurled down the slope of popular government, it was for her a question of immediate life or death to begin to fill up the abyss that separated the multitude of her igno-

---

[6] Charles E. Chapman, *A History of the Cuban Republic* (New York, 1927), p. 111. The discussion in Chapman is based on critical estimates by foreigners and by eminent Cuban educators and is drawn upon largely in the following paragraphs.

rant people from the small group of her cultivated people." [7]

Enrollment reached 256,000, to fall off, after the first enthusiasm passed, to 160,000 with an average attendance of 125,000 in a population of about a million and a half. The daily enrollment in the official primary schools in 1928-9 was 342,502 with an average daily attendance of 257,504 in a population estimated at the end of 1929 at 3,607,919.[8] As reported, the proportion of the population in school is about the same as a quarter of a century ago.

But education under the republican régime does not measure up to the expectations of those formerly in charge. What is actually being accomplished is itself a matter of dispute. The government announcements paint a glowing picture of continued progress. The census of 1919 showed the percentage of those unable to read and write as 49. President Zayas in a message to Congress on April 7, 1924, gave the illiteracy of Cuba as only 27.1 per cent. The Sub-Secretary of Education estimated the percentage in 1930 at about 20.

Official statistics of current educational activities report a number of encouraging factors including increase in the number and salaries of teachers, emphasis on rural education, and a greater number of young women studying pedagogy in the normal and university courses. Fifty-four per cent of the 1,450 women studying in the University of Havana in 1929, in addition to those studying in normal courses, were preparing to teach.[9]

Criticisms by representative Cubans not in politics pre-

[7] Quoted by Aurelio Hevea, "General Leonard Wood and Public Instruction in Cuba," *Inter-America,* October, 1920, p. 4. Hevea gives an appreciative estimate of the educational work done under the American intervention.

[8] There are private, field, night, business, and penal schools giving elementary instruction which enroll about 45,000 pupils. The statistics for 1928-9 are from Republica de Cuba, *Comision nacional de estadistica y reformas economicas* (Havana, 1930).

[9] Republica de Cuba, *Comision nacional de estadistica y reformas economicas,* pp. 1-2.

sent a different picture. It is charged that no reliance should be placed upon the government statistics. Secretaries of Public Instruction, it is asserted, have been regularly dilettantes in education, and hampered in any good programs they have advocated by political influences which have made any real progress impossible. Private critics declare that over half of the Cuban population is now illiterate, that 68 per cent of the children do not enter school, that only one child in a hundred gets as far as fifth grade, and only one in 215 goes through the primary schools. Though appropriations have been generous the increase, and some assert even the maintenance, of school equipment has been negligible at least until very recently.[10]

Whatever allowances must be made for overstatement by both sides to the controversy, it is plain to any one who lives in the island that the Cuban educational system is still inadequate to reach the great mass of the population. The sharp break between the conditions in city and country, the neglected character of the physical equipment including both buildings [11] and school materials outside the larger towns, the inadequate pay of the teachers and the casual character of instruction and discipline make it abundantly evident that Cuba still has to create an efficient system of education, and that if progress is being made it is slow and at a disproportionate cost.

Among the countries less advanced in education, Guatemala may be taken as an example. It is not a republic in which there has been lack of realization of the handicap on national development involved in widespread illiteracy.

---

10 Chapman, op. cit., pp. 592-596. An illuminating discussion of the educational conditions in Cuba with striking comparisons with those in other Latin-American countries is given by Carlos M. Trelles, "Primary Instruction in Cuba," Inter-America, Vol. VII, No. 5 (June, 1924), pp. 401-443.

11 Of the 3,809 buildings used as schoolhouses in 1930, only 194 were government property, 48 belonged to municipalities, 1,763 were given rent free by private interests, and 1,814 were rented.

The proportion of the public budget devoted to education is greater than that in any other Central American state except Costa Rica. The mountainous character of the country, the consequent lack of easy communication, the large portion of the population of Indian stock which does not speak Spanish and finally the lack of adequate financial resources have all played a part in retarding the educational program.

The movement in favor of greater support for popular education, supported by the Liberal governments which came into control in Central America in the seventies of the last century, had its reflection in Guatemala in the establishment in 1873 under President Rufino Barrios of a national system of education, but later developments led to cutting down the funds for schools and even to closing many of them. At the end of the century, shortly after the establishment of control by Manuel Estrada Cabrera in 1898, a new impetus was given the educational program. In 1899, the President established the Festivals of Minerva to dramatize interest in schools. Some twenty-three temples of Minerva were erected at which annual festivals are held where prizes are given to teachers and pupils, degrees conferred, and other educational honors announced.[12] Cabrera, during his long period of control lasting over twenty years, established many schools and emphasized their practical character.

In the courses of study, agriculture had a prominent position. The schools were, as a rule, set up in the larger towns and made no thoroughgoing attempt to reach the Indian population. As a consequence the enrollment reached only 3.2 per cent of the total population, or it has been calculated about 16 per cent of the population of school age which, by law, included all those between six and fourteen. Even these figures do not indicate the inadequacy of the educa-

---

[12] Similar activities were later set up in Salvador and Panama.

tional establishment for enrollment was far greater than average attendance.[13] Illiteracy under these conditions continues a major national problem in which advance has been very slow if indeed existent. A comparison of the census figures for 1893 and 1921 shows that in the interval the percentage of those above seven years of age who were illiterate fell in thirteen departments but rose in nine. If the department of the capital be omitted, the figures show that conditions were no better at the last than at the preceding census and in the northern districts decidedly worse.

Children in attendance at school were fewer in 1920 than in 1903. From that year on, however, the Department of Education reports improvement. In 1926 attendance averaged ninety thousand as compared to less than fifty thousand in 1903. This represents rise of attendance from one thirty-ninth to one twenty-fifth of the population, but a condition still far distant from the one-fifth of the population which it is accepted should be in school if a high degree of illiteracy is to be avoided. Between the censuses of 1893 and 1921, it is doubtful, considering the conditions under which the enumeration took place, whether any reduction in illiteracy occurred.[14]

Interest in higher education on the part of the better-to-

---

[13] In the urban schools foreigners, especially Belgians, have at times been employed in an effort to raise their standard. Little success has attended efforts to reach the Indian population. Well-informed Guatemalans frequently express the opinion that in all educational activities a disproportionate part of the available funds is spent on administration rather than instruction and that the curriculum still emphasizes branches which even if they were generally taught "would educate the Indian rather than prepare him for a more civilized existence."

A comprehensive study of education in Central America from which the statements cited on Guatemalan education previous to 1917 are summarized is H. E. Jensen, *Education in Central America* (unpublished), Latin American Section, Survey Department, Interchurch World Movement (New York, n. d.), on file with the Committee on Coöperation in Latin America, 419 Fourth Avenue, New York.

[14] *Censo de la poblacion de la republica levantado el 28 de agosto de 1921*, pp. 67-70; *Memoria de los labores del ejecutivo en el ramo de educacion publica, 1927-28* (Guatemala, 1928), p. 224.

do classes in the Caribbean has always been marked and in recent years has led to sending a large number of students to colleges and universities in Europe and the United States. Those studying in American higher educational institutions in current years are reported as indicated in the table following:

STUDENTS FROM CARIBBEAN COUNTRIES IN THE COLLEGES AND
UNIVERSITIES OF THE UNITED STATES [15]

Country	1928-9	1929-30
Bahama Islands	1	3
Bermuda	11	21
British Guiana	13	12
British Honduras	5	3
British West Indies	47	35
Colombia	49	77
Costa Rica	22	25
Cuba	111	144
Dominican Republic	5	5
Dutch Guiana	...	2
Guatemala	13	18
Haiti	15	14
Honduras	12	17
Jamaica	11	16
Nicaragua	8	18
Panama	83	91
Porto Rico	250	260
Salvador	5	10
Trinidad	2	4
Venezuela	26	30
Virgin Islands	3	5
West Indies [1]	41	67
TOTAL	733 [2]	877 [2]

1 Unspecified.
2 Does not include "Latin-American Unspecified."

As is to be expected a large number of these young people, in 1929-30 almost half, came from Porto Rico and Cuba where American influence is strongest. Unfortunately, it appears that only a small proportion of these students

15 Compiled from a pamphlet published by the Committee on Friendly Relations among Foreign Students, 347 Madison Avenue, New York.

planned to return to their home countries in educational
work. While they do represent an increasing intellectual
contact among American communities and therefore contribute to a better understanding of the bonds which bind
these states to one another, they do not contribute as much
as might be desired to the general educational uplift of the
communities from which they come. Much the same comment is frequently made by Latin-Americans concerning the
graduates of their own higher educational institutions.
Their graduates tend to pass into professional careers other
than teaching with the result that the educational gulf between the mass of the population and the better educated
classes continues.

Conditions such as now exist in education in the Caribbean region few will consider acceptable whether the standard of popular education which most thinkers in the
Americas have advocated be accepted or not. Only in
exceptional cases does the school system make an attempt
to reach the children of the masses and in no case does it
do so to the satisfaction of the more progressive groups of
the various countries. Even the training given to the sons
and daughters of the well-to-do does not bring into being
a class prepared to take an active part in economic development or in working out a stable public policy related to local
conditions.

A review of the figures available shows only two republics
in all of Latin America with a percentage of illiteracy less
than 25, Argentina and, in the Caribbean group, Costa
Rica. Cuba reports 27 per cent of illiterates but in the
other republics the proportion runs uniformly over 50 per
cent and in one case almost to 87 per cent.

In cases of this sort unfavorable circumstances are less
serious if substantial improvement is being made. In most
cases it is not possible to ascertain whether progress is occurring. In Porto Rico and some of the European colonial

areas, the school systems and attendance indicate encouraging advance. Among the republics, Costa Rica stands out above the others in its emphasis on education. If the figures reflect conditions, Cuban progress is also notable. Panama, it appears, is making headway against a heavy percentage of illiteracy. For the other republics either no information is available or it is not encouraging. In the weakest units it seems clear that there is no substantial progress. So far as information is available, as perhaps is to be expected, literacy and educational advance are both more marked in countries and in portions of countries where the percentage of European stocks is high.

The effect which conditions such as these have on the prospects of the Caribbean units in the near future is patent, though often overlooked. One of the essentials, if these units are to raise themselves to circumstances comparable to those of the more advanced nations of the temperate zones, is improvement of their social conditions and especially among these, the conditions affecting education. So long as the printed page remains unintelligible to over half the population, national activities must continue to be of the simplest sort. Even the transforming industries to which it seems the Caribbean countries may be limited, cannot develop and the building up of economic resources in the hands of the local population is seriously retarded.

The effect of a predominantly illiterate population in public affairs is equally important. If Caribbean states are to have democratic governments in reality and not only in the theory of their constitutions, education of their citizenship is a prime essential. Here lies the weakness of their repeated declarations in favor of "constitutional governments" now crystallized into the treaties by which a number of them have attempted to regulate their relations to each other, and given support by the declarations and practice of the United States. Actual participation in public affairs by the people at large, even in the choice of public officers, is much more difficult to obtain than we are often disposed to admit. In a country where half or more of the population cannot read or write and in which a considerable additional number rarely do so, it is obvious that voting tends to become a form rather than a function. "Republican government" and "democratic control" in the Caribbean states will continue to be, as they have been in the past, ideals to be striven for and not blessings attained until the level of education along with the general standard of life can be substantially raised.

CHAPTER V

SUGAR

In the history of the Caribbean, sugar has played a leading rôle. It was the first important money crop in the export trade, its production brought periods of unexampled prosperity to one region and then to another, control of the sources of supply became one of the causes contributing to international conflicts, and the decline of the Caribbean sugar market, because of development of competition in non-American areas, caused an economic depression widespread and long continued. Renewal of production under the special influence of a rapidly expanding American demand has accounted for the advance of the greatest Caribbean contributor to foreign trade, and current overproduction has had a far-reaching effect on its prosperity.

Sugar was not indigenous to the new world. It appears to have had its origin in Asia. Before the Christian era, cultivation of cane was well established in India whence it spread to Asia Minor and to Europe. Crystalline sugar seems to have been first made in India. By the seventh century, it was produced in Persia, and in the Middle Ages the best sugar came from Egypt. The Italian commercial cities during the period of the crusades spread its use over the Mediterranean region.

When Portugal and Spain rose to the position of world powers they extended knowledge of sugar cane to the western countries of which they took possession. The Portuguese introduced it into Madeira in 1420 [1] and to the other

---

[1] National Bank of Commerce in New York, *The World's Sugar Supply* (New York, 1917).

Atlantic islands later discovered. The Spanish colonized the Canaries in 1496 and introduced sugar there. These areas soon became steady producers at costs with which the eastern Mediterranean areas could not compete.

Sugar cane found its way to America early in the era of discovery. Columbus is reported to have made an unsuccessful attempt to establish its raising in Santo Domingo in 1493. Better fortune attended an enterprise there in 1506 and sugar soon became an important local crop. Within the next generation cultivation was introduced in other West Indies and became established in what is now northeastern Brazil.

This mainland industry outstripped that in the islands in the first century of European colonization. One hundred and two mills were in operation in Bahia and Pernambuco in 1590, and ten years later the sugar exports reached 15,000 tons. Brazil was then by far the leading American supplier of sugar to the European market.

Meanwhile cultivation was spreading in the West Indies, where British, French, and Spanish interests in turn were to take the lead in the three centuries following.[2]

The British cultivation first became prominent in Barbados which later yielded place to Jamaica. Lesser amounts were produced in the scattered smaller islands under British dominion the number of which was, as the years passed, increased by cessions by the French. These British sugar colonies developed characteristics which placed them in sharp contrast to those established to the northward.

Except for a brief period in the sixteen hundreds, there came to the British West Indies but few settlers of moderate means intent on casting their lot permanently in America. "Instead the islands became the goal of spendthrift bankrupts eager to recoup their wasted fortunes, of

---

[2] See a brief description of the shifts in sugar production in George M. Rolph, *Something about Sugar* (San Francisco, 1917), pp. 119-127.

penniless younger sons of gentility desirous of amassing
means sufficient to become landed proprietors in the homeland, and the dumping ground for the riffraff of the parent
country." [3] Due to the rapid increase of wealth in England
in the seventeenth and eighteenth centuries capital was
easily available for sugar ventures. The typical development was soon a large-scale undertaking, dependent on slave
labor. Such small holdings as existed tended to disappear.[4]
Another feature in the development of the sugar industry
in the British islands was the special favor amounting to
a monopoly of the home market which it long received.
Taken together these circumstances made the settlements
fragile, almost artificial. Their economic life had a remarkable but not a virile growth, and when the special
advantage which had promoted it was removed hard times
became as marked as the former prosperity had been.

As it became recognized that the colonies were to be exploitation rather than settlement areas fewer free immigrants arrived. The number of white persons in many of
the islands steadily decreased, after the first inflow, both
relatively and absolutely. Steady importation of Negroes
for plantation work helped to emphasize the disproportion.
Miscegenation occurred to a degree seldom found in British
settlements.

Operations resulted in high profits, and owners tended to
return to England leaving their properties in the hands of
local agents who were neither good guardians of their clients'
interests nor progressive in adopting improved planting
and manufacturing methods. Monoculture was increasingly
characteristic of the islands. Except in Jamaica and in
the colonies ceded by France after the Seven Years' War,
sugar came to be the only important article of export. This

---

[3] Lowell Joseph Ragatz, *The Fall of the Planter Class in the British
Caribbean, 1763–1833* (New York, 1928), p. 3.

[4] Barbados was an exception. White resident proprietors long were
characteristic of the colony. *Ibid.,* p. 4.

tendency to abandon supplementary crops was in some cases stimulated by poorly thought out legislation in the home country, such as the law taxing indigo which killed a prosperous industry of Jamaica and the charges placed on West Indian coffee, which were adopted to lessen its competition with tea.

Even so, of course, the British West Indian sugar industry could prosper so long as the conditions existing at the time of its first success continued. As long as the sugar market was undersupplied, as long as other areas in the empire and elsewhere remained low in production or were shut out of protected markets, profits would be high though landlords were absentees, agents inefficient or even dishonest, and management antiquated. The West Indian planters could live extravagantly and buy their way into Parliament, there to protect their privileged positions.

But economic conditions refused to stay *in statu quo*, and as the seventeenth and especially the eighteenth centuries progressed, the British sugar interests went through a succession of periods of prosperity and hard times. These were in part due to the unsound economic basis on which the sugar industry rested.

Competition from non-British areas in the Caribbean increased, especially in the second half of the eighteenth century from Santo Domingo. The outbreak of the American Revolution cut off a highly valued outlet for sugar, rum, and molasses, and after the winning of American independence restrictions on the commerce continued. New varieties of cane of high sugar content, introduced about 1790 into the French and shortly into the British colonies, increased the yield and for a time the profits, but later had an adverse effect on prices. Non-British sugar from the West Indies began to be smuggled into the British market, through passing first into West Indian ports, and shipments from the East Indies began to come into the home market and cut down the advantages of the long-established American trade. The wars of the period of the French Revolution and the Napoleonic period depressed business though for a part of these years prosperity reached a high level, perhaps the highest which the West Indian sugar industry ever enjoyed. The temporarily favorable conditions were largely contributed to by the fall of Haitian production due to the revolution in the island.

The breakdown of the foundation of the industry increased as the nineteenth century advanced, though there were occasional brief periods of good times. Acquisition of new sugar producing areas in the West Indies and in the Orient as a result of the French Revolution and the Napoleonic wars emphasized competition within the empire. Cuba and Brazil increased their production on fresh lands which gave greater yields than were obtainable in British areas, and shipments thence were given the advantage of direct entry to foreign markets. In 1822, the British West Indies succeeded in securing the abolition of restrictions on their trade with the United States, but the advantages they still continued to enjoy over East Indian sugars in the home market were gradually pared away and disappeared entirely in 1836. Shortly afterward foreign sugars for refining and export were granted free entry into British ports. Beet sugar production which had been negligible early in the century—only 7,000,000 pounds were produced west of the Rhine in 1812—was giving promise of serious competition which might destroy the Continental market.

All in all, the outlook at the end of the first quarter of the nineteenth century was discouraging indeed for the British West Indian planters but the worst blow was still to come. The movement for emancipation rapidly gained strength in the 1820's, and in 1833 a law with compensation and apprenticeship provisions was passed to become effective August 1, 1834. The old sugar régime was at an end. The fragile prosperity which had brief periods of promise has never thereafter been reëstablished.[5]

Satisfactory statistics for the British West Indian sugar trade during the period previous to emancipation are not available. Contraband trade enters the figures reported, for foreign sugars were cleared through colonial ports and marketed as British grown. The trade with the non-British areas, especially that to North America, is not satisfactorily reported. Figures of shipments to Great Britain give, however, a fair idea of the general course of development.

To those familiar with the now greatly increased supplies which find their way to world markets the total sugar yield of the British Caribbean possessions even in their most prosperous period is unexpectedly small, but its importance is to be judged not by comparison with present-day output but in relation to the world supply of the time and the position which sugar then held in the total colonial commerce.

Failure to adopt new methods of production, the limited areas suitable for planting, exhaustion of some of the longest exploited areas, and until the closing years of the eighteenth century the use of cane of low sugar content all contributed to make the increase in yield less than it otherwise might have been. In 1763, the shipments to England totaled 1,288,135 [6] hundredweight. Thereafter the general tendency was upward until 1774, when smaller shipments began, making the total in 1780 little more than in 1763. The average English import of West Indian sugars in 1793-5 was 2,105,567 hundredweight, and in 1801-3 it stood at 3,591,508. In 1809, it was down again, reaching only 2,288,656 hundredweight, but in 1828 it

---

[5] The authoritative account of the developments above summarized is Ragatz, *op. cit.*

[6] Calculating the hundredweight at 112 pounds, this is equal to 72,130 short tons or about 64,400 long tons or metric tons.

reached record amount at 4,068,058,[7] including in the latter year the shipments from Berbice and the rapidly increasing Demarara yield. Then decline began again.[8]

For the last century, however, British Caribbean sugar yield has not developed marked variations. Guiana, Trinidad, and Jamaica have increased their production, and the same is true to a lesser degree of Barbados, but the smaller islands now produce only about half as much as they did two generations ago. At one time in the early nineties the total yield rose to about 300,000 long tons, but in current years stands at about 225,000.

French production of sugar in the West Indies prospered from almost the establishment of the colonies. The trade policy adopted was liberal when contrasted with that of Great Britain, and the character of the settlers assured a greater initiative in developing their holdings. The early colonists were seldom persons of means and they came to make the colonies their permanent residence. Plantations were better managed by resident owners than were the British developments. Cost of production was less and the restrictions on trade were not burdensome. Even direct trade with foreign countries was allowed before that step was taken by the British. In 1763, before the American Revolution, special arrangements were made to foster the sugar and rum shipments from French colonial ports to the British mainland colonies.[9]

The greatest sugar development in areas under French control occurred not in the older colonies but in Santo Domingo where large estates came to be the rule as in the British colonies and where as time went on the plantations

---

[7] About 222,811 short tons or somewhat less than 200,000 long tons or metric tons.

[8] From *Statistics for the Study of British Caribbean Economic History, 1763–1833,* compiled by Lowell Joseph Ragatz (London, 1927).

[9] Ragatz, *The Fall of the Planter Class in the British Caribbean, 1763–1833,* pp. 136-137.

were worked by slaves driven so hard that the labor supply was kept up only by the steady importation of large numbers of African blacks.

As has already been indicated the first successful cultivation of sugar cane in the new world occurred in this island,[10] but possession of all the island was then nominally in the hands of Spain.

French settlement did not begin till 1629, over a century later, and at first was confined to Tortuga, a small island off the coast. There developed the famous settlements of the buccaneers. These men at first were not pirates as the name later came to indicate, nor were they settlers interested in sugar production. Spain did not recognize the settlements in Tortuga and the west portion of Santo Domingo as carrying title to the land to France until the treaty of Ryswick in 1697.

Development of the French holdings was then pushed, especially after 1725. Within fifty years the colony became the best-known tropical settlement of the world and the greatest of sugar producers. About 1790 there were 792 sugar estates in operation.[11] By 1791, exports of sugar from the French colony reached 177,230,000 pounds,[12] or 88,630 short tons, an enormous amount for that early time.

But the treatment of the blacks and the reports of revolutionary activity in France brought on a slave revolt which made the fall of the colony and decline of its economic importance as spectacular as had been its rise.[13] With the

10 H. P. Davis, *Black Democracy* (New York, 1929), p. 12.

11 Ragatz, *The Fall of the Planter Class in the British Caribbean, 1763-1833*, p. 204.

12 Davis, *op. cit.*, p. 25. "Legal exports from St. Domingo in 1784 included 602,343 cwt. of clayed sugar; 716,512 cwt. of muscovado...." Ragatz, *The Fall of the Planter Class in the British Caribbean, 1763-1833*, p. 204, note 2.

13 See Theodore Lothrop Stoddard, *The French Revolution in San Domingo* (Boston, 1914).

ending of French control, sugar manufacture rapidly declined. The plantations were invaded by tropical undergrowth, irrigation works fell into disrepair and the factories became ruins. Shipments of sugar fell to insignificance, both in the total from the Caribbean and in the exports of the new state set up by the revolt. In fact, on balance it came in some years to import more sugar than it shipped abroad.

French sugar production in the West Indies came to be confined to that from the older colonies, Guadeloupe and Martinique. Both these are so small in area and limited in lands suited to plantations that they contribute now only negligible amounts to a greatly increased world trade. On the whole the local industry is, however, a prosperous one due to liberal trade arrangements on sugar cane products with the mother country. Rum shipments in current years make up a large part of the exports. Over the past seventy-five years, the total tonnage of sugar produced has varied from about fifty thousand to almost a hundred thousand tons.

Production of sugar in the Spanish colonies came to have importance in local economic life and in international trade comparable to that in British and French areas, only at a surprisingly late date. In fact, the great Spanish sugar industry in the Caribbean came into the lead so late that it may almost be said to have been the heir rather than the competitor of the sugar industry of the other European countries.

Cuba and Porto Rico both developed slowly. Few settlers went to the islands and those who did so engaged in mining and stockraising. A generation after the discovery, those in Cuba totaled probably less than three hundred, and as late as 1576 there were only three crude mills producing sugar of a very inferior quality. In 1617, after over a hundred years of Spanish exploitation, there were only some thirty-seven mills.[14]

Sugar cultivation continued to advance but did not attract great attention. It was not until about the middle of the eighteenth century that the mother country came to realize the value of Cuba and, in less degree, the value of Porto Rico. Up to that time the larger island was a neglected colony with a mild slavery system, often unable to pay the cost of its own government without aid from the mother country.

But a change was coming. In 1740-60, the Real Compañia Mercantil de la Habaña enjoyed extensive rights in the island and did much to improve its condition. In the period, eighty new sugar mills came into existence. Later the restrictions on the slave trade were reduced. Sugar production and foreign trade both showed a prompt response. After a brief ten months' occupation by the British in 1762, Havana was returned to Spain, and there soon followed the opening of its trade to eight ports in the homeland and a general liberalization of the regulations affecting commerce.

Sugar production now took on a new lease of life. Before 1765, shipments had been insufficient to supply even the demands of the mother country.[15] They now rapidly increased and the latter part of the eighteenth century was a period of great economic activity.[16] The American Revolution brought a new impetus to Cuban development, followed by a check during the period of the Napoleonic wars which for the time damaged the sugar market but proved only a temporary setback. At the end of the century, the competition of Santo Domingan sugar had ceased and though British efforts to stop the slave trade—the continuance of which was believed essential to the continued

---

[14] Hubert H. S. Aimes, *A History of Slavery in Cuba, 1511–1868* (New York, 1907), pp. 11-15.

[15] Albert Galloway Keller, *Colonization* (Boston, 1908), p. 330.

[16] Aimes, *op. cit.*, p. 34.

sugar production—were a cloud on the horizon, the general outlook continued favorable.

British West Indians shortly began to lose their long established hold on their home market and were forced to give up the advantage of slave laborers. Spanish immigrants by the early forties were arriving in increasing numbers, and French, British, and Americans were coming to the now specially favored Spanish areas where slavery was still allowed, bringing capital, mechanical abilities, and improved machinery further to develop the sugar industry.

Improved methods of production cut down dependence on slave labor. In 1825, some three hundred slaves were needed to produce four hundred tons of sugar. In 1849, the same amount could be produced with one hundred fifty Negroes.[17] Sugar estates steadily grew in size and value of equipment. A good yield on a large estate before 1845 was from four hundred to six hundred tons. Single units soon thereafter came to produce four thousand tons. British duties on Cuban sugar were removed in 1846, with a great increase in demand and sharp rise in prices, and the rapid development of the United States gave the American market a new importance.

Spanish domination of Caribbean sugar production was beyond question at the middle of the nineteenth century. It totaled 368,000 metric tons—300,000 in Cuba and 68,000 in Porto Rico. This was more than all other areas in the Caribbean together; in fact even Porto Rico produced more than any two of the non-Spanish areas.

The Cuban advance continued. At the beginning of the ten years' war of 1868-78, the yield reached 850,864 short tons. The revolt did not affect the sugar producing regions seriously though this record was not exceeded until 1891, when a favorable trade agreement with the United States

---

[17] *Ibid.,* p. 157.

once more pushed up demand and production. In 1894, the total was 1,197,587 short tons, and Cuba alone produced about four times as much as the British and French possessions.

But the War of Independence was now at the door, and the years following 1895 cut the yield to a quarter of the record figures of 1894. In 1897 and again in 1900 the total crop gave only about 240,000 short tons.[18]

Before taking up a discussion of the Caribbean sugar developments of the last generation, a word should be said of the industry in the areas which in the earlier part of the nineteenth century established their independence. All of them have long established sugar industries but ones for which the foreign market has not been of great importance except in the Dominican Republic. There a sizable industry has developed in the last quarter-century. In the calendar year 1905, the sugar shipments totaled 52,986 short tons. The subsequent development has made sugar decidedly the most important commercial crop and it constitutes in current years about 60 per cent of the exports. Production reached 368,000 long tons in 1927-8.[19] In 1929 it was 322,088 long tons.[20]

Haiti, once so important in its yield of sugar, has not reëstablished the production of the colonial period. Only one company now produces raw sugar for export, and refining in the island dates from 1928. Less than 15,000

---

[18] These figures are from *The Cane Sugar Industry*, U. S. Department of Commerce, Bureau of Foreign and Domestic Commerce, Miscellaneous Series, No. 53 (Washington, 1917), p. 400, and from *Statistique de la production du sucre brut dans les cinq parties du monde*, De Bayser and Co. (16 Rue du Louvre, Paris, n. d.).

[19] In most of the other independent areas the sugar industry is chiefly important for domestic supply though some shipments abroad are regularly made. The *Commerce Yearbook, 1929*, Vol. II (Washington, 1929), reports the following exports: Venezuela, 8,000 tons (1927); Haiti, 13,000 tons (1928); Guatemala, 9,000 tons (1928); Honduras, 25,000 tons (1928); Nicaragua, 6,000 tons (1927); Salvador, 8,500 tons (1927).

[20] *Report of the 23d Fiscal Period Dominican Customs Receivership, Calendar Year, 1929* (Washington, 1930), p. 81.

tons are exported in current years, almost all to British ports.

Porto Rico, on the other hand, has greatly increased its production since the establishment of its connection with the United States, especially since the grant of free entry into American ports to which practically all of the production entering export goes. The total shipments reached 68,909 short tons in 1901 and 605,620 in 1928. They fell, under the influence of the crisis of the following year, to 471,244 tons.

For an appreciation of the conditions under which Cuban and other Caribbean sugar production has occurred in the twentieth century, it will be an advantage to sketch the advance which had been made in world production at its beginning and the peculiar conditions which then surrounded the market. Perhaps the position of none of the great staples illustrates so well the degree to which production and prosperity in the regions supplying world trade may be influenced by the commercial policies of the great consuming nations. The history of British Caribbean sugar is an example of long standing but hardly a more striking one than that of the development of the portion of the industry which produces sugar from beets.

In the first quarter of the nineteenth century beet sugar began to be offered in continental markets but only in relatively small amounts. By the middle of the century, however, production had been stimulated by bounties and tariffs, and in 1852-3, 202,810 tons were marketed. Cane sugar supplied still 86 per cent of the total. Thereafter to the end of the century,[21] the cane sugar yield increased, but beet sugar production grew still more rapidly. As a result, in 1899-1900, in the total world sugar production of 8,291,800 tons, cane sugar made up only 34.7 per cent. Fifty years

---

[21] Except in the years in which production was affected by the Cuban revolution.

before, beet sugar was still not a serious factor, but it had now come to take almost two-thirds of the market.

The continental European countries, by a system of tariffs on imports and direct and indirect bounties on export, had not only succeeded in supplying themselves but had become heavy exporters of beet sugar. Germany, France, Austria-Hungary, and Russia all had crops of about a million tons. Colonial cane sugar furnished only a minor fraction of even the British supply. The mother country purchased increasingly from the Continent where sugar could be purchased at exceptionally low prices, lower than the cost of production. The bounty competition had become so keen, in fact, that support of the beet sugar industry was a serious drain on the treasuries of the producing countries.[22] Production in Java, in the Far East, was steadily growing in the meantime, and the yield of cane sugar there had become greater than that in Cuba.

The conditions of the sugar market were highly unsatisfactory. The continental countries had come to pay for the prosperity of their beet sugar industries from the yield of general taxation, their local prices of sugar were high, the British cane sugar producers were continually complaining of their "abandonment" by the mother country. The Far East was supplying itself and becoming a heavy exporter of cane sugar. Cuban production was for the moment at a low ebb though this and the other Caribbean areas had still an active market in the United States in which the dumping of bounty-fed sugars by the European countries had only in 1897 been stopped by the adoption of a countervailing tariff.

The lead in remedying these circumstances was taken by Great Britain. As early as 1886, a conference had been held in London which, however, brought no relief to the

---

[22] The legislation for encouragement of beet sugar production and the Brussels convention are discussed in Rolph, *op. cit.,* pp. 128 *et seq.*

British Caribbean producers. Later British opinion became more aroused, and in 1895, after a Royal Commission had reported on conditions in the West Indies, the first remedial measures were adopted.

The continental countries were meanwhile tiring of their expensive support of their sugar industries, and in 1898 Belgium called a conference to study what could be done, but without concrete results. Another met at Brussels in 1901. It also seemed headed for deadlock when Great Britain, now greatly concerned in the effect of the abnormal conditions in her dominions, threatened to exclude bounty-fed sugar from her markets if an agreement were not reached. The chief beet sugar producers then agreed to the Brussels convention signed March 5, 1902,[23] to which a number of other countries later gave their assent. It abolished all bounties. Great Britain and the Netherlands agreed that while the arrangement lasted they would not give preferential treatment to their colonial sugars. This was half a victory for the Caribbean sugar interests. They no longer found competition artificially supported but were still at no advantage in the home market. The convention with modifications was subsequently continued for five-year periods, but Great Britain retired from it on September 1, 1913, though observance of its provisions was continued for a time thereafter.

Though the Brussels convention eliminated the worst features of the artificial conditions previously prevailing it did not create a free world market for sugar. Continental countries continued their tariffs to protect local beet production. Cane sugar plantings in the Far East, especially in Java, increased, Cuban sugar production rose for the time under favorable conditions discussed below, and production in British areas taken as a whole showed an upward tendency. Consumption also rose and kept the world

---

[23] To go into effect September 1, 1903. *Ibid.,* p. 145.

market relatively more stable than previously. The World War period, however, has been followed by a recrudescence of public policies stimulating production, and improvements in manufacture which have brought back dislocations of the market and distress in the Caribbean sugar industry which recall the conditions in the closing years of the past century.

During the war, when European beet sugar production was seriously cut down, the cane sugar industry enjoyed a number of very prosperous years. After the war, higher tariffs were adopted to revive beet production and assure, in various areas, national self-sufficiency of sugar supplies.[24] At the same time, laws were adopted favoring colonial production. France and Portugal made colonial sugars free of tariffs. In England, where sugar had entered practically free before the war, legislation establishing "imperial preference" became marked. The dominions followed the lead and also adopted measures for protection of their own home production.

Under these stimuli, world sugar production, which was 18,484,889 long tons in 1914-5, rose to 27,082,706 long tons in 1928-9.[25] The crops had outrun world demand. Stocks were held on the market in amounts never before reached, and prices fell below the level at which many producers could make a profit.

The crisis affected Caribbean producers acutely. Operations in the British colonies became increasingly difficult in spite of the fact that the mother country had created

---

[24] Measures of this sort were adopted by Germany, Austria, Czecho-Slovakia, Hungary, Belgium, Italy, Spain, Portugal, Rumania, Sweden, and Denmark. The increases averaged 7 per cent for raw and 52 per cent for refined sugar, over the prewar duties. Central and South American countries except Peru also adopted high import tariffs on sugar. *The Planter and Sugar Manufacturer,* October 20, 1928.

[25] Farr and Company, *Manual of Sugar Companies, 1929* (New York, 1929), p. 16. Willet and Gray report 27,246,372 long tons in 1928-9 and 26,702,632 in 1929-30. Quoted in *The American Sugar Refining Company Annual Report, 1929* (New York, 1930), p. 15.

a preference on empire sugar equivalent to 80.3 cents per hundred pounds,[26] and Canada gave the Caribbean colonies a preference of a dollar a hundredweight.[27] How critical the position of the producers is in current years it is difficult to judge, for there has hardly been a period in the last hundred years when local sugar interests have not avowed that they faced imminent disaster, but it seems beyond doubt that conditions are now less favorable than at any other time in the last quarter century. The West Indian Sugar Commission has reported that if the existing conditions in the world market persist and the present preference be withdrawn without the substitution of some other substantial relief practically the "entire West Indian production of export sugar will, after the 1931 crop already planted, rapidly disappear." [28]

While this is probably too pessimistic a view, there is no doubt that the older high-cost plantations are in difficult straits and barring the receipt of special favors cannot continue in production at current price levels. Various expedients for relief are being urged upon the British parliament, including the calling of a special international conference such as the Brussels convention to endeavor to break down the artificial stimulation of sugar production behind tariff walls, and the creation of special preference for empire sugars at least equal to that now granted the British Caribbean yield in Canada.

The first of these proposals, however rational, meets the contention that if adopted other countries would be forced to "sacrifice" a domestic industry and to forego the large income their treasuries now receive from the sugar industry.

---

[26] *Report of the First West Indies Conference Held in Barbados, January-February, 1929* (London, 1929).

[27] *Canada, The Customs Tariff and Amendments with Index to September 15, 1928* (Ottawa, 1928), pp. 215-221, quoting *West Indies, Agreement with Certain Colonies in the, 1926*.

[28] *Report of the West Indian Sugar Commission*, Cmd. 3517 (London, 1930), p. 5.

The increase of "preference" meets the objection that it would still further increase the tax burden of the British public. Even the existing preference rates on sugar are alleged to cost the British taxpayers about $30,000,000 a year.[29]

The actions which may be taken by British authorities to improve the position of Caribbean sugar raisers will affect only a minor portion of the total crop. A special position has already been created, through legislation in the mother country, for the French planters. Other producers, with the exception of one, continue to sell their crops at home or on the world market in which they hold no favored position.

This exception is Cuba which enjoys special privileges under the Reciprocity Treaty of 1903 with the United States. Even while bounty-fed sugars were still being thrown on the world market, the chief shipments from the island went to its northern neighbor and constituted about half of the sugars, beet and cane, which it imported.[30] The beet sugar imports into the United States rapidly fell off after the Brussels convention,[31] confining the foreign competition in the American market to cane sugars. But the treaty of 1903, which granted Cuban shipments to the United States a 20 per cent reduction from the normal rates applying to those of other origins, gave Cuba practically a monopoly of the American import trade—a

[29] The recent parliamentary debates on this subject are summarized in the *Times* (London), March 25, 27, 28, and April 3, 1930.

[30] Tables showing this condition are found in *Statistical Abstract of the United States, 1905* (Washington, 1906), p. 452, for figures from 1896-1905.

[31] Shipments from Germany had reached the highest totals among American beet sugar purchases. They were 1,511,402,000 pounds in a total of 1,865,577,000 in 1897. Beet sugar imports were 908,683,000 pounds in 1901 but in 1904 after the adoption of the reciprocity treaty they were only 2,414,000 pounds. The beet sugar imports in the late nineties were of course affected not only by the bounties, but by the countervailing tariff of 1897 and by the Cuban War of Independence.

monopoly of imports into the only great near-at-hand market, the most rapidly expanding one of the world and one which came to consume almost a fourth of the sugar production of all countries. This was a new state of affairs highly advantageous to the Cuban industry, of course, but one which placed other Caribbean areas except Porto Rico at a disadvantage, for they were forced to offer their sugars on the already greatly limited general world market. The degree to which this exceptional market became an influence in the Cuban sugar industry and its relative lessening in importance in the postwar period is shown in the following table:

CUBAN TOTAL RAW SUGAR EXPORTS AND EXPORTS TO THE UNITED STATES

Year	Total Exports, Short Tons	Exports to United States, Short Tons	Per Cent to United States
1900 [1]	348,000	348,000	99.98
1905 [1]	985,000	985,000	99.99
1913 [1]	2,443,000	2,204,000	90.21
1925 [2]	5,441,000	4,040,000	74.25
1926 [2]	5,149,000	4,199,000	81.54
1927 [3]	4,510,000	3,615,000	80.15
1928 [4]	3,967,000	2,870,000	72.34
1929 [5]	4,808,000	3,689,000	76.74

[1] U. S. Tariff Commission, *Reciprocity and Commercial Treaties* (Washington, 1919), p. 329, quoting *Cuba: Comercio exterior.*
[2] *Commerce Yearbook, 1926* (Washington, 1927), Vol. II, p. 174.
[3] *Ibid.,* 1929, Vol. II, p. 195.
[4] Cuban statistics from Guma-Mejer quoted in *The American Sugar Refining Company Annual Report, 1928* (New York, 1929), p. 17.
[5] *Ibid.,* 1929 (New York, 1930), p. 18.

The changes which were occurring took place under the influence of shifting tariff rates which after the war bore more heavily on Cuban sugar notwithstanding the continuance of the reciprocity treaty and under the influence of the growth of the supplies raised under the American flag. The proportion of domestic and colonial "free" sugars in the supply of the United States steadily rose while at the same

UNITED STATES TARIFF RATES ON SUGAR [32] AND PROPORTIONS OF

Tariff Rates in Cents per Pound for Raw Sugar 96°	Consumption, Long Tons	Per Cent by Duty Paid		
		Free	Cuba	Full Duty
1897–1898 .... July 24, 1897 Full duty: 1.685¢	2,047,344	32	13	55
1902–1903 .... Porto Rico: free after July 25, 1901 Philippines: 1.26¢ after March 8, 1902 Cuba: 1.348¢ after December 27, 1903; full duty, 1.685¢..	2,549,643	41	34	25
1908–1909 .... August 5, 1909 Philippines: free to 300,000 tons Full duty: 1.685¢ Cuba: 1.348¢	3,257,660	50	44	6
1913–1914 .... March 1, 1914 Full duty: 1.256¢ Cuba: 1.0048¢ Philippines: free after October 4, 1913	3,760,827	45	54	1

[32] The tariff rates on imported raw sugar since 1789 have been as follows:

Period	Rate
July 5, 1789-Aug. 11, 1790............1.000	cents per pound
Aug. 11, 1790-May 14, 1800............1.500	" " "
May 14, 1800-Apr. 28, 1816............2.000	" " "
Apr. 28, 1816-July 15, 1832...........3.000	" " "
July 15, 1832-July 31, 1846............2.500	" " "
July 31, 1846-Mar. 3, 1861.............30	per cent ad valorem
Mar. 3, 1861-Aug. 6, 1861.............. .750	cents per pound
Aug. 6, 1861-July 15, 1862............2,500	" " "
July 15, 1862-July 1, 1864............3.500	" " "
July 1, 1864-July 15, 1870.............4.000	" " "
July 15, 1870-Mar. 4, 1883............2.750	" " "
Mar. 4, 1883-Oct. 2, 1890.............2.240	" " "
Oct. 2, 1890-Aug. 28, 1894............free	
Aug. 28, 1894-July 25, 1897..........40	per cent ad valorem
July 25, 1897-Dec. 17, 1903..........1.685	cents per pound
Dec. 18, 1903-Mar. 1, 1914............1.685	" " "
Mar. 1, 1914-May 28, 1921............1.256	" " "
May 28, 1921-Sept. 23, 1922...........2.000	" " "
Sept. 23, 1922-June 17, 1930..........2.206	" " "
June 18, 1930......................2.500	" " "

Since Dec. 18, 1903, Cuban sugars have paid 20 per cent less than the normal rate. (Figures from Farr and Company, *op. cit.*, p. 50, and Tariff Act of 1930, 71st Congress, 2nd Session, H. D., No. 746, p. 46.)

CONSUMPTION PAYING VARIOUS TARIFF RATES IN CERTAIN YEARS [33]

Tariff Rates in Cents per Pound for Raw Sugar 96°	Consumption, Long Tons	Per Cent by Duty Paid		
		Free	Cuba	Full Duty
1919–1920 .... Virgin Islands: free March 31, 1917 Full duty: 1.256¢ Cuba: 1.0048¢	4,084,672	34	52	14
1921–1922 .... May 27, 1921 Full duty: 2.00¢ Cuba: 1.60¢ September 22, 1922 Full duty: 2.206¢ Cuba: 1.7648¢	5,092,758	42	57	1
1927–1928 .... Full duty, 2.206¢ Cuba: 1.7648¢	5,542,636	52	47	1
1930 June 18, 1930 Full duty: 2.50¢ Cuba: 2.00¢				

time Cuba with the advantage of the tariff reduction established in the treaty was able practically to drive all other foreign sugars from the American market.

The favorable position in which Cuban production was placed by the treaty was far from that of a supplier enjoying a free market, however decided the advantage enjoyed over sugars from other countries. The American tariff even with the reduction provided by the reciprocity treaty was by no means low when reckoned to an ad valorem basis, and it stood in sharp contrast to the low rates charged on most

[33] Table compiled from statistics of Willet and Gray quoted in *The American Sugar Refining Company Annual Report, 1928*, p. 21. Sugar testing 96° by the polariscope is the basis on which the tariff charges are reckoned. The per cent of consumption listed as "free" includes domestic production of beet and cane sugars.

of the foodstuffs and raw materials imported from Latin America. In fact, almost from the beginning of the history of the United States tariffs on sugar had been relied upon as a source of revenue and had brought in very high returns with the growth of population and rapid rise in per capita consumption.[34] But the general rates charged were low in comparison to those obtaining in Europe, and especially after the establishment of the reduction on Cuban sugars promised a rapid rise in purchases from the island.

Cuban production showed a remarkable response. Only twice in the colonial period had it ever reached a million tons, and in 1895-6 it had sunk to 212,051 tons. By 1901-2, it had risen again to over a million, almost to the colonial record, and continued to expand under the impulse of the treaty rates. By 1906-7, the total was 1,427,673 long tons and the grindings of the December to June season of 1913-4, just before the outbreak of the World War, brought in 2,597,500 tons.

Under the better guarantee of order in the new régime, local and foreign capital, the latter largely from the United States, had made heavy expenditures in the sugar industry. Equipment was modernized and the center of activity tended to shift from the western provinces to the formerly little exploited eastern end of the island.

During the years of the European war, high prices and the temporary opening of a large market in Europe due to the destruction or immobilization of some of its most important beet sugar producing facilities gave the Cuban industry another great impetus to expansion. Production rose from 2,592,667 long tons in the crop year 1914-5, to 3,971,776 tons in 1918-9—almost four times the yield of 1901-2.

---

[34] Per capita sugar consumption in the United States was 40.7 pounds in 1871-5; in 1896–1900, 62.2 pounds; in 1921-5, 104.4 pounds; in 1925, 114.2 pounds—the record figure. It was 110.1 pounds in 1928. *Statistical Abstract of the United States, 1929* (Washington, 1929), p. 702.

At the latter date, the war was over but the new equipment had not yet produced to capacity. European production was soon put on the way to being reëstablished and the buying power of the world was for the moment high but soon to fall off bringing a sharp reduction in prices. At one time Cuban raw sugar had risen to 22.50 cents per pound, but was quoted after the "crash" at 1.813 cents.[35] Many operators were forced into liquidation and the financial outlook of the industry became anything but encouraging. Still the fields and mills kept on producing great yields of sugar, which in 1924-5 and 1928-9 were reported at over five million long tons.[36] These were quantities far beyond the peace time capacity of the American market to absorb and ones which could not be sold at profitable rates elsewhere.

A high level of production, extended manufacturing capacity, reëstablishment of competition from European beet fields, and decline of the world's buying power—these and other less obvious adverse factors have brought to Cuba the most serious crisis in the history of the sugar industry, a crisis which has affected all activities of the republic. From it have resulted important readjustments in the position of private economic interests and the undertaking by the government of a far-reaching program looking toward the creation of a basis for the national life less dependent on the fortunes of a single industry.

Within the sugar industry itself there has long been a tendency both in Cuba and elsewhere for production to

---

[35] Based on Willet and Gray statistics quoted in Farr and Company, op. cit., p. 41. These prices represent the extreme variations. The yearly fluctuations are much less marked. The wholesale price per pound New York averaged 3.8 cents in 1914. It rose to 7.5 cents in 1919, and to 13.0 cents in 1920 under the influence of the boom. The next year the price was back to 4.7 cents. Yearbook of the Department of Agriculture, 1928 (Washington, 1929), p. 883.

[36] Based on Willet and Gray statistics quoted in Farr and Company, op. cit., p. 16.

pass into the hands of large units. This was true long before the end of the colonial period, but the shift has been accentuated since the independence of Cuba and has been still further emphasized in the years of crisis since the World War. The small inefficient grinding mills, the "trapiches" of colonial days driven by oxen or windmills, cannot compete with the costly but modern machinery which extracts all but a negligible percentage of the sugar-laden juice and works at a fraction of the former cost per unit. Modern sugar making is distinctly a "big business" enterprise.

What the relation of those who produce the sugar cane to the interests which manufacture sugar may come to be is not yet clear and does not seem to have been greatly changed by recent developments. Only a small part of the cane produced is "administration cane" grown by the owners of the mills. The proportion is reported as about 10 per cent. The rest is produced by "colonos" who sell their cane to the "central" under agreements to take their pay in sugar at a certain percentage of the weight of the cane delivered. Up to the present this sort of agreement does not seem to be undergoing modification. "Big business" in manufacture has definite advantages which large units for the growing of cane may not have.

Even the present position of the "colonos," however, is not without some features that have been criticized as undesirable. The location of the land of the "colono" puts some limitation on the market in which his cane can be sold to best advantage and the practice is widespread among cane producers of accepting advances of money during the "dead season" and thus "living on the profits of next year's crop." These are disadvantages, however, which are found in many other agricultural districts and ones which it appears have not been either caused or accentuated by recent developments.

The gravitation toward big units in manufacture brought

about a tendency for the sugar industry to pass into the control of foreigners even before the current crisis. Local capital has been insufficient to set up modern establishments which may cost over a million dollars before a wheel is turned in production. This has meant in Cuba that American interests, the chief investors, have come to control an increasing percentage of the industry. Expansion of this sort was marked during the period when war prices stimulated investment and it has continued in the period of hard times following because many of the weaker mills which borrowed heavily in the boom years have proved unable to weather the deflation period and have passed into the control of American interests.

The developments of recent years have brought a change in the location of the industry which is also not without significance. In Spanish days, sugar was produced in greater proportion in the western provinces. In later years new developments have been chiefly in the east which has been opened up by railroads since Cuba has become independent and the new lands of which give greater yield than those of the longer worked west. It is in this area that American investment has chiefly been made. A map of the more important sugar centrals controlled by American companies in 1929 shows thirty-three in the eastern provinces of Camaguey and Oriente as compared with ten to the westward.[37]

Many calculations have been made of the degree to which Cuban sugar mills have passed into American hands but none are wholly satisfactory though it is beyond doubt that the proportion of American holdings has greatly increased since the winning of Cuban independence and particularly since the postwar deflation period. Before the World War

---

[37] This total of forty-three mills does not represent all the "American controlled" operations but includes the distinctly American interests and represents a larger percentage of the total production than is indicated by their relation to the total number of mills.

it is commonly estimated that over a third of manufacture was in American control. By 1920, some believe that little less than half was in American hands. In current years, estimates run from two-thirds to three-fourths. All figures of this sort are difficult to prove since there is no satisfactory record of the nationality of stock holdings.[38]

Unsatisfactory economic conditions have roused the government of Cuba to consideration of a number of programs looking toward the defense of the sugar industry and the development of other national resources. Attention was first given to the possibility of setting up a control of sugar production in the hope that the low price levels could be raised. The 1925-6 crop was cut down by at least 300,000 tons. Harvesting of the 1926-7 crop was delayed until January 1, 1927, and total production limited to 4,500,000 tons. These measures proving ineffectual, efforts were made without result to form trade agreements with producing groups in other countries looking toward control of the market. A company was formed to control sugar exports. By decree the 1927-8 crop was to be cut to 4,000,000 tons. Some 3,300,000 tons were set aside for sale in the United States and the export company was to sell 600,000 tons elsewhere. This plan also did not end the depression in the industry and governmental restriction of the crop was abandoned by decree in December, 1928, except that the mills were not allowed to start grinding before January 1, 1929. The export sales organization also became inactive.

---

[38] A critical discussion of American holdings is found in Leland Hamilton Jenks, *Our Cuban Colony* (New York, 1928), pp. 281 *et seq*. The list of mills known to be owned by non-American interests also does not give a satisfactory indication of their importance in the industry because of great variation in their production. Most of the larger mills are in American hands. All told there were listed as "active" mills in 1929, 183 establishments of which 162 ground cane in the crop season of 1928-9, but the Central Maria Antonia in Santa Clara which had not ground at all in the previous three years produced only 2,348 bags while the Central Preston produced the enormous quantity of 1,014,425 bags. From statistics published in Farr and Company, *op. cit.*, pp. 92 *et seq*.

Before these attempts to improve conditions had run their course it became evident that a change in the commercial policy of the United States, the chief Cuban market, was imminent which would have a serious bearing on the Cuban industry. Circumstances there in relation to sugar had materially altered since the days when the reciprocity treaty was negotiated.

The growth of holdings in Cuba by Americans in the years following the treaty has made an increasing number of Americans interested in the prosperity of the island. These groups have naturally wished to have low rates of tariff on imported Cuban sugars. On the other hand, there have been developing two groups within the United States which have been interested, in the one case, in the development of a "domestic" sugar industry and, in the other, in the establishment of sugar production in the Caribbean and Pacific territories now under the American flag. The conflicting ambitions of these various groups have greatly modified the influences which are active in shaping the sugar policy of the United States.

At the time when the treaty of 1903 was negotiated, the United States had no important domestic sugar production. The supplies available for consumption were somewhat less than 3,000,000 short tons per year.[39] To this total, the "domestic" cane industry contributed about 350,000 tons and it was not prosperous. In later years, it has not had a healthy growth. It now tends to emphasize the production of sugar or molasses according to the condition of the market and in some years produces less than 100,000 tons.[40] Those who thought that this industry would prove of declin-

---

[39] They averaged for 1901-5, 2,875,638 short tons. These figures and those following are from *Statistical Abstract of the United States, 1929,* pp. 702 *et seq.,* and *Yearbook of the Department of Agriculture, 1928,* pp. 876 *et seq.*

[40] In 1926 the production was 44,000 tons.

ing importance in national supply have had their belief supported by events.

On the other hand, there was already in existence in 1903 an "infant" beet sugar industry which under the stimulus of special legislation showed a tendency to increase its yield. By 1906-10, it was producing more than the unprosperous "domestic" cane fields. In current years, it markets an average of about 1,000,000 tons. It is to a large extent confined to a limited number of districts, is rather irregular in annual yield, and has been criticized because it is alleged that even with the tariff protection which it enjoys it has had to depend to a large extent on imported labor, largely in recent years Mexicans, to maintain even the present level of production. The industry has come to furnish, however, somewhat less than a sixth of the sugar available for consumption in the average year in the United States and its defenders have a considerable influence in shaping the national sugar policy.

But another factor of increasing contribution to the national sugar supply is the industry in the outlying territories, Hawaii, Porto Rico, and the Philippine Islands. While the raisers of cane sugar in these areas do not have full representation in Congress and the permanent position of the Philippine Islands in relation to continental United States still remains undefined, the fact that the production is one "under the national flag" has doubtless an influence in determining the attitude of Congress toward it. In addition, the circumstances that import of these sugars has been made free of tariff charges in the United States has undoubtedly stimulated production. The yield in all three areas has risen rapidly from an average of 598,000 short tons in 1901-5 to 2,514,400 short tons in 1929-30.[41] While the areas available for further expansion in Porto Rico and

---

[41] Estimates of Willet and Gray in *The American Sugar Refining Company Annual Report, 1929* (New York, 1930), p. 15.

Hawaii are limited those in the Philippine Islands are of great extent. All but a small fraction of the exports from the insular areas is imported into the United States. In 1928, the total reached 2,051,756 short tons or little short of one-third of the amount available for consumption for the year. In fact, so large are Philippine possibilities of production that some of the domestic cane and beet producers believe that there as much as in Cuba lies the great "danger" for the "domestic" industry. However that may be, in current years the "territorial" or "colonial" contribution to the sugar supply of the United States is another new element contributing to shaping the national sugar policy in a way less favorable to low rates on Cuban sugar.

Though there is not now any concerted move to modify the terms of the treaty of 1903, the basic tariff rates upon which the 20 per cent preference to Cuban sugar is calculated have been increased under the last three tariffs of the United States, with the result that Cuban sugars entering the United States have had to work against an increasing differential as compared to those produced under the American flag.

Taken as a whole, the outlook has increasingly become one prompting a consideration of means by which the economic basis of Cuban life may be modified through government assistance. Aside from the general disadvantage of dependence on a single crop, a move for diversification is especially justified in a country depending so greatly on sugar production because of the highly seasonal character of the industry in Cuba.

From December to June during the dry season, activity is at its height; there is a scarcity of labor; wages are, for the Caribbean region, very high; the whole country gives the impression of a factory run at high speed. Then comes the "dead" season. Preparation for the next crop proceeds leisurely. There is a great deal of idleness or semiemployment throughout the country. Such a condition would be less keenly felt in a region with a variety of industries, but these Cuba does not have with the result that, taking the year as a whole, the man power of the republic is very unevenly and very inefficiently used.

The government program for diversification of the life of Cuba as announced by President Machado looks toward the creation of a nation of eight or ten million people. A comprehensive road-building program has already been undertaken and the construction of a paved national highway from one end of the island to the other is already approaching completion. From the trunkline, branch roads are to be built, thus opening up the back country the development of which has heretofore been retarded by lack of adequate communication facilities.

There are under way a number of studies of possible improvements in production and marketing of crops already established, such as tobacco, and of crops which are either new or which have lost their former importance, such as coffee and rice. Cultivation of off-season vegetables and fruits is to be encouraged as are also dairying and livestock raising.

Local industries are also to be encouraged, especially the lighter transforming industries which do not require large amounts of power, for Cuba has no source of cheap industrial fuel. To this end the new tariff of Cuba has given greater protection to local industries already established and to others the development of which it is hoped to encourage. Though the tariff has not been in force long enough to show what will be its effect a number of new enterprises have been set up including such lines as dairying, canning factories, textile mills, and paper and paint factories. Tobacco manufacture, production of leather goods, straw manufactures, ready-made clothing, furniture, rope, soaps, perfumes have been longer established and have demonstrated the industrial aptitudes of the local population.

It is still too soon to judge the success of these efforts, but it is clear that if they prove fruitful they will bring a much to be desired stability to Cuban economic conditions. A one-crop economy of a highly seasonal character, dependent in large degree on special favors granted in a single market, is an unsound basis for the national life. The outlet in the American market has been of great economic advantage to Cuba, but that it has been an advantage not without limitations has been amply demonstrated. By helping to keep attention on the sugar industry it accentuated the monoculture which was already characteristic of the island and thus emphasized the importance of what was at the same time the greatest and the weakest feature of the national economy. Cubans are apt to blame the depression through which their country is now passing on the expansion of the sugar industry which was encouraged by the high price levels of the World War. It is doubtless true that the more acute phases of the crisis are the result of the too optimistic hopes which that period raised, but the treaty relation itself had, even before the war, brought the industry to a position where it would soon have had to begin to seek markets elsewhere than in the United States. In addition, the growth of sugar-producing industries within United States territory has changed the prospects of the Cuban industry.

It seems clear that the United States will not again take from Cuba so large a percentage of Cuban sugar as was taken in the period immediately following the treaty of 1903. Possibly even the percentage of American consumption supplied from Cuba may fall, though in this there is not as yet a definite trend observable, and Cuba will, it appears, continue to be practically the only foreign source of supply for the American market.

Adjustment of industry to new standards in Cuba will

be slow and not without hardships, particularly, as in all such cases, for the high-cost producers, but as the years pass it seems probable that sugar may form a less significant proportion of Cuban exports.[42]   Certainly it is desirable that it should do so.   From a national point of view diversification of industries has long been one of the greatest of the island's needs.   If it can be brought about, there can be no doubt that the well-being of future generations of Cubans will rest on a much sounder basis than that of the present or of any time in the past.

Adjustment to new conditions is not, indeed, only a Cuban problem nor one involving the sugar industry alone.   It is the great problem which lies ahead for all the areas of the Caribbean and a problem upon the solution of which depends the prosperity and happiness of its peoples and the stability of its governments.

---

[42] In the period 1927-8, exports of sugar made up 84.6 per cent of the total value of shipments from Cuba.

CHAPTER VI

COFFEE

THREE vegetable products which are the bases of widely used beverages find their way into international trade—coffee, tea, and cacao. Their amounts and values show great variations from year to year, but a rough average of about three billion pounds of coffee worth $500,000,000 are exported for consumption every twelve months, compared with 800,000,000 pounds of tea worth $225,000,000 and 1,125,000,000 pounds of cacao worth $90,000,000—the latter only in part used as the base of a beverage. All of these crops are produced in communities which to a great degree rely upon them for their prosperity. All are crops which require years for new plantings to come into bearing thus making the standard of life in the communities which raise them even more dependent on their success than is the case where a shift of activity among annual crops is possible.

In the production of coffee, the most important of the group in international trade, America is now far in the lead, though coffee culture originated and long had its chief seat in the old world. Few lines of economic production show as interesting changes in the areas of cultivation and in markets. The berry is believed to have had its origin in Africa, in Abyssinia. It was found early in Arabia and is alleged first to have come into general use in Persia.

It made its way into Europe apparently by way of Arabia early in the seventeenth century through Venetian traders, though there is some reason to believe that it may have been known as a curiosity in Italy before the end of the fifteen hundreds. The spread of its use westward and northward is not clearly recorded. In the period 1650-1750, coffeehouses became common in Italy, and the same period saw the adoption of the beverage in France. Captain John Smith before coming to America had made the acquaintance of the beverage, but it was, it is alleged, only in 1650 that the first English coffeehouse opened its doors. Dutch traders brought Mocha coffee home from their voyages to the Near East, as early as 1616, and commercial shipments began in 1640. About 1670, coffee-drinking was introduced into Germany. The first coffeehouse in the country was established by an Englishman at Hamburg in 1679-80. The spread of the use of the beverage was irregular and limited because of its high cost, but by 1750 it had won its way to favor in all of the leading European nations.[1]

The generally accepted story of the introduction of coffee into America is that De Clieux, a Norman noble, carried a plant grown in the Botanical Garden of Paris to Martinique in 1723. Coffee culture spread rapidly in the island and thence, so the story goes, to Santo Domingo, Guadeloupe, Porto Rico, Cuba, and the mainland.[2] The first harvest of coffee from De Clieux's plant occurred in 1726. By 1777, there were 18,791,680 coffee trees in Martinique.

There are many other claims to the honor of having introduced coffee to the new world, some of them disputing the priority of De Clieux. Cultivation is said to have started in Haiti and Santo Domingo as early as 1715, but hardier plants were brought in from Martinique later. The Dutch claim to have introduced coffee to Surinam in 1718, and shipments to the Netherlands are reported beginning in

---

[1] The dates given above are summarized from the discussions in William H. Ukers, *All about Coffee* (New York, 1922). There are many conflicting claims centering about the introduction and spread of the trade. Cacao is reported to have been introduced into Europe from America by the Spanish as early as 1528 while tea was a later arrival, reaching Europe through Dutch traders in 1610. *Ibid.,* p. 25.

[2] Abraham Martinez, *Colombia Yearbook, 1927* (New York, 1928), pp. 135-6, and Ukers, *op. cit.,* p. 7.

1723. In that year the first plantation in Brazil was started at Pará with plants from Guiana but the venture was not a success.[3]

Leadership in American production after the period of introduction was first probably on the mainland in what are now the Guianas and then in the West Indies. It later passed definitely to Brazil, especially to the São Paulo region. Meanwhile, however, the production in the Caribbean area and Mexico has also shown remarkable increase and new world countries now produce close to 90 per cent of the world crop, which in 1928-9 reached a total of 22,085,000 bags of 132 pounds each.[4]

In practically all of the tropic areas of America, coffee is grown to some extent, but two regions stand out as the great producers, Brazil producing about two-thirds of the world's crop and the countries grouped around the Carib-

---

[3] The spread of coffee in the new world is to some degree indicated by the dates of the introduction of the crop, though the developments subsequent to these dates often showed marked irregularity especially in Brazil. Though introduced in the north in 1723 there were only 17,000 trees in Para by 1748, and export from Para is reported only in 1770. By this time cultivation was spreading into the State of Rio de Janeiro from an independent importation from Goa by the Portuguese, but export thence is not reported until 1800. Large crops were gathered in the Rio region only in 1842-43. Thereafter Brazilian expansion in the industry was steady. Some of the chief dates marking the spread of coffee culture follow:

1750–60	The plant was introduced into Guatemala. Intensive cultivation did not begin until about 1875 after which steady advance occurred.	1779	It is reported that Don Francisco Xavier Navarro introduced coffee into Costa Rica from Cuba.
1752	Intensive efforts in cultivation were made in Brazil, in Amazonas and Pará.	1784	The industry was started in Venezuela with seed from Martinique by a priest, José Antonio Mohedano.
1755	Cultivation began in Porto Rico.	1790	Cultivation began in Mexico with West Indian seed.
1760	João Alberto Costello Branco brought coffee to Rio de Janeiro from Goa.	1852	Cultivation began in Salvador with Cuban plants but was slow to develop. The first plantations date from 1876.

These dates are taken from Ukers, *op. cit.*

[4] As reported by the New York Coffee and Sugar Exchange, Inc., C. B. Stroud, Supt., *Supplement* (n. p., n. d.). The average, 1924-8, was 23,179,-000 bags. Reported by the Tropical Products Section, Foodstuffs Division, Bureau of Foreign and Domestic Commerce, Washington, 1930.

bean producing more than a quarter of the total. This latter area tends to contribute an increasing share. In 1900, Rio and Santos coffees accounted for 65.7 per cent of the world crop,[5] in 1909-13 for 69.7 per cent but in 1919-23 for only 62.4 per cent, and in 1930 only 53.5 per cent. Meanwhile the Caribbean shipments, which were 22.2 per cent of the world trade in coffee in 1909-13, were 26.0 per cent in 1919-23 and 25.4 in 1928.

Leadership in production in the Caribbean area no longer rests with the island units but with the north coast of South

PER CENT OF WORLD TRADE IN COFFEE SUPPLIED BY CHIEF AMERICAN AREAS [6]

Country	Average, 1909-13	Average, 1919-23	1928
Caribbean region			
Colombia	4.3	9.1	11.0
Venezuela	4.6	4.4	2.6
Guatemala	3.7	3.5	3.0
Salvador	2.6	3.0	3.6
Haiti	2.7	2.6	2.3
Costa Rica	1.2	1.2	1.2
Nicaragua	.9	.9	1.2
Porto Rico [1]	1.8	.9	.0
Jamaica	.3	.3	.2
Dominican Republic ...	.1	.1	.3
TOTAL Caribbean	22.2	26.0	25.4
Brazil	69.7	62.4	57.8

[1] Fall of yield in 1928 due to effects of the hurricane of that year.

America and the Pacific coast region of Central America. The industry in both these regions has come into real importance only since the middle of the last century. Indeed

[5] Tabulation of the New York Coffee and Sugar Exchange, Inc., *Supplement*.

[6] The figures from 1909-13 and 1919-23 are from M. L. Bynum, *International Trade in Coffee*, U. S. Department of Commerce, Trade Promotion Series, No. 37 (Washington, 1926), p. 3. The figures for 1928 are from information supplied by the Tropical Products Section, Foodstuffs Division, Bureau of Foreign and Domestic Commerce, Washington.

the large-scale production of all American areas is much more
recent than is often popularly supposed and is a development scarcely more than two generations old. The increased
proportion of the coffee entering world trade from American
countries is indicated below.

Colombia, the leading north coast producer, had an export
in the decade 1852-3 to 1861-2 averaging only 940,000
pounds. By 1906, a total of 80,000,000 pounds was
reached, by 1918, 152,076,000, and by 1928, 351,000,000.[7]

The growth in exports in the north coast areas in recent
years is indicated in the following table:

COFFEE EXPORTS FROM THE NORTH COAST OF SOUTH AMERICA
(In pounds) [8]

	1900	1908	1917	1928
Colombia	47,000,000 [1]	79,750,000	150,834,000	351,000,000
Guiana				
British	......	88,700	267,500	513,100 (1924)
Dutch	424,000	310,000	1,600,000	4,908,700 (1924)
French	......	1,100	900	400
Venezuela	86,950,000 [2]	111,326,000 (1909-13) [3]	88,155,000 (1914-18) [4]	112,579,000 [5]

1 Unofficial 1895.
2 1904-5.
3 *Commerce Yearbook, 1926,* Vol. II, p. 611.
4 Exports in these years were cut down by the European War. In the following
year they were 179,414,815 pounds.
5 1927.

Central America has come into importance as a coffee
region even more recently than the north coast of South
America. Costa Rica had known coffee since 1779 and by
1845 it exported 7,823,000 pounds—then leading even
Colombia by a wide margin. Later, coffee began to be important in what are now the chief producing countries of
the group, Salvador and Guatemala. It was introduced into

7 Figures previous to 1928 from Ukers, *op. cit.,* p. 278. For 1928 from
Commerce Yearbook, 1929 (Washington, 1929), Vol. II, p. 172.
8 Compiled from Ukers, *op. cit.,* for figures for 1917 and previous. **For**
later years from *Commerce Yearbook, 1929,* Vol. II, and Bynum, *op. cit.*

Salvador in 1852 and rapidly became a popular crop. In Guatemala and Nicaragua, it came to importance only between 1860 and 1870. By 1912, the total export of the group reached 188,748,000 pounds, of which about three-fourths came in about equal parts from Salvador and Guatemala.[9] Since that date, Costa Rica, which then produced about one-seventh of the total exported, has continued to have an almost stable proportion of the total. Salvador and Guatemala have continued to increase their yields and now market about 70 per cent of the crop exported. Nicaragua has also markedly increased its yield.

COFFEE EXPORTS FROM CENTRAL AMERICA [10]
(*In pounds*)

Country	1912	1927 or 1927-8
Costa Rica	26,984,569	45,000,000
Guatemala (green and in the shell for 1927-8) ...	76,242,064	98,669,000
Honduras	699,426	5,140,550
Nicaragua	13,588,753	39,800,000
Salvador	71,362,620	117,878,000
TOTAL	188,877,432	306,667,350

Besides the production in the Caribbean areas already discussed a lesser amount comes from the islands which at one time were the greatest suppliers. The economic position of the crop there has become less favorable than it was formerly, due to a number of causes such as the growth of competing industries, local political conditions, and the tariffs applied in some consuming areas to coffees formerly enjoying better rates. Prospect for great increases in these

[9] Compiled from detailed tables for 1912-23 for the exports of the five republics as given in the *Revista de agricultura* (San Salvador, June, 1925), and published in the *Pequeño Atlas, Libreria salesiana* (San Salvador, (n. d.).

[10] Figures for 1912 calculated from tables published by the *Revista de agricultura* as published in the *Pequeño Atlas, Libreria salesiana*. For 1927 and 1927-8, the figures are from *Commerce Yearbook, 1929*, Vol. II.

regions is not good. Cuba, once a producer, now imports
large amounts of coffee. Haiti has no organized coffee plantations, and the grading and marketing system has been
poor.[11] Porto Rican production tends to decline. Jamaican
coffee lands are limited and some are approaching exhaustion. The French islands hold no great promise of increased
production, in fact Martinique, an important producer in
the early period of the American coffee industry, is now on
balance an importing area. Dominican exports show
marked irregularity, but have increased fairly steadily over
the period since 1913. Taken as a whole, however, the
West Indies have apparently passed their high point as
contributors to the world's coffee trade.

COFFEE EXPORTS FROM CERTAIN WEST INDIAN REGIONS [12]
(*In Pounds*)

Region	In Given Years	1928
Dominican Republic	1,361,666 (1920)	10,014,000
Guadeloupe	2,144,855 (1918)	1,673,953
Haiti	61,970,094 (1920)	16,324,000
Jamaica	8,246,672 (1919)	8,770,000
Martinique	10,358 (1918)	26,250
Porto Rico	32,776,754	7,837,800
Trinidad and Tobago	73,201 (1920)	265,000

Through peculiarities of soil, elevation, climate, treatment, and stock, the product of the various coffee producing areas has come to have characteristics which have

[11] *Seventh Annual Report of the American High Commissioner at Port
au Prince, Haiti, 1928* (Washington, 1929), p. 9.

[12] Figures for 1920 and previous years from Ukers, *op. cit.*, p. 276.
Other figures from *Commerce Yearbook, 1929*, Vol. II, except Porto Rico
for which see *Twenty-ninth Annual Report of the Governor of Porto
Rico*, Honorable Horace M. Towner (San Juan, 1929), p. 31. The figure
for Porto Rico in 1928 was very low on account of the damage done by
the hurricane of that year. Production has shown a steady decline since
1914. Exports are usually over 20,000,000 pounds. Cuba produces some
coffee but on balance imports over twenty million pounds a year in current years. The crop in Haiti in 1928 was exceptional. It usually runs
about 60,000,000 pounds.

led to their classification by the trade as "Brazils" and "mild coffees." The latter term, in fact, includes all coffees other than Brazils although what are called mild coffees include some "hard" or "strong" grades. Custom, available transportation facilities, commercial connections, and the peculiar qualities of crops from certain localities have influenced the markets for certain portions of the world yield. The trade channels which have thus developed are not unchanging, in fact; in recent years they have in some instances shown marked modification, but they continue to have an appreciable influence on the markets for Caribbean coffee.

Curious cross currents have developed in the trade. Some of these were at least temporarily modified by the conditions arising during the World War which shifted a greater percentage of the shipments of the mild Caribbean coffees to the United States. In the years following, the exchanges have in a number of cases not recovered their former courses, though the proportions going in various directions show such irregularity in recent years that it is not yet certain to what degree the traditional markets have been changed.

Among the customary preferences which still show themselves are those in favor of the Guatemalan product in Germany and England and of Nicaraguan coffee in France, though in recent years American purchases have become an increasing factor in both countries. In Salvador, the greater part of the exports goes to Europe especially Germany, Switzerland, France, and the Netherlands. In 1928, however, the United States had become the largest purchaser after Germany. Costa Rican coffee finds an appreciative market in Great Britain and France.

In the islands the European colonial areas ship their coffee chiefly to the mother countries and their dominions. Porto Rican coffees find an outlet mainly in Cuba and

Spain, though in 1928 over one-third went to the United States. France is far the most important buyer of Haitian coffees taking in some years as much as three-fourths of the total export. The best purchasers in the Dominican republic in recent years have been Cuba, the United States, France, and Italy, with no country taking a definite leadership.

Colombian coffee, which has advanced in amount to a greater extent than that of any other Caribbean area and is now half of that exported from the region, has an increasing popularity in the United States.[13] On the other hand, only about half of Venezuelan exports reach the United States and in some recent years, Cuba, Spain, and France have been heavy purchasers.

The changes in the coffee trade of the Caribbean areas can be appreciated by a study of the demands of the chief market. The United States is the greatest coffee-consuming nation of the world and has been taking an increasing share of the total. In the five-year period before the World War, 1909-13, it consumed an average of 6,828,000 bags, or 38.5 per cent of that entering world trade, while 51.1 per cent went to European countries. Consumption thereafter grew rapidly. In 1919-23, the consumption in the United States was 9,682,000 bags, or 48.8 per cent of the total, and this proportion continues to be about that taken in later years, though with a tendency toward increase. In 1928-9, the arrivals in the United States were 10,477,179 bags, while all Europe took 9,795,490.[14] The United States was thus taking steadily increasing amounts and about half of the total offerings. Coffee is in fact the greatest foodstuff im-

13 "Tabular Guide to Economic Conditions, Colombia," *Commerce Reports,* September 10, 1928. The shares of coffee exports as given for other countries in these paragraphs are drawn from a series of tabulations similar to the above and from *Commerce Yearbook, 1929,* Vol. II. See also the annual reports of the Governor of Porto Rico, and Bynum, *op. cit.,* for comprehensive statistics.

14 New York Coffee and Sugar Exchange, Inc., *Supplement.*

port of the United States, reaching a value not far from $300,000,000 per year.

Along with this development in consumption has gone a change in the origin of supplies of far-reaching significance. The American purchases show a tendency to shift to the Caribbean area. In 1909, 14.4 per cent of the purchases, by quantities, were made in northern South America and

UNITED STATES IMPORTS OF CARIBBEAN AND MEXICAN COFFEE [15]
(*In thousands of pounds—Years Ending June 30*)

Country	1900	1913	1927	1928	1929
British Honduras	21	14	33	5	.....
Costa Rica	17,319	1,474	3,368	4,509	4,551
Guatemala	17,528	18,544	27,825	26,514	21,549
Honduras	580	239	1,642	2,201	1,033
Nicaragua	1,748	2,915	2,673	8,405	9,065
Salvador	6,617	8,756	5,121	12,321	16,397
Mexico	35,328	26,121	22,559	38,876	31,266
Cuba	30	74	9	.....	61
Netherlands West Indies	36	308	36	112	59
French West Indies.....	.....	.....	3	105	.....
Haiti	5,349	2,264	1,428	1,556	867
Dominican Republic ...	480	513	1,442	2,690	2,695
Colombia	20,050	89,685	252,173	264,213	311,518
Dutch Guiana (Surinam)	410	281	11	279	221
French Guiana	.....	.....	.....	46	.....
Venezuela	42,444	49,671	47,765	52,411	65,317
Panama	.....	201	4,655	6,862	698
British West Indies.....	3,542	979	845	624	867
TOTAL	151,482	202,039	371,588	421,737	466,165

Central America. By 1913, 19.7 per cent, or almost a fifth of the American supply, came from these areas, and under the conditions prevailing during and after the World War the percentage rose still higher, reaching 35 in 1918. Subsequently, with the economic reëstablishment of European countries, their purchases increased, but the share of

[15] Data from U. S. Department of Commerce, Bureau of Foreign and Domestic Commerce, *Foreign Commerce and Navigation of the United States,* for respective years.

American demand supplied from the Caribbean still stood at 31.4 per cent in 1929.

Meanwhile the percentage drawn from Bazil has fallen. It was 80.8 in 1909. It declined to a low point of 57 in 1918, after which it rose to 67.9 in 1925. It was 64 in 1929.[16] Though purchases from the Caribbean may not continue proportionally at as high a rate as at present it seems probable that the United States will be a more important factor in the industry there than was the case before the war.

This is especially true in Colombia, now the second coffee producer of the world. As late as 1906, her exports were only about 84,000,000 pounds, of which the United States took 46,000,000 pounds or roughly 55.3 per cent.[17] In 1928, the exports were 351,000,000 pounds, of which the United States took 264,213,000 pounds, or about 75 per cent. In 1929, the American purchases rose to 311,518,-400 pounds.

In the Central American area, the export of coffee rose from 210,137,382 pounds in 1913 [18] to 306,667,350 pounds in 1928.[19] In the same period United States purchases there rose from 31,929,245 pounds, or 17.1 per cent, to 53,952,717 pounds. This was 17.6 per cent of the total shipments.[20]

---

[16] These figures are compiled from the statistics in Bynum, *op. cit.*, and from *Foreign Commerce and Navigation of the United States* for the years cited.

[17] *Foreign Commerce and Navigation of the United States for the Year Ending June 30, 1907* (Washington, 1908), p. 207. The figures of Colombian coffee experts, especially for the early years, are not exact because much was exported through Venezuela, but the general course of development is as indicated. About 6 per cent, it is estimated, went through Venezuela in 1928. Ukers, *op. cit.*, p. 278, and *Commerce Yearbook, 1929*, Vol. II, p. 176.

[18] This figure compiled from figures published in the *Revista de agricultura* (San Salvador, June, 1925).

[19] *Commerce Yearbook, 1929*, Vol. II.

[20] The purchases in the United States rose to exceptional heights during the World War. They later fell in relative importance as European markets became reëstablished.

The United States purchases were almost 80,000,000 pounds in 1929.

Taken as a whole, the Caribbean coffees have now an established market in the United States. It is one which has risen from 151,000,000 pounds in 1900 to 466,165,-000 in 1929.

After the United States, the European countries are the most important markets for coffee. Before the war Germany was the heaviest European buyer, but in the years following France took the lead followed by Germany, Italy, Sweden, Belgium, and the Netherlands. All of the major buyers now take more coffee than before the war, and their demands on Caribbean supplies have shown a tendency to increase.

The prospects for continuance and increase of coffee imports can be judged by considering the population of the chief markets and the tendencies in per capita consumption. From both these points of view the United States promises to continue to be the greatest of coffee markets and any tendency to prefer the grades produced in a certain region will have an important influence on the location and prosperity of its industry. This is of special significance for the Caribbean countries, for if the shift toward preference for milder coffees continues American purchases there may continue to increase in greater proportion than in other areas.

Already the United States is far the greatest coffee consuming nation and ranks high in consumption per capita. The people of Scandinavian countries are individually the greatest coffee drinkers taking in recent years sometimes as much as fifteen pounds per capita. The average American, however, has steadily increased his demands, especially since the war. In 1911-5, the net imports of coffee per capita were 9.65 pounds. In 1921-5 they were 11.67 pounds and in 1927, 11.97. Evidently this rapid increase is one of the most promising factors in the outlook of those supplying the market.

It has been pointed out that the recent increase in coffee consumption in the United States has occurred during the years since the adoption of the amendment to the constitution affecting the sale of alcoholic beverages and that the growth of demand for Caribbean coffees containing a higher percentage of the excitant caffein than do "Brazils" has come in the same period. Whether these facts have any real relation is at least doubtful. The people of the United States were already great users of coffee before the war, and the per capita consumption even then showed an upward tendency. The prosperity of the postwar period may in itself be sufficient reason for the increased demands. The same influence may have contributed to the appreciation of the special qualities of the higher priced milder coffees. These seem sufficient explanations especially since coffee consumption is growing in the other major markets irrespective of whether they have restricted the sale of alcoholic beverages or not.

A group of countries in which coffee consumption has never had the importance which might be expected is the United Kingdom, Australia, Canada, and New Zealand, in which purchases are regularly much less than a pound per capita, except in Canada which takes over two pounds per inhabitant. These are, except for the tea producing areas, the great tea drinking nations of the world, and with the exception of Canada they do not promise soon to become of markedly greater importance for coffee producing regions.

From one point of view the coffee industry of the Caribbean has an importance far greater than is indicated by the value of the export shipments. Coffee is the only one of the major staples of the region which is in major part a product due to local initiative. The crop is raised by

owners of comparatively small plantations and the profits
remain to a large extent in the country where they are made.
There are qualifications to all of these statements. In Colombia there are some large plantations, though none as
large as the greater Brazilian enterprises. The large exports
from this country come from plantations yielding as a rule
not more than thirty-five to fifty bags per year. In many
cases the financing of production depends in large degree
on foreign capital, as for example in Guatemala where German influence continues to be important. In many cases,
too, native producers if they are prosperous tend to spend
their profits abroad so that the effect of their activities on
the economic position of the country is similar to what it
would be if they were foreigners.

Taken in the large, however, it is true that the coffee
industry is the most widely spread, geographically and in
ownership, of any of the major lines of activity contributing
to foreign trade and has for this reason a special interest
for the local population. In most countries of the region
coffee enterprises seem likely to continue relatively small.
The character of the lands planted contributes to make large
plantations unlikely in some areas, and the lack of immigration and the characteristics of the local labor supply also, it
appears, put individual enterprise at an advantage.

The rise in Caribbean exports to the United States, also,
is important not only because of the increase in economic
strength in the local units which it in fact reflects, but because of its influence upon local opinion as to the value of
trade with the United States. Due to the relatively large
ownership of the coffee plantations by resident citizens,
public opinion is favorably disposed toward trade with a
country which increases its coffee purchases.

Official opinion in some of the republics also tends to
be well disposed toward countries which are heavy coffee
purchasers because of the connection, direct and indirect,

between the coffee industry and public finance. If the crops and prices are good, the local tax yield rises, export taxes, if they exist, increase in amount and large purchases of goods from abroad come to be reflected in greater revenue from import taxes. The income from the expenditures of the people in other lines of commerce from which the government obtains support, tends to rise.

The relation of the governments to all the staple industries of the Caribbean has peculiar phases. In the case of sugar the conditions of the world market do not allow the imposition of heavy export taxes, because in an oversupplied market such taxes would seriously discourage production. In the case of fruit exports also, export taxes have been kept low—but not in this case because the market is, as yet, at least, oversupplied. An attempt by one government to tax fruit exports heavily would tend to induce the enterprises to shift their activities to other areas in which taxation was less heavy. In the cases of the coffee and petroleum industries, however, the governments of a number of the Caribbean countries have felt that the industries can be made to contribute directly to public income and have succeeded in collecting important parts of their total receipts from them.

Practice shows a wide variety in the revenue laws applied to coffee. From some of the colonial areas exports do not bear special taxes though in some this is not the case and in a number of the republics coffee shipments pay export taxes ranging up to two dollars gold per one hundred kilos. Guatemala and Salvador, for example, have a very important income from this industry.[21]

The interest which coffee has for the people and govern-

---

[21] In a revenue of $12,411,182 in 1927, Guatemala received $1,865,103 from the coffee export tax. In Salvador in the same year the total income was $10,257,245 to which export taxes, chiefly in coffee, contributed $965,546. As of February 1, 1927, export taxes on coffee were levied in the French West Indies, French Guiana, British Guiana, Dominica, Mont-

ments in the Caribbean is much more widespread than that of any other of the great staples, but it is not generalized over the entire region. Coffee has lost in relative importance in the West Indies except perhaps in Haiti and seems likely to continue to do so. It has gained in the continental areas and in some will continue to do so. Even there, however, it affects as a rule—Guatemala and Salvador are at least partial exceptions—certain districts rather than the people as a whole.

In none of the Caribbean areas is the position of the coffee industry wholly satisfactory. In the West Indies the conditions which have developed would be acceptable if the relative decline in the importance of coffee were a reflection of the growth of other supplemental industries which broadened the economic foundation of the communities. But this is not always the case. The decline of coffee production has too often meant only a decline of one crop while another already established has increased, thus in some areas emphasizing dependence on a few lines of economic production. This is what has occurred in Cuba and Porto Rico. On the mainland, too, increase of coffee culture tends, in the areas of greatest yield, merely to emphasize an already prevailing monoculture.

While Caribbean coffee production has definite advantages from a public point of view as compared to that of sugar, fruits, and oil, it has under existing conditions a peculiar weakness. Prosperity of the industry as in the cases of sugar and oil is affected by a tendency for supply to outrun demand and in many of the producing areas by wide variation in yield in successive years. The overplanting which may flood the market is the more serious because coffee is not an annual crop, with the result that once the

serrat, the Dominican Republic, Haiti, Guatemala, Nicaragua, and Salvador. Florence K. Ioannou and Roberta P. Wakefield, *Export Duties of the World,* U. S. Department of Commerce, Bureau of Foreign and Domestic Commerce, Foreign Tariff Series, No. 42 (Washington, 1927).

capital is invested the owner must continue to raise coffee over a fairly long period to get back his money. The variations in yield from year to year also increase the producer's risk. These circumstances have led Brazil, which has produced roughly two-thirds of the world's coffee, to set up in the period since 1906 various "valorization" schemes to control price through influencing the amount of coffee offered on the market and to level off the highs and lows in prices that are caused by poor and bumper crops. While the Brazilian and mild coffees do not supply exactly the same market they are competitors to a degree which makes any control of this sort have a very real effect on both classes of product.

On the whole the Brazilian coffee control, even if it has applied to only a portion of the crop, has had a very considerable success, though one due to accidental circumstances rather than the measures taken by official authority. There is no doubt that all other coffee producing countries profited by the high price levels which the control helped to establish, without having to share the responsibilities of its financing. But a power to control prices tempts those who exercise it to abuse, and it is clear that prices were arbitrarily raised beyond what they would have been if stabilization were all that was attempted. The result was regularly stimulation of production and approach of a crisis avoided by exceptional circumstances which saved the price control from disaster. Bad crops, frosts, and revival of postwar buying took off threatening crop carry-overs.

But equal good fortune was not met in the crisis of 1929. Under influence of the control, coffee rose to peak prices in 1925, thereafter to decline irregularly to a crash in October, 1929. Brazilian coffees led the advance, but the "milds" followed with a lag of from three to five months. The uncertainty of the market was caused primarily by inability of dealers to find out what were the quantities of coffee stored by the authorities in the warehouses of Brazil. A series of favorable crops preceding 1929 brought the conviction that these withheld stocks were of very large amounts. The bumper crop of 1928 was, after long delay, accepted by Brazilian authorities to have reached 28,000,000 bags. The world consumption is estimated at 22,000,000 bags. Meanwhile coffee produced outside Brazil, which in previous years totaled less than 6,000,000 bags, had been increased under the stimulus of high prices to 9,000,000 bags. The coffee trade under these conditions became convinced that the price levels were unjustified, and at the end of 1929 prevailing quotations had declined from 30 to 35 per cent compared to those of a few months previous.[22]

The repercussion on economic conditions in the Caribbean was far-reaching. The bright outlook and high degree of activity which had prevailed in the coffee regions abruptly came to an end. Colombia, Venezuela, Haiti, the Dominican Republic, and all of Central America, except Honduras, faced a period of hard times the duration of which depended primarily neither on conditions within their own borders nor in the countries where their coffee crops find their markets. If they had previously enjoyed the benefits of the "valorization" activity without its responsibilities, they were not to be so fortunate as to escape the disadvantages of the crisis which it created. Recent history has furnished no example more striking of the economic weakness of monoculture countries and of the dangers which attend efforts to control the prices of growing crops.

---

[22] See discussion by George J. Eder, *Commerce Reports*, Jan. 6, 1930.

CHAPTER VII

THE SHIFTING FRUIT TRADE

WE live in a century in which America is one of the leading factors in both the production and consumption of foodstuffs and find it difficult to realize the extent to which the new world lacked our staple articles of diet at the time of its discovery. When Columbus and his conqueror successors skirted the coasts and made their expeditions inland, they found none of our common domestic animals and none of our staple small grains. Wheat, rye, barley, oats—all these were first planted in the new world by Europeans or were accidentally scattered on the ground from the fodder which had been brought to sustain their animals. Rice had its origin in India. Attempts were made unsuccessfully to introduce it into Virginia in 1647, but at the end of the century—in 1694—its cultivation was established in South Carolina. Several varieties of beans, including kidney and navy beans, are now recognized to be indigenous to tropical America but they had no general use at the time of the discovery. Garbanzos, popularly associated with Mexico and Caribbean countries, soy beans, broad beans, velvet beans, peas, and cow-peas, however, are all old world products.

Nearly all fruits common to our diet also came from the old world. From Asia apples were introduced in prehistoric times to western Europe and from there were brought to the new world at a very early date. Grapes of the sorts with which they were familiar were introduced by the early settlers from Europe but without marked success. The varieties indigenous to America were developed only during the nineteenth century. None of these strains has ever come to thrive widely in the American tropics.

Citrous fruits were natives of Asia. The sweet orange came from China or India. The sour Indian orange preceded it to Europe whence both varieties, it appears, reached the new world, though the earliest actual settlers in Florida reported finding oranges already there. The Spanish settlers are to be credited also with the introduction of peaches to the new world. Coconuts, the basis of the copra trade, may have occurred in prehistoric times on the west coast of Central and South America, but probably came originally from Asia and the Indian Archipelago.

Of the distinctive Caribbean foodstuffs of the present day—bananas, sugar, and coffee—not one was in the new world at the time of the conquest. Only maize, potatoes, chocolate, pumpkins, and squash, among our major vegetable items of diet, were contributed by the new world.

Important among the tropical fruits introduced from the old world which have come to flourish in the new is the banana. It belongs to a botanical grouping including arrowroots, cannas, lilies, and palms. Many varieties of the group found in Africa have no pulp, but bear a fruit resembling a pea-pod full of seeds. The edible banana is a hybridized variety which has pulp but no fertile seeds. It is propagated by planting suckers or sections of the root containing what may be compared to the eyes of the potato.[1]

The introduction of the banana to America was one of the earliest examples of the transplanting of vegetable foodstuff resources. Its establishment in the West Indies is credited to Father Tomas de Berlanga who brought roots from the Canaries to Santo Domingo in 1516. Thereafter, cultivation spread steadily in the islands and to the main-

---

[1] Detailed discussions of the banana and its importance as one of the elements in human food are found in Philip Keep Reynolds, *The Banana* (Boston, 1927), and Frederick Upham Adams, *The Conquest of the Tropics* (New York, 1914). These authorities are liberally drawn upon in the following paragraphs.

land, and in all of these areas the fruit came to furnish a highly valued addition to the local diet.

Of edible varieties of the banana there are many. Three have importance among the world's foodstuffs, though only two have as yet come to figure more than occasionally in international trade. The plantain is a large variety, lacking in sweetness, which is used extensively by the populations of moist tropical countries. Its hard flesh is used toasted, boiled, baked, fried, and as a base for flour. The so-called Cavendish banana grows on a plant eight to ten feet tall. It is produced for the international trade, chiefly in the Canary Islands where heavy winds and restricted planting areas put larger varieties at a disadvantage. It has been introduced experimentally into America where its resistance or immunity to the Panama disease may give it greater acceptance in the future.

The variety leading in production in the Caribbean is the *musa sapientum* of which, again, a large number of sub-species are cultivated and eaten locally. In 1836, a sub-species, the Gros Michel, was taken from Martinique to Jamaica by Jean François Pouyat. Cultivation of this variety has become the basis of large-scale commercial exportation due to the vigor of growth of the plant, and its compact, regular regimes or bunches, one to a plant, which can be easily shipped and which develop good flavor.

Probably the banana is the largest plant without a woody stem. The Gros Michel may reach a height of thirty feet, though the average falls between fifteen and twenty. Its "false stem" is formed of sheathed leaves reaching at the base a diameter of from nine to sixteen inches. It has no tap root, but many radiating small ones like those of a lily or onion. When the plant is about nine or ten months old the blossom shoots. The flower bud falls over and in a period of two or three months the fruit develops in "hands" pointed upward on the pendent stem.

The bunches vary greatly in size, but normally range from six to nine "hands" of bananas. The standard in the industry is nine "hands." Under particularly favorable conditions, single bunches may bear as many as twenty-two hands with three hundred "fingers" and weigh as much as one hundred and fifty pounds.[2] This, however, is rare.

In the present-day fruit trade, the best and heaviest bananas come from Central America, especially the "north coast." The lightest come from Cuba and Jamaica. The variation is due to a number of factors, including climate, length of time during which the soil has been under crop, the water supply by rainfall or irrigation, and the methods of cultivation. These factors are to a degree interdependent. In Jamaica, where the lands have been longer exploited and the growth is less luxuriant, the plants are set closer together than in Central America and cultivation to keep down grass and the "followers" which spring up around the roots is more systematic. Here the planting is planned to secure as many as two hundred or more bunches per acre. In the Central American plantations of most generous yield, the plants are set out in the field at spaces intended to assure that when full grown they will shade the ground sufficiently to keep down the greater part of the undergrowth. The unexhausted soil and plentiful rains which can be counted upon, contribute to make the growth ranker, and the fruit heavier but the number of bunches per acre in these areas may be only one hundred or less.

Commercial harvesting of bananas always occurs when the fruit is still green and relatively hard, for tree-ripened bananas tend to be insipid. The bunches are gathered when

---

[2] The range of weights (pounds) per bunch of bananas, for all classes exported in 1929, is:

Colombia	25–56	Honduras	39–66
Costa Rica	27–59	Jamaica	24–51
Cristobal	26–56	Mexico	41–72
Guatemala, West	36–60	Panama, West	39–66
Guatemala, East	29–58	Panama, East	29–69

"lean" or "full," according to the promptness with which they can be sent to the intended market. The methods of getting the fruit to shipside show wide variety. Small planters' crops and those from large plantations on which the cost of labor or the lay of the land makes it an advantage are "headed" out or brought in on the backs of donkeys or mules to roadside stations from which they can be picked up by carts or trucks maintained over set routes by delivery companies or the larger fruit producers. On the larger and better established plantations, the first step in gathering only involves taking the fruit to sidings of the company railroads which carry it to tidewater.

Though bananas have long been a staple article of diet in the regions where they grow, their entry into international trade in an important way is a development less than half a century old. Tradition has it that the first importation to the United States was one of thirty bunches brought to New York in 1804 by the schooner *Reynard*. Large-scale imports were then impossible not only because the population in the northern consuming markets was small but because transportation was slow and irregular. Sailing ships could not keep schedules, and internal transportation in the consuming areas was so deficient that even if supplies had been available shipments would have been small and the market would have been confined to the seaboard cities.

For another half century, conditions continued unfavorable to any consistent development. Supply was unorganized and northern populations were unfamiliar with tropical fruits. Bananas were curiosities, interesting as table decorations rather than as food, as they continued to be in many districts in Europe even to recent years.

Up to the middle of the nineteenth century, imports of bananas, chiefly of the red variety, occurred irregularly from Cuba. Then yellow bananas began to be sent from the Honduras coast to New Orleans. After 1866, a company known as Frank Brothers made a business of shipments from Panama, but when the French undertook the digging of the canal, their supply of labor was heavily drawn upon and the trade practically stopped in the early eighties.

Credit for the firm establishment of the international banana trade belongs to two men, Minor C. Keith and Captain L. D. Baker, working independently. In 1871, Minor C. Keith joined his three brothers in attempting to build a railway from the Atlantic coast of Costa Rica to the capital, San José. Before the line was completed it became evident that if the capital invested was to bring returns, steps had to be taken to create greater freight traffic than could otherwise be expected. To this end, banana plantations were started. To assure a market when these came to bearing, shipments were meanwhile made from Aspinwall, now Colon, Panama, to New Orleans. Costa Rican shipments began in 1879. The business grew with widening of both markets and sources of supply. Many other competitors entered the field, though Keith had established himself as the greatest factor in the New York and New Orleans banana markets.

One of the major competing interests was that represented by Captain L. D. Baker who on a return from a trip to Venezuela had brought a small shipment of bananas to New York with a cargo of bamboo from Jamaica as early as 1870. The next year he took a full schooner load of bananas and coconuts to Boston, which, it is claimed, was the first quantity shipment to that port. Though the shipments were not uniformly successful, Baker continued his activities and with others formed the Boston Fruit Company in 1885. Thereafter, more prosperous conditions developed in the trade. By the end of the century, about one hundred and fourteen companies had made ventures in the Caribbean fruit business. The majority had passed into "the banana graveyard" but some twenty-two were still active. In 1899, the Keith and Baker banana interests ceased to be competitors through purchase of the former by the United Fruit Company.

The organization of the fruit trade in large units is prompted by a number of the economic conditions which determine its success. When fruit shipments were only a supplemental cargo and northern markets were confined to the coast towns, small-scale operators were under but little disadvantage. As the trade broadened this ceased to be the case. The typical banana producing area is in low lying land within relatively easy reach of the coast, but insalubrious and only thinly populated. To this general characterization, Jamaica, formerly the greatest and still one of the main sources of supply, is, at least as to the number of laborers available, a marked exception. If the supply of fruit is to be greatly increased, it is often necessary in less favored districts to undertake the building of special ports, the draining of large areas and the adoption of measures for importing labor or drawing it from more favored local districts. These are circumstances which give great advantages, in the first stages of operation, to units which can undertake extensive operations with adequate capital.

Bringing the fruit from the coast where it is delivered to the foreign port of entry is also best done by large and well-organized services. They can regulate plantings so that the bananas become marketable in accord with what experience has shown to be the flow of demand. This is especially important in the banana trade, because not even with the best of modern equipment can the fruit be held for long periods as is possible with citrous varieties. On well-organized plantations, one of the tasks of those in charge is to plan the harvesting so that production shall be correctly "timed."

Actual cutting is done on schedule so that the fruit shall pass with the least possible delay from the plantation to the ocean carriers. In the present-day industry, these are large ships operating on a fixed time schedule. Waiting for cargo would greatly increase overhead. The boats must be able to count on regularity of delivery of cargo to them as they call at successive ports. To keep the fruit in condition, the vessels are equipped with special ventilation systems and apparatus for regulating temperature. Special refrigeration machinery is installed in vessels for more distant markets to avoid the loss that would come with premature ripening, which, if it occurred, might run into large amounts, for the modern fruit ship can carry from 45,000 to 100,000 stems per trip.

When the ship has arrived at its port of destination another marketing problem must be solved—that of distribution to the interior consuming areas which now absorb far the greater part of the shipments. For this purpose, special cars and special equipment are maintained for keeping the fruit from heat in summer and cold in winter.

At all of these steps in distribution, the company with large equipment and capital operates at a decided advantage. In fact, many of its functions cannot be performed at all by the small producer and shipper. The economic factors which surround the fruit trade have made it typically a "big business" enterprise, and it seems likely to remain such, though a much larger portion of the fruit entering international trade is purchased from producers who do not market the crop than is popularly supposed.

It is not to be concluded that the growth of the larger fruit companies has meant the disappearance of all smaller enterprises. The growth of the fruit market has in fact made possible activities on the part of small producers and distributors which would not otherwise exist. But these are regularly confined to a single phase of the producer to consumer transactions. In Jamaica, however, a coöperative organization, the Jamaica Fruit Producers' Association, has been built up to serve small producers from delivery to final marketing. Even the largest fruit companies in current years have come to purchase half or more of the fruit they market. The leading interest with the most extensive company-operated plantations and shipping more than half of the bananas entering international trade in 1929 bought half of the fruit shipped, and a leading competitor only produced on its plantations about one-fourth of its total. In only Honduras and Guatemala, it appears, is as much as one-half of the fruit exported grown by the large fruit companies. Elsewhere, their activities are in greater part confined to purchase, shipping, and marketing of the product.

In marketing, too, the trade is not exclusively by the large companies. Smaller vessels call at non-company ports on the Atlantic coast to take fruit to the nearer ports of the United States where the local markets are now of sufficient size to absorb chance cargoes. Such operations on the whole, however, must necessarily make up only a small portion of the total.

The remarkable growth of the American tropical fruit trade has been accompanied by great changes not only in its organization but in its origin and destination. In the earlier period of its growth and up to within the last few years Jamaica was the region furnishing the greatest supplies, but Honduras has now taken the lead. In fact, the fruit industry contributing to international shipments has shown a tendency to expand to all regions of the Caribbean where circumstances favorable to its development exist and in later years to extend to other tropical areas in both North and South America.

Supplies now reach the market from a number of regions not fronting on the Caribbean Sea and from non-Caribbean areas. Plantations on the Pacific coast of Panama are coming into bearing. The west coast of Guatemala already ships to the northern Pacific ports of the United States and further plantations are being established. Mexico is rapidly increasing its exports both by rail and by sea. The development in the El Hule district in Mexico holds exceptional promise.[3] Ecuador ships small quantities to the southern west coast countries and Brazil has a rapidly increasing trade with Buenos Aires and Montevideo as well as with Europe, to which it shipped 1,469,700 bunches in 1929. In the large, however, the tropical fruit trade continues to be characteristically a Caribbean industry and will probably continue to be so because of the peculiar local climatic advantages for production and because of the relative nearness of the region to the great consuming markets.

---

[3] The production in Mexico is one of the most important of recent developments. Bananas have been grown in this area since the colonial period. Lands suitable for banana plantations in Tabasco and Chiapas alone are said to reach 4,143,996 hectares, with large areas in other states. *Foreign Commerce and Navigation of the United States,* U. S. Department of Commerce, Bureau of Foreign and Domestic Commerce (Washington, annually), reports imports of bananas from Mexico as early as 1908, when 120,219 bunches were received. The trade grew steadily to 2,697,272 bunches in 1914, after which, due to the World War, it declined and by 1918 had ceased. Thereafter increasing quantities were again shipped yearly.

The exports to the United States in the year 1922 and following that time as given in *El Economista,* February 1, 1930, have been as follows:

Year	Bunches	Year	Bunches
1922	739,186	1925	3,240,551
1923	2,098,476	1926	4,591,626
1924	3,047,144	1927	5,680,896

In 1928 the shipments to the United States were 5,526,200 as reported in *Foreign Commerce and Navigation of the United States for the Calendar Year, 1928,* p. 228. In 1929, the shipments from Mexico to the United States, as reported by the United Fruit Company, were 5,602,499 bunches. Brazilian exports also have reached large proportions. The shipments in recent years are reported as follows:

Year	Bunches	Year	Bunches
1924	5,547,531	1927	6,021,978
1925	5,349,566	1928	6,192,667
1926	5,561,066		

Memoria de la secretaria de hacienda y credito publico, for the years indicated, and *Informe y cuadros de la direccion general de Aduana, año 1928* (Mexico, April, 1929). See also for tabular analysis, *Instituto de expansão commercial, Brazil* (Rio de Janeiro, 1929).

Between 1900 and 1929, the total banana exports from the Caribbean region and the countries contributing, underwent remarkable changes. Shipments in 1900 were about 20,166,435 bunches, but in the next thirteen years increased in amount almost two and a half times, reaching 48,752,315 bunches in 1913. The years between 1913 and 1929 saw an even greater increase in quantity, the total rising to 88,855,795 in 1929.[4] This was an increase of twice the amount of the total exports in 1900.

The changes in production areas are also marked. They reflect a number of influences, such as the degree of maintenance of peace, liability of certain lands to hurricanes and the troublesome Panama disease, rainfall and fertility of the soil, land values, labor supply, and unfavorable legislation. At the beginning of the century, Jamaica was far in the lead of all other producing areas, shipping almost 36 per cent of the total. Central America and Panama accounted for 57 per cent of the shipments. Within this group, Honduras and Costa Rica were disputing the leadership and Guatemala had not yet come to figure as a producer of tropical fruit.

In 1913, Jamaica showed a good increase in amount but her share of the total had fallen to 22 per cent while Central America and Panama almost maintained the ratio of 1900. Colombia and to a lesser degree Cuba had been added to the list of important producers contributing respectively 13 and 5 per cent. Within the group made up of Central America and Panama, Costa Rica had the greatest increase and was still the greatest mainland producer. Guatemala was already rising in importance.

---

[4] These figures are compiled from a large number of official and unofficial sources. While they are not exact in detail they represent with fair accuracy the growth of the banana industry. They do not include Mexican shipments which were not entered in 1900 but had reached over 2,000,-000 bunches yearly before the World War and as reported by the trade 5,602,499 bunches in 1929. They do not include Brazilian exports reported as 6,192,667 bunches in 1928.

By 1929, the geographic redistribution of the industry showed even more pronounced changes. Jamaica, the former leader, had almost doubled the amount of its 1913 crop, but so rapidly was the industry growing that the island's share of the total crop rose only from 22 to 25 per cent, and the leadership for the year passed to Honduras with a record yield of 28,221,463 bunches. Central America and Panama contributed 54 per cent of the total and Colombia almost 12 per cent. The rank of the leaders in production which had been Jamaica, Honduras, Costa Rica, and Panama in 1900, was now Honduras, Jamaica, Colombia, and Guatemala. The total yield of these new leaders in production had now risen almost four and a half fold. Costa Rica and Panama had fallen to second class, and their production was even showing a tendency to decline in amount.

In the last quarter century, a number of minor producers have entered the field, some of which have become steady contributors of limited amounts of fruit and some of which have been snuffed out after developments which seemed to give the best of promise. Among the latter, the most important was the Dominican Republic. Prior to 1914, the exports showed a marked tendency to rise but the hurricane of that year practically destroyed the crop of the extensive plantation then operated by an American company and production of bananas for export has become insignificant.[5] Another of the enterprises which failed after great hopes that the banana industry might be a means by which an unprofitable colony could be rendered prosperous involved Dutch Guiana. In 1908, the prospects were such that the authorities arranged for facilities to ship up to 10,000 bunches per week, but after four years of effort the enter-

---

[5] The export reported as "plantains" in 1928 was 646,098 kilos. *Report of the 22nd Fiscal Period, Dominican Customs Receivership, Calendar Year 1928* (Washington, 1929), p. 78.

prise was given up because the land of the colony proved to be one peculiarly subject to the Panama disease and hence unsuited to banana culture.[6]

The following table shows the shifts in the chief producing areas since 1900:

BANANA EXPORTS FROM CERTAIN AMERICAN AREAS [7]
(*In bunches*)

Country	1900	1913	1929
Brazil	.....	.....	6,192,667 [1]
Colombia	273,882	6,277,540	10,300,021
Costa Rica	3,332,125	9,366,485	5,784,724
Cuba	845,942	2,327,536	3,682,900
Dominican Republic	317,803	584,061	25,138 [1]
Guadeloupe	.....	.....	24,400
Guatemala	.....	3,444,036	6,545,695
Honduras	4,772,417	8,238,726	28,221,463
Jamaica	7,173,890	11,419,281	22,020,877
Mexico	.....	2,213,510	5,602,499
Nicaragua	1,324,727	1,639,120	4,160,700
Panama	2,125,709	5,185,530	4,722,426
Porto Rico	.....	.....	1,800
St. Lucia	.....	.....	1,800
TOTAL	20,166,435	50,695,825	97,287,110

[1]These figures as reported for 1928.

One of the marked changes in the tropical fruit trade in recent years has been in the destination of shipments. The United States continues to be the outstanding market and is increasing the amount of its purchases but there has developed in recent years a rapidly growing outlet in Europe.

Transatlantic purchases have been less important than might have been expected due to conservative consumption habits and because, until the development of refrigeration

[6] *Unifruitco*, June, 1927, p. 667.

[7] These figures are compiled from a large number of sources. In a number of cases conflicting figures are found. The table is therefore one in which errors may be entered but it may be accepted as indicating general course of development with a fair degree of accuracy.

practice, marketing fruit from America involved a high percentage of waste.

Formerly, the bananas marketed in Europe came almost exclusively from the Canary Islands, four of which now ship the fruit in international trade. The bananas grown there are of the Cavendish variety. The plant is relatively small and is therefore adapted to the scant rainfall and high winds which prevail in the Canaries. The supply has never been large; in fact, even in current years there are only about 10,000 acres planted. These are intensively fertilized, irrigated, and cultivated and carry about six hundred and twenty-five bunches to the acre.

Small shipments of bananas from Madeira to England were reported as early as 1878 and four years later the trade with the Canaries began. In 1884, only about 10,000 bunches of all origins entered the country. The decade following saw demand grow slowly but steadily. The fruit became a regular, though, because of its continued high price, still not important market offering.

In 1896-7, Minor C. Keith began shipments of American bananas on liners to Liverpool but with very irregular success. Better refrigerating equipment for direct shipments from Jamaica to Bristol made possible bi-weekly shipments of 25,000 bunches by 1901 and the following year Costa Rican bananas began to supplement the Jamaican supplies in the British market.

Tropical fruit was at first distributed to the Continent largely through Great Britain. The cross-channel sales were slow to develop and only in 1914 were cargo shipments to Continental ports attempted, though distribution on a luxury basis reached as far as St. Petersburg and Tiflis. Then came the World War which temporarily put an end to the new trade. Postwar development, however, has been in sharp contrast to that in earlier years. European sales have in recent years not only been growing relatively more rapidly than those to the United States, but have been taking more than half of the increase in offerings. Between 1927 and 1929, European sales increased by 7,700,000 bunches. Those to the United States by only 7,400,000.[8]

By 1928, the leading company in the business had thirty-one refrigeration steamships in the trade maintaining a direct service between the sources of supply in the West Indies, Central America, Colombia, and the Canary Islands and the ports of Great Britain, Germany, and Holland. In 1929, the Caribbean producing regions shipping most to the European markets were Colombia, Jamaica, Honduras, and Costa Rica. The chief sources of supply for the American trade were Honduras, Jamaica, Guatemala, Mexico, Panama, and Costa Rica.

The remarkable growth of the tropical fruit exports in value and amount is a development important not only because of its contribution to world trade and the addition of a new food supply to the diet of peoples of temperate climates, but because of its influence on the economic position of the Caribbean states. As has been indicated, only very limited areas profited from export shipments in the early years of development, but one after another new areas have entered the market until the industry now affects the foreign trade of at least fifteen political divisions in the new world.

The industry is the more welcome to Caribbean communities because it promises to be a permanent asset and one

[8] BANANA EXPORTS FROM THE CARIBBEAN REGION
(*In bunches*)

Totals	1929	1928	1927
Total to United States	66,519,773	64,362,671	59,148,953
Total to Europe	26,316,332	20,957,118	18,624,162

As reported by the statistical services of the United Fruit Company. See also *Commerce Reports,* June 23, 1930. Some European countries have recently shown a tendency to adopt prohibitive tariffs on bananas.

which, so far as such things can be forecast, does not seem likely soon to outrun its market, as coffee and sugar have done.[9] Nor does it face the disadvantage of eventual exhaustion of supply as does the petroleum industry. Though it is true that the commercial cultivation of the banana will occur in restricted areas, it occurs in a large number of the Caribbean communities, and its benefits are on that account more general than those of the highly localized petroleum industry or the sugar industry which, though it might be widespread in the Caribbean, is localized in large degree in Cuba because of the commercial policies adopted in the great consuming markets.

There can be no doubt that the growth of the fruit industry has been a factor greatly increasing the economic strength of the Caribbean. When Jamaica had to rely on a decadent sugar trade for its prosperity and when Costa Rica and Guatemala produced for export practically coffee alone, their prosperity depended upon the fortunes of a single crop. This is no longer the case. These examples are outstanding illustrations of the advantage which has come through the development of a second staple. Twelve of the Caribbean communities now have an export banana trade which contributes to their economic strength. The industry has steadily broadened its geographic basis to its own advantage and to that of the countries in which the developments lie. This growth seems destined to continue.

The shift in the markets where the fruit is sold also has a far-reaching influence on the stability of Caribbean economic life. In 1900, all but a negligible percentage of the fruit exports found their destination in the United States. Hard times or adverse tariff legislation affecting

---

[9] Some producers, however, feel that the "saturation point" is approaching, particularly if European countries further develop tariffs on banana imports.

the fruit trade in a single market would have had serious
repercussions on the prosperity of the industry, on local
purchasing power and on public income so far as this was
affected directly and indirectly by the fruit trade. The
present position is much stronger. In 1929, 20 per cent
of the fruit exports were sold across the Atlantic, primarily
in Great Britain, Germany, and the Netherlands. Sales in
all the countries of Europe promise further increase and
unfavorable conditions which may affect the trade in one
country now influence less seriously the industry and the
countries in which it is located.

The broadening of the base on which the industry rests,
through its spread into new producing areas has increased
the yield, minimized the influence of failure of single sources
of supply and moved a number of countries a step away
from the monoculture basis of agriculture. The broadening of markets has brought a variant to the diet of more
northerly communities and stabilized operations in the
industry by lessening its dependence upon the prosperity
and fiscal policy of the major purchasing area.

Expansion of fruit production to other lines than bananas
is much to be desired for the further diversification of local
products. In some lines, though local conditions make possible increased yields, the commercial policy of the United
States which continues to be the chief market for bananas is
not favorable to the development of a large market. This is
particularly the case in the citrous fruits which are grown
in large quantities in the country and which would probably be protected by a practically prohibitive tariff if serious competition with the home grown product developed.
In current years the only item of importance in this group
is lemons of which the equivalent of 634,000 boxes of
seventy-four pounds were imported in 1929. This is above
the average taking. Italy is practically the only supplier.

Grapefruit is imported chiefly from Porto Rico, which

shipped 373,000 boxes of seventy pounds in 1929,[10] and from Cuba which contributed 102,000 boxes. Porto Rico, in 1928, shipped also 10,129,000 pounds of canned grapefruit. The Porto Rican shipments enter the United States tariff free. About a third of the shipments are ultimately marketed in the United Kingdom. Imports from Cuba are almost exclusively from the Isle of Pines and arrive a month or more before the Florida grapefruit are ready for the market. They thus do not compete directly with the American crop. In normal years shipments are about 225,000 boxes.

Shipments of oranges from the Caribbean are not important. Small amounts enter the United States from Porto Rico, Cuba, and Jamaica, but the greater part of the supplies come from Japan, chiefly for the holiday trade.

All these fruits can be produced in quantity in Caribbean countries, and it may be that the small exports now occurring are only earnest of a larger trade which may develop particularly with northern countries which have no local production.

Practically all Caribbean fresh pineapple shipments now go to the United States. Hawaii is the only other American source of supply, but, though nearly half a billion pounds of canned pineapple come from there in favorable years, the shipments of fresh fruit are unimportant. Porto Rico supplied 548,000 crates of fresh pineapples to the United States market in 1929, as well as 2,379,000 pounds of canned pineapple. Other imports of Caribbean pineapples reached 1,449,400 crates, of which Cuba furnished over 95 per cent. Smaller quantities came from Haiti, Costa Rica, and Honduras. This trade also should grow and should extend to Europe. It has the advantage in the American market that except for the limited Porto Rican production there is no American industry supplying fresh pineapples.

---

[10] 452,000 boxes in 1928. The hurricane of September, 1928, damaged the plantations and reduced shipments in 1929.

CHAPTER VIII

THE RISE OF CARIBBEAN PETROLEUM

NEVER before has there been such competition for control of raw materials as is going on in our own day and in few if any lines has this competition been so keen as in the petroleum industry. How great the exploitable resources may be is still a subject for only speculative estimate in spite of the fact that surveys have been pressed forward in all parts of the world.

In recent years, methods of deeper drilling have been developed, deeper oil sands discovered, improved methods of oil recovery worked out and new fields explored. While these have made it clear that there is far more oil in the world than was formerly believed, they have not made it possible to make a valuable estimate of the quantity which may prove industrially available.

Far greater than all other oil developments have been those in the United States. "Rock oil" in small quantities had been used for years before the strike at Titusville in 1859 which brought production in that year to some 2,000 barrels. The next year yielded 500,000 barrels and later developments brought the outrun in 1929 to 1,006,681,000 barrels in a world production of 1,478,400,650.[1] Over two-thirds of current supplies come from the United States.

If production in Latin America be included, the degree to which the world depends on the Western Hemisphere for

[1] *World Petroleum,* Vol. I, No. 1 (February, 1930). The contributions to world petroleum supplies are well discussed in *International Trade in Petroleum and Its Products,* U. S. Department of Commerce, Bureau of Foreign and Domestic Commerce, Trade Promotion Series, No. 80 (Washington, 1929).

petroleum is still more striking. About half of the supplies
which do not come from the United States are from Latin
America and in all but small proportion from the Caribbean. The new world supplies almost 83 per cent of the
total. Control over so large a part of this great source of
power for moving the wheels of industry and driving the
ships of commerce and of war cannot fail to be of far-
reaching significance.

Of the great fields of Latin America, only one—that in
Mexico—had in 1920 come to be an important producer.[2]
The others were either unvisited or only giving first proofs
of their resources.

There had been some interest in possible Colombian developments, an interest perhaps as much political as commercial, for the United States felt that a field so near the
Panama Canal was one in which it had an unusual interest.
American criticism of the operations of the British Pearson
group in the field brought the announcement of its with-
drawal from Colombian activities.[3] No production had
been obtained there, and the Venezuelan fields farther to the
east were only beginning the development which has since
been so remarkable.

What constituted the "Venezuelan field" was unknown
and is still unknown for prospecting continues over a large
part of the national area. Producing wells and proven
properties lie, however, in the northwest and particularly
around and under Lake Maracaibo.[4]

If the United States once looked askance at development

---

[2] A good review of this development is that in the *Mexican Yearbook,
1920-21,* Robert Glass Cleland, Ed. (Los Angeles, 1922), pp. 290-320.

[3] Chester Lloyd Jones, "Oil in the Caribbean and Elsewhere," *North
American Review,* Vol. 202 (1915), pp. 536-544, and *Caribbean Interests
of the United States* (New York, 1916), pp. 282-294.

[4] Small quantities are being produced in eastern Venezuela. See W. C.
Clark, "Maracaibo Fleet Carries 50,000 Tons a Day," *World Petroleum,*
February, 1930, pp. 38-42. Recent developments are described in *World
Petroleum,* March, 1930, pp. 85-87, and June, 1930, pp. 238-240.

on the north coast in other than American hands, such an attitude is no longer evident. The larger early concessions in the Venezuela fields have found their way into the hands of Europeans. The Vigos concession of 1907, south and west of Lake Maracaibo, covered about 4,500,000 acres. The Venezuelan Oil Concessions, Limited, took over in 1915 rights covering the district of Bolivar—about 4,864,000 acres. These properties came to be controlled by the Royal Dutch. The Planas concession in Falcon, covering about 7,000,000 acres, has been controlled since 1918 by the British Controlled Oilfield, Limited. Later, large holdings have been acquired by many American companies. All told, the lands under concession as of January 1, 1927, were about 14,000,000 acres and in 1930 are reported as having been still further extended.[5] These statements are not, of course, indicative of an equal area of oil lands but they show the extent of the territory, rights on which are now held by petroleum interests. The Venezuelan government still holds extensive properties and there are some private Venezuelan enterprises but the best developed areas are in the hands of the Dutch-British interests and American companies.

Who deserves the credit for first foreseeing the possibility that the unpromising lands of this area might become of great economic value no one knows. Asphalt deposits, seepages, and the other indications that oil might be present had long been reported and "wildcatters" had penetrated the region for years before it drew serious attention.

The rush to stake out extensive claims goes back only to 1907. Serious exploration work began only in 1912. By 1918, some sixteen concessions had been granted by the government. The number rapidly increased thereafter and claims now run into the hundreds, with United States citizens the most frequent holders.

Commercial production began in 1917 at Mene Grande,

---

[5] "Venezuelan View of Production," *World Petroleum*, June, 1930, p. 239.

about halfway down the east side of Lake Maracaibo. This yield rose steadily and at the end of the sixth year was about a million and a half barrels. Mene Grande continued to be the only field of importance until 1922, when a gusher came in at La Rosa up at the base of the bottle neck, which flowed 900,000 barrels in nine days. Since then, the chief new producing fields developed have all but one been north of the first strike, lying on the east coast of the lake and at some distance inland on each side of its entrance.[6]

Old oil men who have spent their lives drilling elsewhere have no such tales of success to tell as rise out of the statistics of operation in the latest great field. Their talk is of "dry holes" and "dusters" quite as much as of producing wells. Concentration of ownership of the best properties in the hands of a few companies in Venezuela has enabled them to push operations in fields they had already proven and thus reduce the failures to a minimum. Of 1,659 wells drilled in Venezuela up to June 30, 1929, 1,451 were producers.[7]

Most were large producers yielding from 200 to 5,000 barrels per day. Some gushers have flowed daily from 40,000 to 50,000 barrels.

Under such conditions it is not surprising that Venezuelan production has risen in a spectacular manner year after year. The first reported commercial yield, that of 1917, was 119,692 barrels. Thereafter, it rose steadily, often doubling the record figures of the previous year. It reached 138,914,552 barrels in 1929.

Of the eighteen countries with major producing fields,

---

[6] The exception is the Tarra field southwest of the lake which, under Royal Dutch management, has been under development since 1913. In January, 1930, the company began shipments through a newly opened pipeline capable of handling 20,000 barrels a day. Developments in eastern and central Venezuela yielded about 350,000 barrels in 1929. *World Petroleum*, March, 1930, pp. 85, 97.

[7] Producing wells as of December 31, 1929, were reported as 1,738. *World Petroleum*, March, 1930, p. 96.

Venezuela passed three in the first year of its production. In 1922 twelve still produced more, in 1925 there were only five ahead, and in current years only one—the United States—produces more. Venezuela now produces more petroleum than all other American territory outside the United States. It produces more than all of Europe or of Asia. It would market still greater quantities than it now does if the proved wells were pushed to their greatest production.

The most extensive group of holdings in Venezuela is now in the hands of the British and Netherlands interests cooperating in the Dutch Shell Company. Their operations are carried on through a subsidiary known as the Caribbean Petroleum Company which was formerly controlled by an American interest, the Barber Asphalt Company. Allied with this group, also, is the Venezuelan Oil Concessions, Limited.

These companies produced almost half the oil raised in Venezuela in 1928 and 1929.[8] They hold, it is reported, 50 per cent of the developed production, much of which is closed in, besides owning proved areas which seem to assure a leading position among Venezuelan companies.

American interests in Venezuelan oil are scattered all over the country but the producing properties are few. The Gulf Company of Venezuela and the Lago Company—a subsidiary of the Pan-American—compete with the Shell interests in the Rosa, Ambrosia, Benítez, and Lagunillas fields but their production is from wells drilled not on land but under water, below the shore line of the lake. These two companies and their affiliates produced in 1928, accord-

---

[8] *World Petroleum,* February, 1930, p. 29. Information on oil holdings and other phases of development has also been incorporated in the discussion from the files of O'Shaughnessy's *South American Oil Reports* (New York, monthly) and *Petroleum Refineries in Foreign Countries,* U. S. Department of Commerce, Bureau of Foreign and Domestic Commerce, Trade Information Bulletin No. 623 (Washington, 1929).

ing to returns partly estimated, slightly more than the Shell group. Like the Shell interests, they have developed and proven properties in holdings not now actively exploited from which they could at short notice greatly increase production if world market conditions justified such a policy.

To a lesser degree, the same may be said of a number of other American companies whose holdings are important but which have not yet been opened up to commercial exploitation.[9] Four-fifths of Venezuelan production in 1928 came in fact from two relatively small areas on the east coast of the Lake, the La Rosa and Lagunillas fields. The latter field alone accounted for 60 per cent of the total.

American and British-Dutch interests have recently alternated in production leadership. In view of the great current activity by American companies not now producing, the years to come may see an increase of the American share.

It is probable that the practical monopoly of Venzuelan production by the groups now active will not continue for a number of European companies have begun to show an interest in development. The Société Française de Recherches au Venezuela and the Belgian Venezuelan Oil Corporation began active operations in 1929, and representatives of the Spanish monopoly and a number of French oil groups have visited the fields.

The conditions of work in most of the camps are not greatly different from those in other tropical enterprises, but there are striking exceptions. Few operations the world around are as extraordinary as those of the two leading American producers. Their actively exploited "fields" are under water and their labor force lives largely in ark-like boats which can be easily moved to any portion of the lake where "hands" are needed.

---

[9] Fourteen companies are listed as producers in 1930. The number of registered oil companies is 108. Seven new ones were registered in 1929. *World Petroleum,* June, 1930, p. 238.

Most interesting are the conditions in the Lagunillas field. The town itself, until it was destroyed by fire in 1927, recalled the description by Amerigo Vespucci, whose name came to be applied to America, of villages he reported having seen on his much debated fourth voyage in this part of the world. "We landed," he says, "in a harbor, where we found a village built like Venice upon the water: there were about forty-four large dwellings in the form of huts erected upon very thick piles and they had their doors or entrances in the style of drawbridges which stretched from house to house. . . ." Hence, we are told, came the name for Venezuela, little Venice.

Whether it was here or farther north that Vespucci saw his village—if he saw it—the description fitted the village of Lagunillas and others of the neighborhood. Lagunillas had, it is true, some two hundred fifty houses before its passing but they were still built on piles, the roofs were of the traditional thatch, and between them ran board walks from which single boards reached out to the individual dwellings.

In surroundings reminiscent of the age of discovery went forward some of the most important of Venezuelan oil operations. In fact, the greatest producing field in the country is Lagunillas. Wells are drilled in the bed of the lake under water, currently running from four to thirty feet deep. All the land under water—which at most is only sixty-five to seventy feet deep—can be tapped, it is asserted, by similar means. From the wells sunk the oil is loaded directly into the barges that start it on its way to market.

Ultimately, no doubt, when active exploitation of these fields for quantity production is sought, great storage facilities will be built. In fact, these are already rapidly going up. At the end of June, 1929, American companies had a storage capacity of 14,332,500 barrels as compared to

4,298,500 in the control of British-Dutch enterprises. Refineries also will follow. The Royal Dutch and the Standard Oil have establishments in Venezuela, but these are for the supply of the local demand for petroleum products. At present, Venezuela oil regularly starts for the world market as crude. A subsidiary of the Royal Dutch refines part of the British shipments in an up-to-date plant in Curaçao, Netherlands West Indies, for supply of the Caribbean, South American, and European markets. Another subsidiary operates in nearby Aruba where the American owned Lago interests have also put up a refinery embodying the latest improvements.[10] These plants are now the greatest center of refining activities south of the United States.

Lake Maracaibo, over which the petroleum must all now be shipped, is a pear-shaped body of water with a shallow outlet. Due to the limitations which surround its navigation, the oil companies have had to build up a tanker fleet of special design. The boats should not draw more than 12 feet 3 inches to pass the channel and they must be craft that can buck the northeast trade winds.[11] The first boats tried for the oil trade carried only 4,000 to 5,000 barrels but the larger ones now take as much as 20,000.

Each boat can make from nine to eleven trips per month under favorable conditions, according to which of the transshipping points it serves. The average number passing the channel is about twenty-four per day each way and all the traffic must be in the daylight high water,[12] a period of about three hours. Race for position is avoided by inter-

---

[10] T. Orchard Lisle, "An International Refinery Center," *World Petroleum,* February, 1930, pp. 36-37. See also for discussion of living conditions in Aruba, Charles Rigby, "Food and Water for Aruba," *World Petroleum,* July, 1930, p. 283.

[11] The passage of boats over the bar had created by 1930 a channel which could take vessels loaded to 12 feet, 6 inches.

[12] The government of Venezuela in February, 1930, was installing lighting facilities intended to allow the use of the channel during the night high water.

company agreements under which it is possible for as many as twenty-four ships to leave Maracaibo in line in an hour, keeping their relative positions through the channel passage. From a distance this long procession looks like a leisurely warship parade rather than a group of hurrying cargo boats.

No development such as has been going on in Venezuela, creating a lively demand for labor, can fail to upset local economic conditions.   Maracaibo, formerly only a lazy coffee-exporting town, has become one of the world's great crude oil exporters.   The men who serve the oil companies there and in the fields are a heterogeneous lot drawn from all parts of the Caribbean, from all parts of the world. Some four or five thousand from the north headed the invasion.   They included engineers of a wide range of nationalities.   Laborers from Barbados, Jamaica, Mexico, and Central America elbow each other at their jobs.

But the greatest change in local conditions has been that in the life of Venezuelan laboring classes of the district. Work in the oil fields has meant wages before undreamed of.   Coffee and cacao planters have had their men leave overnight for new jobs, to the decided disadvantage of these old and well established industries.   The peon who supported his family on from 15 to 25 cents per day could now receive from $1.40 to $2.00 for his labor.   He has flocked to the centers where with these wages he can change the family diet from the sugar, yams, plantains, jerked beef, and coffee to which they have been accustomed, to a variety of foods of which he partook before only on feast days, if ever.   He can in his new job buy clothes, house furnishings, and a wide range of other comforts of life and is not slow to seize the opportunity to do so as the imports to the oil district show.

No one can forecast the prospects of a region which in twelve years has become the second greatest producer of the world and still, it appears, could double its output in twelve months if the owners of its wells so desired. Estimates of probable future yields vary greatly and will continue to do so, for they must take into consideration not only the proved resources and what the existing wells can produce but the probable delivery facilities which the operators will bring into existence. These in turn depend on the conditions in the world market. So long as exploitation is carried on in major areas, especially in the United States, under the competitive conditions which currently obtain, an increase elsewhere tends to cut the profits of producers or increase the losses of those in less strong positions. Under such circumstances the practice of "capping in" producing wells in Venezuela will probably continue and perhaps increase.

What the field *could* yield under favorable conditions is also a matter of widely varying opinion. Estimates run at 1,000,000 barrels a day within five years, but no one can make more than a guess for the extent of the Venezuelan resources is even now unknown.[13]

No other oil field in Latin America now yields amounts comparable to those produced in Venezuela though a number are of exceptional promise. Next after that in Venezuela are, at present, the Colombian fields, said to extend over 34,000 square miles. A number of companies, chiefly British and American, have extensive claims but only one, the Tropical Oil Company, a Canadian corporation controlled by American capital, has as yet developed an important commercial production. Its operations are at Barranca Bermeja, about three hundred and seventy-five miles up the Magdalena River. The first commercial production reported was in 1921 when 66,750 barrels were taken out. Distance from markets seriously limited opera-

---

[13] The estimated daily potential capacity of producing Venezuelan wells as of December 31, 1929, was 542,315 barrels. *World Petroleum*, March, 1930, p. 96.

tions until the opening of a pipe line of a capacity of 50,000 barrels a day to Cartagena Bay on July 1, 1926. On July 4, 1926, the first tanker sailed from Cartagena with 87,500 barrels. Thereafter shipments steadily increased and reached, in 1929, 20,384,548 barrels.[14]

The only other important producing field in the Caribbean area is Trinidad which has now for a score of years had a steadily but not rapidly increasing output reaching 8,710,052 barrels in 1929. Nearby Mexico, however, has large oil resources at present checked in development but which some day will again contribute heavily to the trade passing to world markets through the Caribbean. A number of other Latin American republics already contribute to the world's supply, including Peru, Argentina, and Ecuador. Bolivia and perhaps still other countries southward will ultimately contribute, but up to the present time none have given promise equal to that of the north coast.

Here on the northern border of South America is one of the world's greatest areas of future oil supply. Already it is the greatest producer from the resources south of the Rio Grande, and far ahead of any other non-American field. From Caribbean ports are exported over two-thirds of the crude oil which enters world commerce.[15] This is a region upon which the world will rely increasingly for its petroleum supplies.

Perhaps, too, in the opening of these resources lies a new economic outlook for the countries in which they lie. Petroleum may give a source of industrial power for local

---

[14] See "Cartagena and the Petroleum Industry," *Pan-American Magazine,* June, 1929, pp. 374 *et seq.*

[15] The announced exports of crude oil in 1928 were about 216,000,000 barrels but 69,000,000 represented reëxport of Venezuelan crude oil from the Netherlands West Indies. The export of crude oil from Venezuela, Colombia, and Trinidad in 1928 was about 115,000,000 barrels. See an analysis with maps of the contributions to world trade in petroleum, Chester Lloyd Jones, "International Trade in Crude Oil," *World Petroleum,* April, 1930, pp. 129-132.

use and cut down the disadvantages under which the Latin-American states have worked because of their lack of coal. The diversification of industry which is so longed for and so essential, if the Latin-American republics are to be economically stable, may be promoted not only by the addition of petroleum production to their already existing activities, but by the new industries which a plentiful supply of power will make possible.[16]

---

[16] Additional material on recent oil developments is found in *International Trade in Petroleum Products,* U. S. Department of Commerce, Bureau of Foreign and Domestic Commerce, Trade Promotion Series, No. 80 (Washington, 1929). See also *Monthly Foreign Petroleum Statistics* (mimeographed), U. S. Department of Commerce, Bureau of Foreign and Domestic Commerce (Washington); Sir Arnold Wilson, "Oil Legislation in Latin America," *Foreign Affairs,* October, 1929, pp. 108-119; O'Shaughnessy's *South American Oil Reports* (New York, monthly); and *Commerce Reports,* U. S. Department of Commerce, Bureau of Foreign and Domestic Commerce (Washington, weekly).

CHAPTER IX

EXTRACTIVE INDUSTRIES

No review of the development of economic activity in the countries south of the United States can fail to impress upon the mind of the student the marked degree to which the major enterprises are the result of capital and initiative drawn from outside their borders. Dependence on the foreigner not only for markets and supplies other than locally produced foodstuffs but for capital and economic initiative is greater than in the United States or Europe, greater indeed than in the farther states of Latin America. This dependence has increased many fold in the last quarter century and has led to widespread criticism both in the borrowing and in the lending countries.

Often the arguments advanced as to the conditions resulting from dependence on foreign capital overlook the fact that similar conditions have characterized the life of other parts of the world when they have been going through a similar period of development. The United States, Canada, and South Africa are all outstanding examples of countries which, lacking sufficient local capital for the development of their resources as rapidly as has been desired, have in the past called upon the citizens of nations economically more advanced for funds by which their public utilities and other enterprises have been built up and operated. It is only fair to state that in these cases the development which occurred was, to a greater degree than has thus far come to be the case in the Caribbean, carried actively forward by residents and citizens of the "debtor areas," but so far as dependence on the foreigner for capital is concerned the conditions which have arisen are similar.

157

Whether dependence on the foreigner for large amounts of fresh capital will be a characteristic of economic developments in the Caribbean for a period of greater length than elsewhere is an open question. The less sanguine are disposed to believe that in these tropical areas the dependence on more northern regions for initiative and funds to develop the national resources may be permanent. Local ownership of the great developmental enterprises in the region has, it is true, not thus far shown any important development. Whether in the long run it will do so will depend almost entirely on the character of the civilization which comes into existence with changing economic, political, and social circumstances.

Although some of the largest industries financed by foreign capital are constantly reinvesting their capital in the development of the southern republics, and although investments continue to be encouraged by local governments, many of their citizens and not a few liberally minded outside their borders have looked with apprehension upon the rapid developments of the last fifty years as ones which may absorb the national resources and result in draining off the profits of industry to foreign lands in a way which will limit the possibilities of improvement of the general living conditions and the growth of national strength in the "exploited" countries. Some industries financed by foreign capital have not, it is asserted, reinvested a reasonable proportion of their earnings in the countries which have given them their prosperity. They have become "extractive" enterprises which use the states in which they are located as workshops but contribute but little to the local well-being.

There is as a rule no clear distinction which can be drawn between activity which is properly considered extractive and that which is not. If the boundary line lies between the cases which involve movement of money out of a country and those which do not, then all import trade tends to be an "extractive" activity and is objectionable particularly to the degree that it represents luxuries and not machinery or other goods which directly contribute to national economic development. Such imports, however valuable from the point of view of the cultural development of the country, are ones the effect of which in the narrow view is substantially the same as the sending of profits out of the country in payment of interest or dividends on foreign capital. But import trade is not as a rule in mind when "extractive" activities are discussed.

Cases which involve import trade but are more clearly examples of industries of the sort criticized are many of those manufacturing enterprises run by foreign capital within a country, particularly when the raw materials are not locally produced. These may be enterprises the existence of which is in many cases made possible only by tariff legislation and ones which if owned by foreigners, it may be argued, "tend to leave in the country only the expenses of plant maintenance and the wages of labor." Raw materials may be bought abroad and profits may find their way out of the country. The effect of such industries on the national economy is substantially the same as that of enterprises usually considered "extractive" in an unwelcome sense such as mines operated by foreign capital. Even if such undertakings are owned by nationals their effect, if these nationals spend their profits abroad, may be substantially the same as if the ownership were foreign.

It is clear that any country is in a stronger position if it has within its borders capital and enterprise adequate for its development and is thus not under the necessity of "paying tribute to the foreigner." But few countries, especially few developing countries, are in that position and certainly those in the Caribbean are not. They could create conditions which would shut out foreign capital but it is neither their interest nor desire to do so. Their choice as a practical matter, like the choice of other countries at the same stage of development, does not lie between satisfactory advance with foreign or with national capital but between accepting the coöperation of foreign capital and being satisfied with delayed development.

The necessity of making this choice of course does not mean that an industry operated by foreign capital, the profits on which after plant, labor, and extension expenditures are met in the usual course, go abroad, may not properly be called upon to contribute along with other industries to the upbuilding of the country in which it carries on its activities. Tax laws and other measures may require it to do so and in practice have done so to a much greater degree than is commonly supposed. The extent to which both foreign and national capital shall be required to contribute to public revenues is a matter for the national legislature. Upon the success with which the public interest in greater revenue is brought into harmony with satisfactory profits for investors, the economic advance of the country in no small measure depends. If the demands on industry are too low, the development of public services is retarded; if they are too high, capital seeks to escape. This is the common experience of all tax-levying units, but that foreign along with domestic capital is properly required to contribute to public revenues, and that laws may be passed to assure that it shall do so, is accepted both in theory and in practice.

The argument is often made that at least three of the great staples in the Caribbean contribute only a negligible amount to its development. Sugar, fruit, and oil, it is alleged, are all produced in the main by foreign enterprises. They have no interest in developing the communities in which their activities lie, and the profits obtained, instead of finding their way back into local commerce are drained off to the advantage of foreign investors.

The facts are far from justifying such statements. How much individual industries actually contribute to increasing public wealth and public revenue it is always impossible accurately to determine, and the problem is often as complex in the case of "extractive" as of "national" industries. Nevertheless, though the total economic support resulting from the "extractive" industries cannot be ascertained and though what they should contribute must always be a matter of opinion, it is clear that all of them already contribute directly and indirectly in a very substantial way to the communities in which they lie.

Local conditions of production and divergent public policies have made various the means by which the advantage from the industries has been sought for the public. Examples of the means adopted and of the limitations which surround them will be discussed in the following pages from each of the great staple line of Caribbean production.

The sugar industry is the outstanding economic development of the Caribbean. The greatest production is in Cuba where it has come increasingly into the hands of those representing foreign capital. Over two-thirds of the sugar produced in the island and probably much more comes from plants representing foreign capital, predominately that of citizens of the United States. The total American investments are variously estimated, one recent compilation reporting an increase from $220,000,000 in 1913 to $1,525,-900,000 in 1929.[1] A very large part estimated by the Cuban-American Chamber of Commerce at $800,000,000 represents investments in the sugar industry. The United States Department of Commerce estimated the American investment in the industry as $750,000,000 in 1924.[2]

---

[1] Max Winkler, *Investments of United States Capital in Latin America* (Boston, 1928), p. 284.

[2] *Bulletin of the American Chamber of Commerce in Cuba* (Havana, August, 1927).

Others have considered even this figure too high and have argued that even in 1928 it did not exceed $600,000,000.[3] Whatever the amounts of these investments and of the total investments by foreigners in sugar and other enterprises in Cuba it is clear that they do not represent equal amounts of fresh money which has been invested in the island. An author critical of American policy in Cuba estimates that "more than half of the value of the sugar property (owned by Americans) represents reinvested earnings" and that even in the years following the sugar crisis of 1921, the new capital finding its way into the island may average as much as the fixed interest and dividend obligations due to American investors.[4]

If these assumptions be correct, the effect of the development of the sugar industry on the balance of payments in the island is far less than has been popularly supposed. In fact, to the degree that earnings have been put back into the economic development of the island or equivalent amounts have been made available through fresh investments, the effect on the economic position of the republic does not seem to differ greatly from what would have been the case if the enterprises had developed through local initiative.

Cuba has only recently attempted to develop a comprehensive system of taxes which shall assure that the foreign interests in investments in sugar and other industries shall contribute directly in an important way to her revenues and the public improvements which they may be used to promote. Efforts are being made to collect substantial income taxes, but reliance for public income continues to be primarily on

---

[3] Leland Hamilton Jenks, *Our Cuban Colony* (New York, 1928), pp. 284, 299, 339. Mr. Orestes Ferrara, Cuban Ambassador to the United States, asserts that the American holdings in sugar properties in Cuba costing $800,000,000 could not be sold for more than $300,000,000. See his *El Panamericanismo y la opinion europea* (Paris, 1930), p. 251.

[4] Jenks, *op. cit.*, p. 300.

customs revenue which makes up about half of the total.[5]

The income thus obtained has increased as the economic production of the island has risen with the development of industry and its reflection in foreign trade. In this latter, imports have risen from an average of $72,527,000 in 1901-5 to a high point of $557,017,000 in the postwar boom to decline to $211,918,000 in 1928 as a result of unfavorable conditions in the sugar industry. Industries representing foreign investments have contributed to the development of the public revenue in the main through the tariffs paid on their imports and indirectly through the duties paid on imports which the expenditures on plant and labor in the island and the resulting exports have made possible.

The wide development of the fruit industry among the countries of the Caribbean and the different policies followed toward the enterprises in different districts makes generalization as to its contribution to development of the countries in which it lies, difficult. As in the case of the sugar industry in Cuba, the stimulation it has given to exports has greatly increased the buying power of the areas in which it operates and thus indirectly has contributed to public revenue.

This is, of course, the most easily demonstrable advantage. There are a number of others. The large commercial production of bananas has occurred, as a rule, in areas formerly either wholly unproductive or yielding only a negligible economic return and if banana culture is abandoned in them they frequently go back to the jungle. The fruit industry increases national wealth thus in a way contrasted with those which replace some other already established economic activity. Like other agricultural developments it is one which in contrast to the exploitation of

---

[5] In the budget of 1928-9 in a total of $84,400,000. Customs were estimated at $41,173,000. *Commerce Yearbook, 1929* (Washington, 1929), Vol. II, p. 198.

mineral wealth opens up the possibility of indefinite utilization of the land occupied. Its enterprises are not ones which by extraction of fixed supplies lead to their ultimate exhaustion.

Secondly, the agricultural developments are ones which, both in the areas exploited by foreign capital and on the plantations locally owned, increase the demand for labor and the local wages of labor. The population has the advantage of both a large labor market and one which makes possible a higher standard of life. The new conditions are not ones which are comparable to those existing, say, in the favored agricultural regions of the United States, but compared to those previously obtaining in the locality or to the conditions prevalent outside the fruit raising areas, they show a very marked improvement.

Thirdly, there are a number of advantages, some direct, some indirect, which follow the development of the fruit trade enterprises which it is difficult to measure in a concrete way though they have an undoubtedly beneficial economic influence. The establishment of better steamship services to the outside world creates markets for all export products and cuts down the cost of imports. The building of modern ports in regions where such facilities were formerly all but nonexistent has a beneficial influence on the local life. The extension of railway lines for marketing plantation products and for the general freight trade opens up the national resources. The improvement of the general sanitary conditions of the localities and the building of hospitals better the local health conditions and increase the number of those who can engage in sustained economic activity. Finally the increased intercommunication between local and foreign communities which the development of the industry makes possible brings about a quickening of both political and cultural life. Though it has not made the population one of strength in these lines equal to that in more industrialized areas, the fruit trade undoubtedly has put them far ahead of the standard locally attained a generation ago.

It is not possible to state the actual amounts of foreign capital which flow into a country in various enterprises over a period of years even in a single industry. During the years when the fruit trade has been developing, large amounts have been spent in purchase of lands, payment of wages, drainage, irrigation and sanitation projects, and the general overhead expenses of the industry. There have been many unsuccessful ventures, and even the best managed organizations have not escaped unprofitable investments. The losses in these ways borne by the "extractive industries" have been ones which the countries where the investments lie have not had to bear. An indication of the capital expenditures involved in individual instances may be secured from the reports of some of the larger companies. The leading fruit interest which handled in 1929 some 57,000,000 bunches of bananas in a total Caribbean export of about 86,000,000, reported as of December 31, 1929, an investment, after depreciation, in lands, buildings, equipment, cultivation, and minor items in its tropical operations amounting to $115,431,889 or about half of its assets.[6] As in the case of sugar these funds represented both fresh investments and reinvested earnings but take no account of moneys invested in activities which proved unprofitable, the capital involved in which had to be written off. These investments represented properties in seven Caribbean communities. In the same year, this company put into circulation in these countries $42,419,960 of which $28,420,-060 was distributed in wages and $13,999,900 in payment for purchased fruit and sugar cane.

---

[6] These properties were primarily devoted to banana production but included areas devoted to sugar, cacao and minor activities. See *Thirtieth Annual Report to the Stockholders of the United Fruit Company*, pp. 10-11.

The policy adopted by the greater number of the countries which figure prominently in the fruit trade has been to rely on the indirect advantages which development of the industry may bring rather than to secure income by direct taxation. Export taxes which have practically the character of levies on production have been established in some cases but these, in contrast to those levied on coffee, have not yielded important fractions of the revenue. Such taxes on a flat basis in the conditions under which the fruit industry operates in the Caribbean would not only tend to decrease production, especially in times when the prices of the product are low, but have the disadvantage that they would tend to drive the industry away from countries levying them to other districts where such taxes do not exist or are lower.[7]

Of all the staple industries active in the Caribbean, the one most frequently criticized as "extractive" in an unfortunate sense is that producing petroleum. The degree to which the industry should contribute to public revenue has been considered chiefly in the two major producing areas, Venezuela and Colombia. Government policies as to petroleum in both areas have not yet taken final form as is to be expected in regions where large-scale production has been so recent.

There are not a few who argue that national interests and the interests of the world at large counsel a regulation of petroleum development so that this great "wasting asset" may confer its benefits upon future generations as well as our own. The "capping in" policy followed by some of the interests in Venezuela is considered by them to be wise on this account, as well as because pushing production would further embarrass an already flooded market. This prac-

---

[7] An interesting discussion of the effect of these taxes under Central American conditions is found in *Memoria de la secretaria de hacienda y credito publico correspondiente al año 1927* (Guatemala, August, 1928), pp. 19 *et seq.*

tice, however, is dictated by commercial considerations rather than by public policy.

The official policies as to petroleum taxation so far as they have developed present contrasting points of view. The legislation in Venezuela has not emphasized a conservation program. It has favored development in our own time with provisions that the government shall obtain therefrom a substantial income. Concessions are granted for forty years. Three years may be spent in preliminary exploration, at the end of which time half of the concession area is returned to the government nominally as a "national reserve." In practice, however, these lands are leased again or put under drilling agreements for development. Royalties on production are paid in cash or oil as the government chooses. These are at rates much more moderate than have been demanded in Mexico.

As a result of the development under this policy, both export trade and government income have increased apace. In 1913, before any petroleum industry existed, export trade reached a value slightly less than $29,000,000. By 1926, it was $76,000,000, but except for petroleum exports it was still $29,000,000. In other words, the new industry accounted for the entire advance in the national exports.

Over the same period, too, public income has greatly increased and the petroleum industry has directly and indirectly contributed a large part of the additional resources. This has been particularly the case since 1923. Oil royalties then reached less than 2,000,000 bolivars but in 1927 they totaled 20,014,000, or more than a sixth of the estimated national expenditures of 112,000,000 bolivars. In 1929 royalties had increased as compared to 1927 by 11,856,928 bolivars, thus totaling 31,870,928 bolivars.[8]

The indirect increase of revenue through petroleum operations is probably even greater. It is not possible to reckon

---

[8] *World Petroleum*, June, 1930, p. 240.

this amount exactly, but since the chief sources of revenue are customs taxes and consular fees, it is evident that anything which increases the local buying power, such as increase in the export trade, will be reflected in increased imports and increased government income. In the five-year period 1911-15, before the petroleum trade made its appearance, the average value of imports was 87,515,000 bolivars. In 1926, the value was 367,403,000 bolivars. As a consequence, the tariff dues and consular fees which have found their way into the treasury have greatly increased. In the budget of 1929-30 they stood at 89,237,500 bolivars and were almost half of the total estimated national receipts.

In Colombia, as in Venezuela, income from petroleum promises to contribute in an important way to the public treasury. The government revenue from petroleum in 1928 was approximately $1,000,000 and will doubtless increase as production rises.[9] It was estimated at $2,500,000 in 1929.[10] Here, too, the indirect benefits coming from the investment of increased amounts of capital in the industry and the general stimulation of economic activity are present, though because of the lesser development and its more recent date the reflection in the foreign trade is less marked.[11]

Colombian policy as to oil resources tends to develop more conservative characteristics than that of Venezuela and has at times threatened to limit production by restrictive provisions which would discourage full commercial development.

The advantages which the development of an "extractive industry" like petroleum production brings to any country can never be calculated with exactness since they lie not

---

[9] Abraham Martinez, *Colombia Yearbook, 1927* (New York, 1928), pp. 209-284; *Commerce Yearbook, 1929*, Vol. II, p. 173.

[10] *Fifty-sixth Annual Report of the Council of the Corporation of Foreign Bondholders for the Year 1929* (London, 1930), p. 118.

[11] It is also less distinguishable from the impulse given to economic development by other lines of activity for the foreign trade of Colombia has increased in recent years in other lines than petroleum to a degree not equaled by the trade in Venezuela.

only in the cash return which the industry makes to the tax collecting agencies of the local and central governments, but in the general impulse to economic development through the expenditures for materials and for labor. The benefits to Venezuela and Colombia are the more difficult to estimate because the industries are so new that these reflexes are ones which may not yet be fully reflected in the national economic life.

The importance of these influences is always to some degree a matter of opinion which is apt to be colored by the position of the writer. If he is connected with the producing interests, he is apt to emphasize the contribution to economic development made through the general impulse to trade and to be critical of legislation intended to insure the local government an income drawn directly from the profits of operation or dependent upon the degree to which production is pushed. On the other hand, a writer with strongly nationalistic leanings may neglect the indirect and intangible advantages which the development may bring and may emphasize the necessity of making the "wasting asset" contribute to national development. He may argue the advisability of conserving the natural resources rather than giving impulse to their full development and exhaustion. Whether the opinion is that legislation adopted affecting development is inadvisable or laudable depends frequently upon which of these points of view is held.

The best illustration of the position in which public authorities stand when they determine the conditions which must be complied with in the development of the petroleum industry comes from the experience of Mexico. Mexican production began in 1901 and grew steadily and rapidly thereafter. The republic became the second producer of the world and its yield in 1921 had risen to 193,398,000 barrels. Thereafter, a decline even more rapid than the development set in, and in 1929 the petroleum raised totaled only 44,689,879 barrels, putting the country in fourth place among producers with a yield less than one-fourth of what it had been seven years previously.

This spectacular rise and fall were explained by a number of factors, most important among which is the policy of the Mexican government toward petroleum development, especially as reflected in the long drawn out controversy as to the title to oil lands and in the taxation policy adopted. The purposes of the legislation are declared to be "to encourage the petroleum industry of the country and [to provide] that its development takes place within the established rules and in accordance with scientific technical procedure, in order that the country may obtain from these natural riches the maximum benefits derived from the maximum profits which the invested capital will obtain for itself and for the persons and countries from which it comes." [12] But the effect of the policies adopted has been neither to encourage the production of petroleum nor to bring steadily increasing returns to the national treasury. Drilling has fallen off and though the income from petroleum taxes was once high under the influence of the great demand during and following the World War, it has now become almost negligible.

So far as the tax yield other than that from increased customs measures the national return, Mexico received but little from the petroleum industry in the years when it was becoming established. [13] There was no special taxation applying to it before 1912. Production and later export taxes have since been levied. In the period from 1911 to

---

[12] José Colomo and Gustavo Ortega, *La Industria del petroleo en Mexico* (Mexico, 1927), p. 4.

[13] The following estimate of the relation of the petroleum industry to economic development in Mexico is based on a study by Enrique C. Creel, "Petroleo," in *El Economista*, November 16, 1929, pp. 10 *et seq.* A similar study by representatives of the producing companies would doubtless find that the stimulus given to general economic development by the petroleum industry was greater than here stated.

1926, the production tax yielded 332,398,225 pesos, the export tax from 1921 to 1926, 95,681,101 pesos, a total of 428,079,326 pesos.[14] This is about 17 per cent of the official valuation of the oil output during the period. The tax rates on production and export now in force are estimated to run about 52 cents per barrel and the combined yield of the two has fallen to less than 10,000,000 pesos per year.

Official data are not available as to the other taxes on the petroleum industry but a statement prepared by the Association of Producers of Petroleum in Mexico for the year 1926 indicates a payment by seven companies during that year of 14,624,603 pesos in such levies.

Benefits to Mexico other than federal taxes from 1901 to 1926 are estimated to include 25,000,000 pesos in state taxes, 42,599,045 pesos in rents and royalties to landowners, 982,738,283 pesos spent in the country in producing petroleum, 100,000,000 pesos saved in fuel to the railroads and industries of the country in twenty-five years and 50,-000,000 pesos in freights for the railroads, increase in land values and profits for the consumer, a total of 1,629,416,654 pesos.

Evidently Mexico has been able to profit very materially from the development of the petroleum industry. As one Mexican authority states, with the yield of only the production and export taxes levied between 1911 and 1926, the entire foreign debt of that time could have been paid off buying the bonds at their market price.[15]

---

[14] These figures are from the study by Creel above cited. Colomo and Ortega report that in the period 1912-27, the two taxes named yielded 448,368,990 pesos. The Mexican Ministry of Industry, Commerce and Labor announced that in 1928 the revenue from petroleum levies was 11,275,430 pesos and in 1929, 8,637,336 pesos—5,259,156 from the tax on production, 3,358,927 from export taxes, and 19,243 from import taxes. He estimated that the production and export taxes in 1930 would total only about 7,000,000 pesos. *World Petroleum*, March, 1930, p. 77.

[15] Creel, in the discussion cited above. The same author calculates the profits of the operating companies from figures of cost of production in

But while Mexico was able to make her petroleum taxes one of her chief sources of income the policies adopted have shown, particularly in later years, that control over the extractive industry may be pushed so far that production may be checked and decline with a serious falling off in public revenue and in expenditures by the industry in the country. The high taxes and other factors of operation which companies have had to face have prompted them to turn their attention to other areas such as Venezuela and, at least until recently, Colombia, where public policy has been of a more liberal character.

Least criticized as "extractive" among the four staples is the coffee industry. After sugar, it has longest contributed in an important way to the export trade though much more recent in its great development than is ordinarily supposed. It yields a product for which neither large initial investments nor highly organized and expensive marketing organization is necessary and to a greater degree than any of the other three it is an industry in which the capital invested represents local initiative.

In more recent years, foreign influences, both in the production and in the financing of the crop, have tended to increase, and when large profits have been made, as has occurred in the recent period of high prices, a considerable but unascertainable portion of the profits has "gone abroad" either in payment for luxury goods imported or in direct expenditures abroad by those who have profited from their enterprises. On the whole, however, though the coffee industry is probably now more "extractive" than formerly the criticism of the development has been negligible.

Taken in the large, much of the comment as to the disadvantages which attend the development of the so-called

---

Mexico, prevailing freight rates to New York and prevailing prices in New York. He concludes that the profits up to the end of December, 1926, were $1,010,852,520.

extractive activities is exaggerated and does not rest on an analysis of all the factors which should be considered. In a developing country, profits, or their equivalent in fresh money for new enterprises, tend to be reinvested or invested within the national borders. The impulse to put capital back into local development, depends not so much upon the nationality of the owner of the capital as upon the character of the local civilization, the attractiveness of living conditions, the general social development of the country, the stability of local political and economic factors, in short upon the sum of circumstances which makes a country stable, strong, and prosperous. The obligation in every area to contribute to its upbuilding rests upon all capital, domestic and foreign. The problem of those who determine public policy is not to determine whether invested capital, foreign and domestic, is taxable but what standard of contribution should in both cases be adopted so as to stimulate further investment in the country and thus bring about the full development of the natural resources.

CHAPTER X

DIVERSIFICATION OF CARIBBEAN PRODUCTS

PROMINENT among the handicaps of the Caribbean area has been its economic dependence upon a restricted list of export products. Though through their history some of these areas have radically changed the items which have held the more prominent positions in their shipments to other countries, none of them have developed a varied line of industries, and when new crops have appeared it has usually been to replace ones formerly significant.

In the colonial period the Spanish possessions were restricted in their exports as in their production for domestic consumption by rules laid down by the mother country. Though these were often disregarded within the colony and though smuggling by Spaniards and foreigners cut down the rigors of the system set up on paper, progress was seriously handicapped. Even the legal commerce was limited through the long-continued requirement that the trade go in fleets, the number of vessels in which was strictly controlled, and be with the mother country only. While the early colonial policies of the other European powers have been less criticized, they were none of them of such character as to encourage the free development of the tropical colonies to which they here applied.

Independence and the adoption of more liberal standards have not demonstrated that the disadvantages were wholly due to the former restrictive measures. Modifications in production and export have occurred, but diversification of products has not been marked.

In some cases, the changes which have been made have

been forced upon the American areas by the rise of new sources of world supplies. Indigo, which formerly figured prominently in Caribbean exports, has become insignificant through the transfer of the industry to the Far East and more recently through the rise of synthetic dye materials. The trade in cochineal, palo tinto, and Brazil wood, formerly relied upon for carmine, black, and red coloring agents, has become negligible. Leadership in cacao production has passed from Central America and northern South America to the African Gold Coast, rubber supplies are now drawn primarily from the Far East, and Caribbean sugar, once relied upon to supply the European market, now serves in all but minor degree only American demands. The trade in the staple has greatly increased and is greater than ever before, but is now limited by the commercial arrangements which have cut down the areas in which it can develop to advantage.

For one reason or another, Caribbean products entering world trade in large amounts remain few. If it be accepted as fundamental that for a state to be strong either economically or politically it is highly to be desired that the national life be based upon a variety of activities, it will be useful to see whether, in the past quarter century during which the advance of production and foreign trade has been so remarkable, there has also occurred a broadening of the economic bases of national prosperity, a progress toward that economic stability which, if not the condition of political stability, is at least one of the factors contributing greatly to make it possible.

A study of this subject at best involves dealing with a number of variable factors. If market values of export shipments be used as a measure, some distortion of the result occurs through the shifting of price levels caused by varying yearly supplies and the competition which must be met from new production areas. The change in the pur-

chasing power of money in the world as a whole during the
postwar years also tends to exaggerate the increases and
decreases though this variant is less marked, when considering the foodstuffs and raw materials of the Caribbean area
than when applied to highly manufactured goods. Adjustments to rectify factors of this sort are practically impossible in studying countries of such wide variety as those
under review. It will be assumed that the value figures
show with a fair degree of accuracy the character of the economic developments which are there in course.

Statistics upon which comparisons can be made are available for four of the major island areas. Cuba, far the most
important in the value of its exports, which reached 37 per
cent of the total for the Caribbean area in 1927, had in
1900 three important items shipped abroad. Sugar made
up about two-fifths, cigars about a fourth, and leaf tobacco
about a fifth. Tobacco products outranked sugar in value.
The years since the beginning of the century have seen a rise
in values of leaf tobacco exports, while those of cigars have
hardly held their own in the face of high tariffs and the
spread of machine manufacture. At the same time, sugar
and molasses exports have increased from a value of 18.5
million dollars in 1900 to 263 million in 1927. As a result
the two lines of activity, production of sugar and tobacco
products, which accounted for 88.3 per cent of exports in
1900, account for 92.6 per cent in 1927, but of this
total 81.4 per cent is now of sugar products alone.[1] The
accentuation of sugar has made the island more dependent
on a single crop. The tobacco industry is unprosperous in
current years and gives no promise of great expansion.
Other crops contribute only minor fractions of the export
trade and are less important now in percentage than they
were at the opening of the century.

---

[1] The comparisons here and in the following paragraphs are based on
statistics in *Commerce Yearbook, 1929* (Washington, 1929), Vol. II.

Porto Rico, even under the stimulus of free entry into the United States for its products and with the active efforts which have been made for diversification, shows a similar development—a remarkable rise in the value of its exports from about eight and a half million dollars in 1901 to over one hundred and three million in 1928, but with an increasing emphasis on one crop, sugar.[2] Though the island was, under the Spanish régime, primarily a coffee area, the production of the berry has suffered from the loss of its former protected markets and the necessity of meeting Brazilian and other coffees in the tariff-free United States market. Though the exports of coffee showed a tendency to rise during the first period of American control, they never kept up with the advance in sugar and reach now less than half of the amount before the World War. Cigar manufacture, in spite of free entry of Porto Rican products into the United States, has run a similar course and now averages only about the same in amount as in 1910. Sugar has crowded other crops to the rear. Its exports were worth four times those of coffee in 1910 but total almost six times as much in current years. Sugar is now more than half of Porto Rican exports. Its increase has emphasized dependence on a single crop.

The economic position of Jamaica shows dependence on the sugar and fruit industries in high degree, though the number of subsidiary crops is larger than in some comparable areas. The island was long identified with the sugar industry and its subsidiary, rum production. It reached its highest yield in the former in 1805, and in the latter in the following year. In these years, practically all

---

[2] The figures for Porto Rico are taken from *Twenty-ninth Annual Report of the Governor of Porto Rico, Honorable Horace M. Towner* (San Juan, 1929). The exports showed a marked falling off in 1929 to a value of $81,722,870, due to the damages caused by the hurricane of September 18, 1928. Because of this factor the comparisons for other crops also disregard the returns for 1929.

of these products consumed in the mother country came from the West Indies. After the abolition of slavery, Jamaica passed through a long period of decline which has later been relieved by the growth of the fruit trade, in which bananas and coconuts are the outstanding factors. These products first passed sugar and rum in value in 1893-4 and are now the mainstay of local prosperity. The recently established preferential treatment for sugar and other items in British markets promises to improve conditions. Coffee, dyewoods, cacao, ginger and other spices, honey, and hides are already supplementary items in export which give the island a more diversified production than most West Indian areas.[3]

The two republics on the island of Haiti have for their goods no tariff-free entry into the United States market, no special tariff status there as has Cuba, and no colonial advantages such as Jamaica enjoys. They have had less well assured public order than the other three units, a circumstance which has held back the investment of foreign capital and thus the development of large industry. Their laws governing land titles and various other features of local legislation are not favorable to large-scale operations. The efforts of the local governments to encourage diversification of products have been until recently negligible or nonexistent.

Though the circumstances under which production occurs are different from those in the other units, the tendency toward a monoculture basis for agriculture shows itself here also. At the beginning of the century, sugar and cacao were both prominent Dominican products. The former led in 1900, the latter in 1910. Recent years show a tendency to emphasize sugar production, and in 1927 sugar exports were valued at over twice those of cacao. Tobacco runs a poor

---

[3] Frank Cudnall, *Jamaica in 1928* (London, 1929), pp. 100-136, and *Commerce Yearbook, 1929*, Vol. II.

and irregular third.   Almost four-fifths of all exports are of the first two items.[4]

The statistics available for Haiti do not allow a satisfactory analysis of the course of its trade.   Even if they were available over the period they could not be accepted as an indication of normal development, due to the upset political conditions which have obtained.   The preponderant position in exports is held by coffee which in the period 1916-7 to 1927-8 was shipped in fairly stable amount averaging above twenty-eight million pounds per year.[5]   It made up about 81 per cent of the exports in value in 1928. Raw cotton exports have shown an increase in quantity in recent years as have also, in lesser degree, the sugar shipments.   On the whole, Haiti is still a country in which diversification in the economic life of the country does not make itself evident.[6]

In Central America, coffee and bananas play a rôle similar to that of sugar and coffee in the West Indies.   All except Salvador now have an export banana industry.   All export coffee, though Panama is just beginning to do so in fair amounts.   Three are distinctly one-crop countries.   Coffee is regularly about 85 per cent of the exports of Guatemala, but there is some indication that the rising banana production may give it a second important crop.   Salvador depended on coffee to furnish 75 per cent of her exports in 1901 and more than 90 per cent in 1929.   Of the shipments from Honduras in 1927-8, about 81 per cent were bananas, and the share of this crop in the total has not shown a tendency to decrease.   In the stablest of Central American countries, Costa Rica, and in the one recently the most dis-

---

[4] For statistics on Dominican production and export see *Report of the 22nd Fiscal Period, Dominican Customs Receivership, Calendar Year 1928* (Washington, 1929).

[5] Exports fell off in both quantity and value in 1929.

[6] For statistics on Haitian production and export see *Seventh Annual Report of the American High Commissioner at Port au Prince, Haiti, 1928* (Washington, 1929).

turbed, Nicaragua, the two crops—coffee and bananas—
contribute heavily. Over the last quarter century, coffee is
gaining over bananas and apparently these two crops are
both increasing their percentages of the total at the expense
of the other contributing items. Together they made up
80 per cent of the exports of Costa Rica in 1903, 85 per
cent in 1913, and 91 per cent in 1927. Similarly these two
crops were 38 per cent of Nicaraguan exports in 1901, 56
per cent in 1912 and 61 per cent in 1927.[7] There is a fair
export of cabinet woods from Nicaragua but one which
does not show promise of increasing its percentage of
the total.

Taken as a whole, Central American exports show the
same concentration on a few crops which is found in the
West Indies, and here, too, the tendency seems to be for this
condition to become accentuated.

An estimate of the course of developments in the two
republics of northern South America is less easily made.
Their resources, especially those of Colombia, are more
varied than those of most of the Caribbean states, and
developments are current which have upset the traditional
lines of activity and promise to do so increasingly. Both
republics at the beginning of the century were primarily
exporters of coffee. About half of the shipments of both
in 1913 were of that article.[8] Colombia has increased her
coffee shipments which have had a growing popularity in
the United States market. It is now the second coffee
producer after Brazil. Of the total export value in 1928,
66 per cent was coffee. Evidently Colombia has, in current
years, become decidedly more a monoculture country as far

---

[7] For statistics on Central American trade see yearly issues of the
Commerce Yearbook, Vol. II.

[8] This and the following statements are based on Tabular Guides to
Economic Conditions, issued by the U. S. Department of Commerce,
the issues of the *Commerce Yearbook,* Vol. II, and on tables in *Fifty-
sixth Annual Report of the Council of the Corporation of Foreign
Bondholders for the Year 1929* (London, 1930), p. 121.

as export trade is concerned than ever before. That this is true is further borne out by the fact that hide shipments, which once were almost a fifth of the export value, have fallen to less than a thirtieth, though the quantity has remained about stable in recent years. Bananas also have fallen in their percentage of the total exports, though their amount has shown a good increase.

Movements now occurring in Colombia indicate that diversification may be much easier here than in the smaller units with more restricted natural resources, and it may be that this diversification is already under way. The most marked development of the last few years has been in petroleum which did not figure in production till 1922, but has since risen from 323,000 barrels to 20,384,548 barrels in 1929.[9] Public improvements, especially those in transportation, now under way also indicate that the development of the natural resources may help to bring about a diversification of Colombian exports.

Venezuela, like Colombia, but to an even greater degree, has had its economic life modified by new factors in the last quarter century. In 1913, coffee was 55 per cent of its exports and cacao 16 per cent. In recent years, both of these products have only fairly maintained their values while the shipments of coffee have shown a tendency to fall off in quantity, and those of cacao have not shown any steady increase. In proportion to the total export trade, however, both these items have shown sharp declines. In 1927, coffee was less than a quarter of the total and cacao only about one-seventeenth. Hides, formerly the third item, had also, in relation to the total, registered a sharp decline. The new factor in foreign trade was petroleum, here as in Colombia. From 120,000 barrels in 1917 the yield rose spectacularly to 138,914,552 in 1929. Oil has replaced coffee as the chief export and in 1927 made up 62 per cent

---

[9] It was 19 per cent of the export values in 1929.

of the total. Petroleum is evidently to be a new basis for Venezuelan development and may as in Colombia be the basis of other economic developments which will strengthen the national position.

From a review of the export trade currents of the last quarter century, it is clear that with the exception of the petroleum developments in northern South America there have been no great new factors modifying the conditions previously existing. Sugar, coffee, and fruits with the addition of petroleum on the north coast, continue to be the staples in the major areas. There has not developed any great differentiation of products either in the region as a whole or in the larger units. In fact, the dependence on a few crops which limited the outlook at the beginning of the century seems to have been emphasized rather than decreased.

So far as the prosperity of a country is dependent on increased production of goods which can be exchanged in world markets, the past quarter century has seen marked progress in the Caribbean. But so far as it is conditioned on the production of a wide variety of products, which by their diversity shall insure against the hard times that follow failures of foreign markets, poor crops or too abundant crops, the past twenty-five years give little cause for satisfaction.

The need of new crops to supplement the few on which the life of the Caribbean communities now depends is frankly recognized within them, but the exploitation of the established and traditional products, especially those which lend themselves to large-scale operations, has thus far been so attractive and in some cases so profitable that the development of new lines has been neglected or at least overshadowed.

The experience of all countries which have sought diversification shows how much easier it is to diagnose what is needed than to bring about the adoption of the remedy and to create the new markets which will give the efforts to establish new lines of production a solid foundation in profits.

Though the staple products show a tendency to monopolize production and though some of the minor lines seem to be losing the relative importance they once had, it cannot be concluded that there is no promise of diversification. It may be that the current emphasis on a few lines represents only a step in a general readjustment to new economic conditions and that there will develop, or are now in course of development, a fair number of supplementary lines of production which will contribute increasingly to export trade and make the local markets less dependent on imports. This may be true at least in the larger areas with a variety of soils and other natural resources. The smaller islands are in less favorable position and as a rule seem destined to remain as they are at present—producers of a very restricted number of products raised by populations of low cultural and economic status.

What can be done in developing new products depends not only on what crops the local population proves able and willing to cultivate, but in many cases upon the advance which science may make in the control of the plant diseases and insect pests which have frequently made unprofitable over a series of years crops which at first have seemed to show great promise.

Efforts to diversify crops and to find means to fight the pests which have limited the production of both old and new ones have been well sustained in some of the British colonies and in Porto Rico. With the encouragement of the British colonial governments, a number of minor crops have come to figure in foreign trade. Though some of them are specialties which must have a restricted market, they represent an improvement in the general trade of the community through the increase of their export values or decrease in dependence on foreign supplies.

In the exports of Jamaica and Trinidad there have come to figure a fairly wide variety of specialties of these sorts, and the same is true to a lesser extent in some of the other British islands. These articles include ginger, nutmegs, pimento, honey, arrowroot, coconuts and copra, sponges, sisal, tomatoes, limes, and various spices. Some success is reported also in spreading the culture of crops of wider demand, such a cacao, cotton, coffee, and rice.

In Porto Rico, consistent efforts have been made by the local authorities and those of the United States government to widen the number of crops and particularly to improve the character of the tobacco leaf and of its preparation for market. Conditions of coffee production have been improved. Demonstration farms are maintained to try out new methods and to facilitate their adoption by planters. Steps are being taken to introduce jaragua, a natural, tick-free pasture grass, already well established in Colombia and Brazil, on large areas which have heretofore been practically waste land. In efforts of this sort, the governments of Venezuela and Colombia have given their coöperation to the officials of the United States. Improved varieties of sugar cane have been introduced, and the local cultivation of potatoes and raising of poultry are being encouraged.

Most marked among the developments toward diversification in Porto Rico have been those involving the fruit trade. The export trade in fruits at the beginning of the century was negligible. It totaled for all varieties in 1901 only $109,801. Since that time it has steadily grown, reaching a value of $7,538,794 in 1928. The greatest advance has been made in the shipments of grapefruit which now make up about a third of the total value of fruit shipments. Second are the shipments of pineapples, followed by oranges, canned fruits—chiefly pineapples, and coconuts. Minor fruit products of various sorts have developed, including the production of orange and grapefruit juice, lemons, limes, and strawberries. Market gardening, both for the local market and for export, has made a promising beginning.

Along with the newer agricultural activities should be mentioned the development of industrial lines. These include tobacco products, men's clothing, fine needlework, and women's wear.

It is too soon to judge the degree to which these developments are earnest of a diversified economic life. Even in their present position the prosperity of some of them is to a great degree due to the special relation in which Porto Rico stands to the American tariff and therefore not evidence that equally favorable results can be obtained elsewhere. Porto Rico, like Jamaica, still needs great development of the newer lines before the dominance of the leading products in agriculture will have ceased to be a weakness.

The best example of what is being done among the independent communities to bring about diversification of production is found in Cuba. The advance has been largely a by-product of the hard times currently affecting the sugar industry. Between 1924 and 1929, the nominal return to Cuba from its sugar exports fell from $374,496,287 to $188,635,735 though the amount of sugar sold was more than a billion and a half pounds greater in the second year than in the first. As a result, the amount of money available to the people for the purchase of imported goods was sharply cut down. Necessity forced greater attention to the possibility of producing locally what had formerly been bought abroad.

Many staple articles of diet, such as rice, beans, dried beef, codfish, and lard, continue to be imported in enormous quantities, but the cultivation of other foodstuffs and manufacture of simpler articles for local consumption, formerly neglected, have greatly increased, though in many cases the totals of production cannot be accurately measured.

Progress in various lines is uneven and has in many cases been stimulated by tariff legislation, the long-time effect of which it is too soon to estimate. There can be no doubt, however, that already Cuba is self-sufficient to a much greater degree than formerly and that there is good prospect of still further advance.

The country people who formerly considered the "dead season" between harvests as a vacation period have taken up a larger number of subsidiary activities which make them less dependent upon goods from other countries. In a period of hard times imports would naturally fall, but the figures of production which are available and the testimony of those best familiar with Cuban conditions indicate that not a few of the declines are due as much to the substitution of goods locally produced as to reduced purchasing power in international markets. The growth of some of the minor export lines also gives promise.

Corn imports have fallen steadily and are now virtually at an end. Shelled Cuban corn is available at prices so low that some feel production will be discouraged. It is being used in large amounts for human food and to fatten hogs and cattle and green corn is becoming increasingly popular in the national diet. Potatoes, especially off-season crops, are claiming increasing attention. In 1925, the export of potatoes was only 80,000 barrels. In 1929-30, it reached 700,000 barrels. A large range of miscellaneous fruits and vegetables are being raised in increasing amounts for local consumption and export. A domestic canning industry has been established since the sugar slump, the chief products of which, from six factories, are canned tomatoes and pineapples. Rice growing is being encouraged by the government. Producers believe the island may become self-sufficient in supply. It now imports about $18,000,000 worth of rice per year. Cuba has been a heavy importer and consumer of coffee. Local production has been stimulated by a protective tariff, and the island promises to raise its own supplies by 1936.

Cuba was formerly a heavy importer of fresh beef and consumed large quantities of tasajo, dried beef, imported from South America. Livestock raising has greatly increased, both on large ranches and by small farmers. Beef prices have fallen, live cattle are now exported, and the imports of dried beef, with the growth of domestic manufacture and the cheaper supplies of fresh meat, have fallen. Poultry raising has become popular and contributes in an important way to the meat supply. The national bill for imported eggs is no longer presented. In 1924, eggs worth $3,230,113 came in from abroad. In April of that year, this item claimed $271,175. But in April, 1930, imports reached only $44. Local eggs were sold in the interior at two cents apiece.

The Cuban farmer is learning to keep a milk cow and a few pigs fed on the corn and cane which his fields produce. Dairying on standards such as those familiar in the United States is making its appearance. In 1930, there were sold on the market two and a half million pounds of domestic cheese of sorts like those imported, and the amount of "country cheese" reached a total much greater than ever before. Within three years, producers believe, Cuba will be a cheese-exporting country. The production and consumption of butter, especially in the country districts, is rapidly growing, and milk of good standard is readily obtained. With greater production, butter imports have now fallen to insignificance.

In many lines of lighter manufactures, also, recent years have shown marked advance. Cuban operatives have shown good adaptability in the making of men's and women's clothes. Cheaper grades of men's suits are now supplied in all but small part from local factories. Women's wear and fine needlework are turned out in increasing amounts. Hosiery and rayon goods are successfully produced.

The leather industries are yielding good returns not only in the larger towns but in the interior villages. The imports declined from a value of $8,000,000 in 1924 to less than $2,000,000 in 1929, though local production of both fine and cheap grades showed good increases. Furniture imports have had to meet a growing competition from local manufacture. Cement production has shown great increase. A large number of specialty lines formerly figuring in the import statistics are now practically exclusively supplied from local factories.

In the large, the differentiation of local industry which has occurred in Cuba in the last six years, competent observers feel, is unquestionably a matter for national congratulation. The republic in this period of adversity, and it appears to a degree because of this period of adversity, is making rapid strides toward building up a self-contained national economy. "A Cuban can not only eat well but dress well on domestic production." [10]

Not the least favorable circumstance in the new developments is their influence upon the national standard of life. The diversification of economic activities which is now in progress is one which brings more continuous employment to the population, especially in the country districts, and a greater variety in diet and clothing. These changes, desirable in themselves, may be forerunners of a general improvement in the living conditions of the common people who have heretofore shared in only minor degree the benefits of the great economic advance which has occurred in the last generation in the island.

---

[10] The information on which the discussion of recent developments in Cuba is based was secured through the coöperation of Mr. Frederick Todd, Commercial Attaché, American Embassy, Havana.

The importance of discovery of means to combat the diseases which affect both new and established lines of agricultural production in American tropical areas is hard to overestimate. Large amounts of money have been spent by the leading fruit interests in fighting the diseases affecting their products, and the research laboratories of the sugar companies have also done excellent work. Projects are under way for the creation of more far-reaching research organizations with government support.

The best known of the disasters which have affected production is probably the Panama disease which has rendered some of the areas formerly profitable for the banana industry of lessened value, but this is only one of a long list of pests affecting less outstanding crops and preventing the development of others which are now of insignificant yield.

The sugar industry seeks cane yielding higher percentages of sugar and cane immune to the ravages of the "gumming disease," the "mosaic disease," "root disease," "dry top rot," the "frog-hopper," and other pests.

Cacao growers must fight the diseases known as "witch broom" and monilia, and lime growers have to contend with the "wither-tip." Cotton plantations in new areas have also suffered severely. A few years' plantings in new areas have yielded extraordinarily favorable results, only to be followed by the appearance of pests of peculiarly virulent character which have not only wiped out profits but brought plantings definitely to an end. The list of promising undertakings which have met bitter discouragements after success has seemed well assured can be almost indefinitely expanded.

One of the serious handicaps for economic development by differentiation of crops lies in the character of the labor supply. At first sight such a statement does not seem justified for there are to be found here densely populated areas and ones in which the problem of unemployment is ever present, or the population is forced to live on such a low standard of life that basic wage costs, it appears, should be low. From some of these areas, such as Barbados, a fairly steady supply of labor should be available for new enterprises, but it has not been available at wage costs which make competition possible with producers in the Far East or indeed in Africa. Importation of East Indian labor has been tried in certain of the British colonies in the Caribbean. On the whole, it no longer seems to be in favor with the colonial authorities and is not encouraged by the Indian government.

Chinese and Japanese laborers have not come in in large numbers. There are a few thousand Chinese in the British colonies and possibly an equal number in the mainland areas. In Cuba, there is an appreciable number of Chinese in and around Havana. The republic has an exclusion law applying to the Chinese but until recently it has not been effectively enforced. As late as 1924, there was a net immigration gain of 3,061 Chinese immigrants. The Chinese population of Cuba contributes to the diversification of Cuban production through its activity in truck gardening, especially in the neighborhood of the capital. On the whole, however, immigration from the Far East is not important. There is good reason to believe that the diversification of the labor supply is one means by which the lines of local production in a number of Caribbean areas could be increased, but the political questions which it has been felt would arise and the disadvantages which might come from the addition of another factor to race relations already not of the simplest character have thus far deterred the local governments from adopting general programs for encouragement of Oriental immigration.

Strengthening the economic basis of a community's life through increase in the number of its staple products for domestic consumption and export may be supplemented through a diversification of the markets in which it sells its goods. A development of this sort may lessen the effects on the local industry of bad times which affect the markets of the customer countries. It will also increase the number of people who are possible buyers and lessen the effect of the adoption of unfavorable tariff rates in any individual country.

Review of the developments in the course of trade since 1900 shows some interesting shifts in the markets of certain of the Caribbean countries, but these have in some cases involved substitutions rather than the adding of new markets to ones already established. One of the most interesting of these changes is that in the coffee trade elsewhere discussed. Canadian and British preferential treatment of West Indian colonial products has made their markets broader. Dominican sugars have widened their markets, and to some extent the same thing has occurred in those of Cuba. Though the sales continue to be predominantly in the United States, about one-fifth of the exports in some years finds a market elsewhere.[11] The expansion of the fruit trade in the European and Canadian markets has also been marked since the World War period. Caribbean petroleum, with the establishment of local refining facilities, tends to find new outlets.

Diversification of local manufacturing industries has only recently claimed consistent attention. The lack of industrial power resources, the nonindustrial character of the labor supply, and the fewness of locally produced industrial raw materials have all been limitations on the development of industry and some of these factors, it seems, will be permanent handicaps. Water powers have been little relied

---

[11] In 1927, about 22 per cent of the Cuban exports of sugar were sold outside the United States, and in 1929, 23 per cent. *The American Sugar Refining Company Annual Report, 1929,* p. 18, quoting Cuban statistics by Guma-Mejer.

upon.[12]   Undeveloped waterfalls are not in positions which promise that they can soon be utilized.   The rise of the petroleum industry has not yet brought into existence local manufactures depending upon oil for power.   For the near future, at least, it seems that the only manufacturing activities that are likely to develop are the lighter transforming industries dependent as a rule on foreign raw materials.   Tariff legislation, looking toward building up production in such lines, has been receiving greater attention in recent years and in Cuba, at least, has already appreciably affected imports in a number of lines.[13]   Such activities, as a rule, are destined to flourish chiefly in the supply of the local markets and only under the protection of tariffs.

Accepting the preponderance of the traditional lines of production, their current tendency to increase in importance, the problems that have had to be faced in fighting plant diseases, the limitations on the labor supply, the need for broader markets, and the very limited success which has attended efforts to establish local manufactures, what are the prospects for better diversification of activity?   Can the minor lines of production be expected in the long run to become of greater importance and are there others untried or now only in the field of experiment which may make the outlook brighter?

[12] WATER POWER IN THE CARIBBEAN REGION

Region	Developed Horsepower	Potential Horsepower
West Indies	19,350	150,000
Central America	38,400	5,000,000
British Guiana	.....	2,500,000
French Guiana	.....	500,000
Colombia	114,000	2,500,000
Venezuela	13,000	3,000,000
TOTAL	184,750	13,650,000

Compiled from *Commerce Yearbook, 1929,* Vol. II, p. 734.
[13] *Commerce Reports,* October 15, 1929, p. 195.

At first sight it seems that the increase of the sorts of agricultural products raised should be easy. A large number of specialized products are already widely raised in small amounts such as ginger, kola, sarsaparilla, nutmegs, allspice, arrowroot, and lime juice. All such products, however, have a restricted market. Their sales are not easily expanded, and even a moderate increase in supply might push prices down to levels at which profits would disappear. But there exist also a large number of products already grown locally or which, it may be, can be grown, which are not equally subject to such limitations and which, if marketing facilities can be found and production put on a basis to compete with other tropical areas, should have good prospects.

Among these are citrus fruits. These can be grown in the Caribbean area cheaply and in large quantities. The market in the United States, except when they come from Porto Rico, is now closed to them because of the prevalence of pests which might spread to the American producing areas. Even if these were eliminated, no satisfactory outlet is to be expected in the United States, for if competition became serious, legislation would doubtless be passed to protect domestic production. A minor market already exists in Canada and the northern European countries are a promising potential outlet as is indicated by the recent expansion of the sales there of bananas. Fruit shipments other than bananas are already being made from Argentina, Chile, Uruguay, and Brazil to northern markets, and the possibility of developing a similar trade from the Caribbean is attractive.

A number of tropical fruits now little exploited have some promise.[14] Experiments are already under way in

---

[14] Extensive experiments with new crops which are being conducted by the United Fruit Company at Tela, Honduras, are described by Wilson Popenoe and Alfred F. Butler in an article on the Lancetilla Experiment Station in the Spanish edition of the *Pan-American Bulletin*, June, 1930.

the production of Asiatic varieties of mangoes. Alligator pears, the mamey, and a large variety of other tropical fruits little known in northern markets could be made valuable additions to the diet of more temperate regions if communications, marketing facilities, and freedom from pests can be assured. The latter form a serious, though perhaps not insuperable, limitation upon development of trade in these lines with the United States. If they can be eliminated, their import would not have the disadvantage of direct competition with a local industry which limits the prospect for citrous fruits. In northern Europe, where similar conflicts of interest are not present, it may prove possible to develop satisfactory sales.

Off-season vegetables already enter into export trade in a small way. Early potatoes, onions, eggplants, and melons are shipped from Cuba to the north. Pineapples and grapefruit, both canned and fresh, are a regular export from Porto Rico. Off-season tomatoes come in considerable quantities from the west coast of Mexico and could be cultivated in a number of Caribbean regions. Plantains, a variety of banana lacking in sweetness but widely used in the Caribbean as a vegetable, already find their way to the United States to centers in which Latin Americans are well represented and could be shipped in large quantities if they could be popularized as a part of the northern diet. Cassava has some promise both as a foodstuff and as a material used in manufacture of textiles.

A number of more staple foodstuffs already widely used can be raised in far greater quantities than at present but have now to contend against a high cost of production as compared to that in the competing areas. Cacao was once relatively much more important in the Caribbean than it is now that West African sources of supply have taken the lead. Rice production can be increased indefinitely but the prices offered in the Far East have made the prospects discouraging. Dates might possibly be grown but no advance in this line has yet occurred. Coconuts grow well and already are produced in quantity, especially in Jamaica, where they are one of the chief crops. Costs of establishing a coconut walk seem low and once established it practically takes care of itself for half a century, but the operating expenses are now higher than in the Far East. If the world continues to demand increasing quantities of vegetable fats for food and industrial purposes, the by-product copra may become a Caribbean staple. Success in such lines as these depends not on the ability to produce them in the Caribbean so much as on the ability to cut down the cost of production.

There are also among those who have studied the outlook some who believe that coffee still holds great possibilities in spite of the fact that the market is now embarrassed by overproduction.

Certain industrial materials are also looked upon as promising. Among these is henequin fiber or sisal, the material from which a large part of the binder twine of the world is made. Formerly it was practically a monopoly of Yucatan but is now grown successfully in the Mexican states of Vera Cruz and Tamaulipas, on the west coast of Africa and in Cuba. There are many Caribbean regions in which the crop could be established. Experiments are being carried on in raising the oil palm, that dual-purpose tree yielding distinct oils from the pulp and the seed of its fruit. Certain cabinet woods, especially Spanish cedar and mahogany, are also being grown experimentally.

But most of the developments indicated are still of the future and those that are not have to overcome established dietary habits in markets to be established, or marketing problems or plant diseases, or high production costs or, what may be the most serious limitation of all, the inertia and prejudice which all new ventures encounter. The best promise lies, it appears, in developing new tropical and subtropical foodstuffs in which the Far East, even with its low labor costs or because of its distance, cannot compete and which cannot be produced in the great northern industrial markets.   At best, it seems that for the near future the economic basis of Caribbean prosperity will be narrow, though the developments of recent years show that it can be made less insecure by broadening the markets on which the staple products are offered and by encouraging new local industries for supplying local demands and in some cases special foreign markets.

CHAPTER XI

CARIBBEAN COMMERCE

In the years following the discovery of the new world, economic developments in the Caribbean received only slight attention. For more than a century and a half, a period equal to that in which the United States has been an independent nation, there was only a negligible advance. The number of settlers of European stock was low, there were no important discoveries of precious metals,[1] and trade in the staple commodities which the region later came to produce in such large quantities was restricted. Holdings were coveted by northern Europeans in part because they gave an opportunity to prey on the Spanish trade, not primarily to and from the Caribbean, but that which went farther west to Mexico at Vera Cruz and south to Peru by way of the isthmus.

It was over a hundred years after the landing of Columbus, before England and France made their first permanent settlements in the Caribbean and even these were freebooters' outposts rather than genuine colonies. In 1595, Sir Walter Raleigh, on the way to Guiana, stopped at Trinidad and claimed it for Queen Elizabeth. A French expedition to Guiana made the first permanent settlement there in 1604. The next year, the English visited Barbados which later became their first prosperous colony. Before the middle of the century, one outpost after another was established in the West Indies by the French and English, and in 1655 the British drove the Spanish from Jamaica.

---

[1] The gold mines of Colombia are a partial exception. It is claimed that during the entire colonial period they yielded over 800,000 kilograms. Abraham Martinez, *Colombia Yearbook, 1927* (New York, 1928), p. 197.

In this century and a half in which Spain had had almost a free hand, the only promising economic development was in the English colony in Barbados. Spain had done little herself in the first discovered of the new American regions. For the first half century her colonial policy was for the time generous. The conditions under which trade could be carried on were regulated after 1503 by the Casa de Contratación but up to 1542 its policies were not seriously restrictive.

In that year, its functions were recast. In the same period viceroys were being appointed for Mexico and Peru, and in general a more detailed system of control was being elaborated. The desire of the government for revenue from the colonies was growing, and the attention of the officials to regions where it could be secured became keener. Agricultural areas were neglected and the limitations on commerce, restriction of emigration, and exclusion of foreigners cut down the initiative for colonial activity. The first hundred and fifty years brought little progress in the Caribbean areas which continued under Spanish control.

For still another century and a half, from 1650 to 1800, in fact, Spanish Caribbean activity continued low. The restrictive trade policy encouraged contraband, which in some periods contributed to the life of the colonies as much as legal trade. But through the period up to 1800, the old policy on one point after another was abandoned. By the Treaty of Utrecht, in 1713, the English secured the right to sell slaves to Spanish-American colonies and to send a single merchant ship of five hundred tons in the Porto Bello trade. Both concessions were soon abused. In 1748, the annual fleets of Spain serving Caribbean trade were abolished. In 1764, the year after the English had established themselves in a fleeting ten-months' possession of the "Pearl of the Antilles," monthly packet boats were dispatched to Havana. The next year, West Indian trade was opened to all Spaniards. These were forward steps and the trade with Cuba and Porto Rico soon reflected their influence. The yearly arrivals of vessels in Havana rose from six in 1765 to over 200 in 1778. Duties at the port tripled, exports increased fivefold.[2] Other colonies also began to be treated more liberally. Restrictions on intercolonial trade were lessened, and the more liberal commercial policy which had already shown its effect in the islands was, in 1778, extended to the north coast of South America and to Central America. Still when three hundred years of Spanish control of her new world colonies came to an end, though they had not been without benefits, the record, from an economic point of view, was far from satisfactory.

The English and French rivals, meanwhile, in their much less important holdings, had pushed agricultural development. Barbados had advanced its sugar trade, reaching the height of its prosperity about 1670. Jamaica proved an even greater asset. However, by the last quarter of the eighteenth century, the conditions of the English colonies were less favorable. Prohibition of refining sugar in Jamaica, the trade limitations of the Navigation Acts, and the loss of markets through the American Revolution all made their outlook less bright.[3]

French struggle for position in the Caribbean, and indeed in all of what is now known as Latin America, involves a history of great promise and great misfortune. On the whole, the rivalry with the English, in spite of agreements solemnly entered to avoid it, was practically continuous and resulted unfavorably to France. The internal management of the French West Indian colonies, too, up to the first decade of the eighteenth century, was from an economic point of view highly unfortunate.

---

[2] H. C. Morris, *The History of Colonization* (New York, 1908), Vol. I, p. 268.

[3] See Lowell Joseph Ragatz, *The Fall of the Planter Class in the British Caribbean, 1763-1833* (New York, 1928), especially pp. 37-141.

But better days were coming. The history of the French West Indies in the eighteenth century furnishes a brilliant contrast both to the prospects preceding and to the disaster which was to follow. At the beginning of the period, the outlook was far from favorable. By the Treaty of Utrecht, the highly lucrative slave trade which had been carried on by the French Guinea Company had to be surrendered. But far-reaching changes in French commercial policy counterbalanced this loss and so stimulated production that the colonies became the envy of all Europe. The sponsor of these measures was John Law whose name was to go down in history connected with financial plans anything but sound. But for the islands, the system of economic and political control which he set up was liberal to a degree before unknown and successful beyond the highest hope of even his most ardent supporters.

Under Law's initiative, colonial duties on exports to France were reduced, export from the mother country to the Antilles was made free. "Colonial products" resold to other countries paid only a tax of 3 per cent, and with some exceptions special privileges of trading companies were suppressed. Coffee and cotton were introduced as crops to supplement sugar. Liberal standards were set up in colonial administration.

The economic response to these progressive measures was without precedent. Plantations flourished and under a generous land policy were rapidly extended. The virgin soil of the islands yielded crops which brought in unheard-of profits. A steady inflow of "black ivory" from Africa increased the labor supply, and the demand for white employees for the managerial positions grew almost in proportion. French coastal cities rose in commercial importance, and shipping in the West Indies trade reached greater and greater tonnage.

In San Domingo, the greatest of the French West Indian

colonies, the sugar exports increased eighteenfold between 1711 and 1778, reaching a value of over $35,000,000, an amount then of much greater significance than at present. French colonial commerce far outstripped that of England, and its "foreign commerce became almost entirely connected with this island." [4] San Domingo alone, in 1783, produced "nearly as much sugar as all of the British Caribbean colonies combined." [5] Up to the close of the seventeen hundreds, French economic development in the Caribbean was one of its most brilliant features.

Before sketching the great changes which came to affect Caribbean economic development in the nineteenth century, the conditions at the close of the previous period may well be summarized. At the end of the first three hundred years of European colonization, the Caribbean region presented socially, politically, and economically highly irregular conditions. To it had come marked changes in the character of its populations. The natives of the island areas had practically disappeared. The European immigration which in some restricted areas had at first shown a tendency to grow had not continued to do so. In the island areas, the number of Africans had steadily increased and already in many far outnumbered those representing other races. On the mainland European blood had become in large degree mixed with that of aboriginal stocks.

Economic progress which had occurred in the region as a whole was disappointing. In the least favorable position was Central America, farthest from Europe and with its economically most valuable regions facing the Pacific. Its trade outlets to the European world were precarious, infrequent, and highly expensive. The trade routes which the

---

[4] A. H. L. Heeren, *Geschichte der europäischen Staaten* (Gotha, 1829-83; continued by F. A. Ukart and W. von Gresebrecht), p. 297, cited by Henry C. Morris, *History of Colonization* (New York, 1908), Vol. I, pp. 400-401. From Morris' discussion the preceding paragraphs are summarized.

[5] Ragatz, *op. cit.*, p. 126.

mother country had been willing to allow up to almost the
end of the period had passed north of it to Mexico or south
of it by Porto Bello to Peru. In addition it had little to
sell. Coffee culture had only just made a beginning in
Costa Rica and played no part in the other states. Tropical
fruit was still raised only for the local demand. These
colonies were truly the "orphans of the conquest."

What is now Colombia was still a region in which a small
population of Spanish inheritance was practically shut off
in the interior with difficult access to the outside world by
the highly unsatisfactory communications down the Magdalena River. The European population of what is now the
republic of Venezuela was in greater degree within reach of
the coast but under Spanish policy had had no satisfactory
economic growth.

The West Indies, though like the mainland lacking in
precious metals, had after a long period of slow development come into much more intense exploitation, but even
there prosperity was irregular. English and especially
French island possessions had at the end of the period a
much greater economic yield than those controlled by Spain.

European political control was still unquestioned.
Within the colonies, popular participation in government
had hardly made a beginning and public policy continued
to be determined in Europe. The large numbers of blacks
which had been imported into the islands for their economic
exploitation lived under conditions which in some of the
areas made slave revolt a danger as events were to prove,
and the political conditions on the mainland were such that
once change in governmental arrangements became an
issue Spanish control could not be maintained. Up to the
closing years of the eighteenth century, however, few
could foresee the rise of movements which were to revolu-
tionize the Caribbean political outlook.

A revolt started by the blacks in Haiti in 1791 resulted,

after vacillation by the French authorities on proposals to free the slaves, in setting up a Negro republic under a constitution of 1801. Later, Haiti extended its control for a time over the entire island. The Spanish mainland colonies declared opposition to Napoleonic control of the mother country and later came out for independence. By 1826, all the mainland possessions of Spain had been lost. After the middle of the century, Spain reëstablished control of her colony in San Domingo only again to relinquish it. Sweden sold its diminutive colony on St. Bartholomew to France, and at the end of the century Spain lost the last vestige of her once great American empire.

Political changes of such sweeping character might be expected to have far-reaching effects on economic development. They did so, but not in the way which those who led the revolutions establishing the new states expected. Economic advance did not follow independence. Inexperience in government and civil dissension which arose from it proved a heavy drag upon enterprise. In the mainland areas, export and import trade showed improvement as the years passed and at the end of the nineteenth century, if comparisons be made on percentages of increase, the advance in some cases was marked, but it was so because foreign exchanges were at the beginning so insignificant. The actual bulk increases were discouragingly small and in some cases for decades the exports and imports of many regions showed no definite progress. Petroleum production had not begun.

A satisfactory review of the advance through the period is not possible, but the general trend may be illustrated by examples. In some of the states of Central America, conditions were least encouraging. Commercial statistics were irregularly and incompletely published and in some cases were lacking for decades at a time. Colombian imports between 1832 and 1870 showed an increase in value of only about $3,400,000 and between 1870 and 1898 increased less than $6,000,000 to reach a total at the time of the Spanish-American War of only $11,083,000.[6]

Such progress as did occur in the development of resources was largely in the island areas which remained under European control and was greatest in regions not formerly in leading positions. Haiti, the leading French colony of the previous century, after its establishment of independence fell to a position of economic insignificance, and the other French colonies played no important rôle. The British colonies had the advantage of better public order than the mainland states, but the public policies adopted by the home country which had formerly put them in a privileged position did so no longer. Short rations and even famine appeared in the British islands at the opening of the nineteenth century. Later slavery was abolished, British preferential tariff rates disappeared, sugar production declined, beet sugar competition increased.

Jamaica, the most valued among the British colonies, went through a long period of difficult years especially after the abolition of slavery, in which sugar production, its chief industry, experienced a steady decline. Not even an increasing trade with the United States in newer lines was able to make conditions satisfactory. Sugar export fell by more than half between 1866 and 1897.[7] The imports in 1900 were only 2,305,000 dollars greater in value than they had been a half century earlier.[8] Other islands showed no more encouraging advance.

---

[6] *Colombia; A Commercial and Industrial Handbook*, U. S. Department of Commerce, Bureau of Foreign and Domestic Commerce, Special Agents Series, No. 206 (Washington, 1921), p. 313, and *Statistical Abstract of Foreign Countries*, U. S. Department of Commerce and Labor, Bureau of Statistics (Washington, Oct., 1909), p. 60.

[7] *Statistical Abstract for the Colonial and Other Possessions of the United Kingdom, 1863-1877* (London, 1879), in House of Commons, 1879, Vol. 75, pp. 72-73, and *Ibid.*, 1883-1897 (London, 1898), in House of Commons, 1898, Vol. 100, pp. 40-41.

[8] *Statistical Abstract of Foreign Countries, 1909*, Parts I-III, p. 50.

The only West Indian units, which in the nineteenth century were partial exceptions to the general malaise, were Cuba and Porto Rico. The fresh lands of Cuba particularly and the fact that it continued to use slave labor long after it had elsewhere been abolished, enabled the Spanish producers to meet unfavorable conditions which their neighbors could not.

In 1800, Havana had exported only 20,000 tons of sugar and in 1820 but 50,000.[9] More Negroes were steadily imported after the abolition of slavery in the British colonies, and the rapidly advancing market in the United States emphasized the advantages to be drawn from exceptional labor conditions.

In 1840, beet sugar was only 4 per cent of the total production of 1,288,000 tons from cane and beet. It steadily rose to 34 per cent of the total in 1870.[10] This competition continued. Before the disappearance of slavery from the West Indies cane sugar had fallen to about one-half of the world production.[11] The tariff and bounty

[9] George Thomas Surface, *The Story of Sugar* (New York, 1918), p. 28.
[10] National Bank of Commerce in New York, *The World's Sugar Supply* (New York, 1917), p. 9. For the decline of the plantation system in the British West Indies, see Ragatz, *op. cit.*, and his *Statistics for the Study of British Caribbean Economic History, 1763-1883* (London, 1928).
[11] George M. Rolph, *Something about Sugar* (San Francisco, 1917), p. 135, quoting figures by Willet and Gray gives a table from which the following data are compiled.

Year	Cane Sugar, Tons	Total, Tons	Per Cent Cane Sugar
1852–3	1,260,404	1,463,214	86.0
1864–5	1,446,934	1,996,727	73.5
1874–5	1,903,222	3,206,221	59.4
1883–4	2,210,000	4,695,300	47.0
1887–8	2,541,000	4,908,200	51.7

Subsequently the proportion of cane sugar rose, and by the end of the first decade of the following century beet sugar contributed about the same proportion as in 1870 in a very greatly increased yield. On the average for 1909-13 in a total of 28,800,000 short tons of beet and cane sugar the former accounted for 8,800,000 short tons or about 30.5 per cent. *Commerce Yearbook, 1926* (Washington, 1927), Vol. II, p. 609.

policies adopted by the countries of continental Europe gave no encouragement to those interested in production of the leading Caribbean staple. Still Cuba could compete and make profits.

The gradual abolition of slavery in the eighties allowed solution of the labor problem without greatly decreasing the yield. On the whole, it showed an upward tendency until 1895, when the new revolutionary activities, this time affecting the western sugar producing area to a degree which previous disturbances had not, temporarily dealt a serious blow to the island's prosperity from which recovery occurred only after the winning of independence.

The nineteenth century, which had brought such remarkable advance in economic lines in western Europe and the United States, had left the Caribbean behind in the march of progress. Independence in the republics had not brought the free institutions of which the heroes of the revolution had dreamed. "Free" trade had not brought them economic independence. Commercial favor had been lost to the colonies. Retrospect in the closing years of the century gave little cause for optimism and current conditions were no more encouraging.

Stability in public affairs was conspicuous by its absence. Porto Rico, Jamaica, and the smaller colonial possessions were at peace, but budgets were frequently unbalanced or only balanced by grants in aid. Cuba was again in insurrection against the mother country in a struggle which was to end in intervention by the United States. The Dominican Republic was dragging through the last years of the long dictatorship of Ulises Heureaux. Its trade was languishing, its credit destroyed. Already the horizon was darkened by heavy debt and damage claims which shortly threatened to bring independence to an end. Haiti, in the interval between two of the longer dictatorships, was going through a series of violent changes of administration.

Rumors of European intervention were being heard, and foreign claims were accumulating and soon to become a major international issue.

The mainland showed conditions hardly more encouraging. Venezuela had just come out of the boundary dispute with Great Britain in 1896 and was being led by the new President Castro into a series of altercations with European powers which were settled, like the controversy with Great Britain, only through the good offices of the United States. Colombia, which in spite of lack of capital and poor transportation facilities had begun to show some signs of progress, was having a period of hard times in the nineties caused by the growing competition of Brazilian coffees. The revolution of 1895 was followed by another of disastrous character in 1899, and the republic embarked on a policy of currency inflation which completely upset its economic organization.

The Central American states also were going through a series of unfortunate experiences. Guatemala, the most populous, had had a series of leaders who brought the finances of the country into very serious condition. It passed, in 1898, under the control of the dictator Manuel Estrada Cabrera who was to set up an arbitrary government which proved unable to check the rapid dilapidation of the public finances. In Nicaragua, the sixteen-year period of domination by Zelaya had begun in 1893, to continue until public finance and private enterprise became so disorganized as to bring the country into serious conflict with the United States. Honduras was still a pawn in the disputes of her more powerful neighbors and powerless to deal with her already overwhelming public debt held by the British bondholders. In Salvador, the government had been overthrown by a *coup d'état* in 1890, a revolution had again upset it in 1894, and it had yielded to force again in 1898. A period of peace was just ahead but recent history gave little reason for confidence in its coming. Costa Rica alone gave reasonable promise of orderly progress. It had passed through a series of administrations in which control of the army had played an important part but there, at least, peace had come to be reasonably assured, and the prospect for economic development of the limited natural resources was good.

The unsatisfactory political circumstances which were prevalent throughout the Caribbean were reflected in the conditions in public finance. In the last decade of the nineteenth century, the budget of not a single colony was in a satisfactory position, and all but one of the independent units went into default in the payments on its public obligations. The exception was Haiti in which, however, the currency and economic activity were perhaps in conditions as little satisfactory as anywhere in the entire area.

In private enterprise, the outlook, at least at first sight, was equally discouraging. Local capital could develop resources only with great difficulty. Even though the revolutions often did not involve heavy casualties, they discouraged the development of property, interrupted business, and in many cases upset the value of the currency through issues of unsecured paper which introduced unforeseeable risks in commercial transactions. Profits tended to be invested abroad or to be put into landholdings, which, though yielding a low return, were at least not subject to great disturbance by revolution. Foreign capital came into the region for investment only under exceptional conditions. In 1900, there were only some $50,000,000 of American capital invested in Cuba.[12] Negligible amounts only had entered other Caribbean units. Even as late as 1913, the total British investments, then the largest factor in the foreign capital account in the region, were only some $416,-

---

[12] Harry T. Collings, *Die Kapitalexpansion der Vereinigten Staaten in Lateinamerika* (Jena, 1927), p. 7.

000,000 of which $222,000,000 were in Cuba. American holdings at the same date were about $285,000,000 of which $220,000,00, it is estimated, were in Cuba. Outside of Cuba the total foreign investment probably did not amount to much over 350,000,000 dollars.[13]

International trade movements in the last two decades of the century gave ground for a fair degree of encouragment. They were the only easily visible favorable factor. Satisfactory figures over a period of years are not available for all the Caribbean units, but a fair indication of what was going on can be made for 1880 and 1900, except in the case of Cuba, which in both years was recovering from the effects of long drawn out revolutionary activity. Imports for the rest of the Caribbean in the first year had a value of somewhat over $90,000,000 and at the second were worth slightly over $100,000,000. Exports had a more satisfactory growth. They totaled a little less than $100,000,000 in 1880, but about $133,000,000 at the opening of the century.[14]

Jamaica, among the colonies, showed some improvement under the influence of an expanding fruit trade. Colombia, Costa Rica, and Guatemala, among the republics, made the best advance. Elsewhere, in Central America and on the north coast of South America, commercial exchanges showed little improvement between 1880 and 1900, and in many of the smaller island colonies, the total values of imports and exports were less at the end of the century than they were twenty years before.

---

[13] These figures are compiled from tables in Max Winkler, *Investments of United States Capital in Latin America* (Boston, 1928).

[14] These figures are only approximations. It is not possible to secure trustworthy data for the years indicated in some instances and there is considerable variation from year to year reported in some units. The statistics on which the estimates are based are drawn in the main from the *Statistical Abstract of Foreign Countries, 1909; Statistical Abstract for the Principal and Other Foreign Countries, in each year from 1901 to 1912* (London, 1914), and the issues of the *Statesman's Yearbook.*

Though the coming of a new day for the Caribbean was by no means self-evident in 1900, influences were already at work which it is now easy to see must profoundly modify its development. Most important among these was the increasing industrialization of the world which would bring about a greater demand for raw materials and for foodstuffs for the populations gravitating toward the cities. This would create a greater demand in Europe for the things which the Caribbean could produce, and, as shipments of these increased, result in greater local buying power.

But the similar industrial development in the United States would be of even greater influence. There free land practically disappeared with the end of the century. Industry was to take a more prominent part in the national life. It was to expand rapidly into the south and west. Twenty years before, only somewhat over a quarter of the population had lived in towns of over twenty-five hundred inhabitants. In the next twenty-five years, over half would do so. The national wealth of the United States was in the same period of twenty years to increase almost fourfold. The republic was to become the greatest creditor nation of the world, and a large portion of the capital invested abroad was to be directed southward. The foreign trade of the United States was to have a remarkable increase from about two and a quarter billion dollars to a high point of over thirteen and a half billion dollars and later to reach a steadier base at between nine and ten billion dollars. Development of this sort could not fail to have a far-reaching economic influence in neighboring areas.

Other influences, some of them rising within the Caribbean region itself and some of distant origin, were to stimulate its activity. Within the republics, there were to come into being, slowly but surely, political conditions more favorable to stable economic development. The Spanish-American War, then just terminated, was to result in an independent

Cuba, producing, under a reciprocity treaty with the United States, five times as much for world trade as in colonial days. The Panama Canal was to be dug, putting the neglected Caribbean on one of the world's great trade routes and bringing the Pacific coast of Central America into more direct contact with western civilization. The fruit trade, already growing, was to have greater significance. It was to increase communication facilities by steamship lines, railroads, and radio stations, bring the sanitation of extensive areas and the establishment of modern hospitals. Central American and Colombian coffees were making irregular headway. Oil fields were to be developed, first off the northern border of the Caribbean and later in the Caribbean region itself. Instead of the cul-de-sac which it had been for the four hundred years since the conquest, this area was about to find itself in the full stream of world affairs and approaching the position of an American Mediterranean.

The influence of the new conditions on Caribbean advance shows itself in all branches of economic life but in none so strikingly as in foreign trade.

The trade development since 1900 falls into two periods: that from the opening of the century to the years preceding the World War and that during and following the war. The great increases in trade values noted in the tabulations are ones which, for years following 1913, must be considered, keeping in mind the changes which have occurred in price levels. Particularly in the value of imports into the Caribbean, the higher values do not represent a proportionate increase in the quantities of the various items that make up the total. On the other hand, the increases in values of exports require less adjustment to make them comparable to the prewar figures, since in many of the foodstuff and raw material items exported in large quantities, the prices per unit have increased much less than in the articles which enter imports. Even making allowance for differences in

IMPORTS OF CARIBBEAN COUNTRIES
(*In millions of dollars*)

Region	1880	1900	1911-13 Average	1928
The Islands				
The Major Islands				
Cuba	...	71.6 [1]	125.5	211.9
Dominican Republic	1.7	3.2	8.1	26.8
Haiti	7.0	6.9	9.1	20.2
Jamaica	7.1	8.2	13.8 [2]	29.1 [3]
Porto Rico	...	8.9 [4]	39.5	92.3 [4]
Trinidad and Tobago	.1	11.5	13.7 [2]	24.7 [3]
The Lesser Islands				
American				
St. Thomas ⎱ .... St. John ⎰	...	.7	1.0 [5]	1.7
St. Croix	...	.9	.7 [5]	.8 [5]
British				
Bahamas	.8	1.4	1.9 [2]	8.9
Barbados	5.6	5.0	6.5 [2]	11.1 [3]
Grenada	.6	1.1	1.3 [2]	2.0 [3]
Leeward Islands	2.2	1.6	2.8 [2]	4.1 [3]
St. Lucia	.6	1.9	1.4 [2]	1.1
St. Vincent	.7	.4	.6 [2]	.9
Turks and Caicos	.1	.1	.1 [2]	.2 [3]
Dutch				
Curaçao and Dependencies..	2.2	...	1.9	57.1
French				
Guadeloupe	11.3	8.9	7.9	14.5 [3]
TOTAL, Islands	...	132.3	235.8	507.4
Central America, Panama, and British Honduras				
British Honduras	.9	1.0	3.2	4.5 [3]
Costa Rica	3.6	6.3	9.2	17.9
Guatemala	3.5	4.1	9.4	24.1
Honduras	1.7	1.6	4.3	12.6
Nicaragua	1.4	2.5	5.5	13.4
Panama	...	...	10.3	16.7 [6]
Salvador	2.2	2.5	6.1	19.2
TOTAL, Central America, Panama, and British Honduras ..	...	18.0	48.0	108.4

IMPORTS OF CARIBBEAN COUNTRIES—*Continued*

(*In millions of dollars*)

Region	1880	1900	1911-13 Average	1928
Northern South America				
Colombia	10.1	10.7	22.8	123.3
Guiana				
British	9.6	6.6	8.0	11.9 [3]
French	1.5	1.8	2.2	2.2 [3]
Dutch	1.5	2.4	3.4	4.2 [3]
Venezuela	14.4	8.5 [7]	18.9	69.0 [3]
TOTAL, Northern South America	...	30.0	55.3	210.6
SUMMARY				
The Islands	...[8]	132.3	235.8	507.4
Central America, Panama, and				
British Honduras	...	18.0	48.0	108.4
Northern South America	...	30.0	55.3	210.6
TOTAL, Caribbean		180.3	339.1	826.4

1 *Statistical Abstract of Foreign Countries, 1909*, Parts I-III, p. 148.
2 1913.
3 1927.
4 From *Twenty-ninth Annual Report of the Governor of Porto Rico, Honorable Horace M. Towner.*
5 *The Virgin Islands of the United States, A General Report by the Governor* (Washington, 1928), p. 89.
6 *Commerce Yearbook, 1929*, Vol. II, p. 505.
7 Venezuela was going through a difficult period at the beginning of the century. The imports in 1898 (listed above) were worth $8,500,000. In 1903 they totaled $5,400,000.
8 The total of 1880 is omitted because satisfactory figures for Cuba and Porto Rico cannot be given.
The figures cited for 1880 are from the *Statesman's Yearbook* for various years, the *Statistical Abstract of Foreign Countries,* 1909, and the *Statistical Abstract for the Principal and Other Foreign Countries, in each year from 1880 to 1889–90* (London, 1892), in House of Commons, 1892, Vol. 87. In some cases a choice has been taken because the figures reported are not uniform in different authorities. Except where otherwise indicated the figures for 1911–13 and 1928 are compiled from *Commerce Yearbook, 1929*, Vol. II, pp. 684, 768-769.

the value of money, the growth of Caribbean trade since 1900 is remarkable. In dollar values, imports into the Caribbean as a whole almost doubled in the period before the war, and by 1928 were over four and a half times as great as in 1900, reaching a value of $826,400,000. Exports grew even more rapidly. They more than doubled in the prewar period, and in 1928 were over five times as great as in 1900, totaling $923,700,000.

Exports of Caribbean Countries
(In millions of dollars)

Region	1880	1900	1911-13 Average	1928
The Islands				
The Major Islands				
Cuba	...	45.2 [1]	153.2	278.1
Dominican Republic	1.6	6.0	11.3	28.8
Haiti	6.0	13.6	15.7	22.7
Jamaica	7.0	8.3	13.8 [2]	29.1
Porto Rico	...	8.5 [3]	47.3 [3]	103.5 [3]
Trinidad and Tobago	.1	12.0	13.7 [2]	24.7 [4]
The Lesser Islands				
American				
St. Thomas	...	...	...	...
St. John	...	...	...	...
St. Croix	...	.6	.3 [5]	1.0 [5]
British				
Bahamas	.5	1.0	1.9 [2]	8.9
Barbados	5.6	4.2	6.5 [2]	11.1 [4]
Grenada	.8	1.5	1.3 [2]	2.0 [4]
Leeward Islands	2.8	1.3	2.8 [2]	4.1 [4]
St. Lucia	.9	.4	1.4 [2]	1.1
St. Vincent	.7	.4	.6 [2]	.9
Turks and Caicos	.1	.1	.2 [2]	.2 [4]
Dutch				
Curaçao and Dependencies..	...	...	.9	54.0 [4]
French				
Guadeloupe and Martinique	12.4	8.2	9.4	16.1 [4]
Total, Islands	...	111.3	280.3	586.3
Central America, Panama, and British Honduras				
British Honduras	1.0	1.1	...	4.5 [4]
Costa Rica	2.7	6.3	9.7	20.6
Guatemala	4.3	7.3	12.9	28.2
Honduras	2.2	2.5	3.1	23.1
Nicaragua	2.0	2.8	6.1	11.7
Panama	...	...	3.4	4.1 [6]
Salvador	4.4	4.2	9.1	25.5
Total, Central America, Panama and British Honduras	...	24.2	44.3	117.7
Northern South America				
Colombia	13.4	18.6	28.7	113.9
Guiana				
British	12.7	7.9	9.6	15.7 [4]

EXPORTS OF CARIBBEAN COUNTRIES—*Continued*

(*In millions of dollars*)

Region	1880	1900	1911-13 Average	1928
French	1.0	1.2 [4]	2.3	1.2
Dutch	1.4	4.7 [4]	3.4	2.2
Venezuela	10.9	84.2 [4]	25.6	7.7
TOTAL, Northern South America	...	219.7	69.6	37.6
SUMMARY				
The Islands	...	586.3	280.3	111.3
Central America, Panama and British Honduras	...	117.7	44.3	24.2
Northern South America	...	219.7	69.6	37.6
TOTAL, Caribbean [7]	...	923.7	394.2	173.1

1 The exports from Cuba at this time were exceptionally low because of the effects of the then recent revolution. The figures quoted are given in *Statistical Abstract of Foreign Countries, 1909*, Parts I-III, p. 148.

2 1913.

3 *Twenty-ninth Annual Report of the Governor of Porto Rico, Honorable Horace M. Towner*, p. 36.

4 1927.

5 *The Virgin Islands of the United States*, p. 89. The figure in the column for 1928 is for 1926.

6 *Commerce Yearbook, 1929*, Vol. II, p. 505.

7 For the general sources of the statistics for 1880 see note at the end of the table for imports.

Analysis of the changes that have occurred in the more important commercial areas reflects the influences which have transformed the Caribbean economic outlook. Cuba continues to be the most important unit, as it was both a quarter and a half century ago. It outdistances all others with a total foreign trade of $490,000,000 in 1928. Its relative importance, however, has declined. Its commerce was 32 per cent of the total, in 1900, even though it was at that time still suffering from the effects of the War of Independence. Its commerce had decreased to 28 per cent in 1928.[15]

The five republics of Central America, though they are

15 In this year also its trade was below that of previous years. It reached $1,351,000,000 in the boom of 1920 but has in more recent years steadily declined with the unfavorable conditions in the sugar trade.

geographically in many respects a unit, offer contrasts in economic conditions which make grouping them together to some degree artificial. In commercial advance, however, they have all gone through similar experiences in the last half century. In spite of defective government and limited resources, their trade showed some advance even in the last twenty years of the nineteenth century. Its total rose from about $27,000,000 in 1880, to about $42,000,000 in 1900 —an increase of somewhat more than 50 per cent in twenty years.[16] The better showing after the turn of the century is due to a number of causes important among which were the opening of the Panama Canal, the accentuation of the fruit trade, and the favorable prices for coffee which were brought about partly through the influence of the Brazilian arrangements for affecting the market. In the thirteen years between the opening of the century and the World War, the trade of the group doubled in value, and between 1913 and 1928, it more than doubled again, reaching $226,000,000 in 1928.

Nicaraguan foreign trade reached in 1928 slightly over $25,000,000, the lowest total for any country of the group. It has shown sharp variations, but has increased fivefold since 1900. Coffee in most years is the most valuable item and averages about half of the total value. Bananas are about one-fourth. Honduras, in many ways the weakest republic of the group, has had in the last quarter century one of the most striking of economic developments. Its trade was about $4,000,000 in 1900, but reached almost $34,000,000 in 1928—an increase of over eightfold. It is distinctly a banana country with the commercial production confined to the north coast which has but little economic connection with the Pacific section in which the majority

---

[16] These statements are approximate. The figures are not in some cases available for all the units for both years and those for 1882 or 1901 have in those cases been used.

of the people live. The banana exports in 1927-8 were about 80 per cent of the total shipments.[17]

Salvador, between 1900 and 1928, increased the value of its trade over six times, chiefly due to greater exports of coffee and the higher prices for that staple on world markets. Guatemalan trade increased almost fivefold due to the same influences, though the growth of banana shipments on the Atlantic now has brought them to about one-tenth of the export values. Costa Rican trade also shows almost a four-fold increase since 1900. Formerly Costa Rica was one of the leading countries in the export of tropical fruit. Lately these shipments have declined in amount though their value has increased. Coffee, on the other hand, has maintained itself in quantity and has had favorable prices. Bananas and coffee were of about equal value in the exports in 1913, but the latter, in recent years, is about twice as important as the former and accounts for roughly half of Costa Rican exports.

Taken as a whole, Central American trade since the beginning of the century has increased fivefold. It has not markedly increased its proportion of the whole. It was about 12 per cent of the total in the Caribbean in 1900 and about 13 per cent in 1928.

The north coast of South America has begun to come

---

17 In considering these trade values and those of other units it is to be kept in mind that the value of money underwent great modifications due to the European war. A rough comparison of price levels of imports and exports taking 1913 as a basis may be made from the index numbers compiled for United States trade in *Statistical Abstract of the United States, 1929,* p. 464. The prices of United States exports in 1928 are estimated as 125 as compared to 100 in 1913. The similar figure for United States imports for 1928 is 126. Hence an increase in the dollar value of Central American foreign trade from $80,000,000 in 1913 to $187,000,000 in 1927, does not represent an equivalent increase in the movement of goods. The change in the quantities of the great staples moved in the export trade is shown in the chapters discussing them. For a valuable analysis of the effect of changing dollar values in our Latin-American trade see George J. Eder, "The Actual Growth in Our Latin-American Trade," *Commerce Reports,* July 21, 1930.

into its own. For a large part of the colonial period, it was a region of which much was expected by the European powers, but to their continued disappointment. The Guianas are still a region in which advance is unimportant. Farther westward, however, the new conditions of the last quarter century have materially changed the outlook.

Colombia in 1900 was still commercially stagnant. It had a foreign trade of about $29,000,000, only about $5,000,000 greater in value than twenty years before. But a more active period was ahead. By 1913, the total was $50,000,000, and in 1928, $237,000,000, an increase as compared to 1900 of eightfold and the greatest of all the major areas. The advance was due chiefly to the increased growth of coffee, export of which had risen in value so that it had come to be more than four times the value of all exports in 1900. In recent years, it is close to four-fifths of all the national produce marketed abroad.

Slower to come and even more markedly in one line has been the advance in Venezuela. The exports showed sharp variations in value from year to year and were worth less than $11,000,000 in the eighties. By 1898, they reached a value of almost $15,000,000, but the disturbances of the first years of the century brought them to less than $8,000,-000. By 1913, they had reached $29,000,000. The boom following the European war carried them to $52,000,-000 in 1919, but in 1921 they had fallen again to $29,000,000. From this time on, oil export was showing good gains and carried the total values higher and higher, reaching $84,000,000 in 1928. Oil represented over 60 per cent of the exports; indeed but for the gain through the oil trade Venezuelan exports show only a small increase in value in current years over the returns of 1913.

Taking the export trade and the imports, which to a large degree it makes possible, together, the commercial advance of Venezuela is marked. The foreign trade was worth about $25,000,000 in 1880, about the same in 1898, and only $13,000,000 in 1903, though the next year it recovered to $27,000,000. By 1913, it has risen to $36,-000,000, chiefly due to increase in coffee exports. With the oil trade it developed to $153,000,000 in 1928, a more than fourfold increase in fourteen years.

Taking the countries of the north coast together, they show a remarkable advance. They contributed 19 per cent to Caribbean commerce in 1900 and 25 per cent in 1928.

But what is to many people the most surprising feature of an analysis of the advance of Caribbean trade is the showing made by the island areas other than Cuba. In 1900, their combined trade was somewhat greater than that of Cuba, as it continues to be. Like Cuba, this group has greatly increased the value of its exchanges but has lost slightly in percentage. It still continues to contribute more than a third of the total commerce though among its units prosperity is highly irregular. The greatest advances have been due to the expansion of activity in sugar and fruits in Porto Rico, in petroleum in the Netherlands West Indies and Trinidad, in sugar in the Dominican Republic, and in fruit in Jamaica. The lesser islands, though they show in most cases increases in the value of their trade, have become decidedly less important factors in the total commerce.[18]

The international trade of the Caribbean has become a factor in world commerce of far greater importance for its peoples and for the world at large than it was at the beginning of the century. It is an index of the degree of local prosperity and affects far distant inland areas which

[18] The relative percentages of the total trade give an interesting tabular contrast:

Region	1900	1928
Cuba	32	28
Other Islands	36	34
Central America	12	13
Northern South America	19	25

formerly contributed to it and benefited by it only in an incidental manner. It reaches out to foreign lands with which contact was formerly negligible. It has not only become greater but stronger as it has come to be relied upon by other regions as a source of supply and as an outlet for their products.

But this commerce continues to have two weaknesses which were characteristic even in the period when it reached but a fraction of its present value. It continues, so far as it involves exports, to be predominately one in a very limited number of lines. Sugar, coffee, fruit, and oil—markets for these four staples control the prosperity of the Caribbean. Secondly, this is commerce which depends upon the tariff policies adopted in the leading markets. The European colonies and Porto Rico could not have developed as they have done without special treatment in the national customs laws. Cuba has grown through the special favor extended by the United States. The independent states would find their outlook far less bright without the free entry for their coffee, fruit, and oil which they enjoy in some markets and the low rates granted them in some others.

CHAPTER XII

UNITED STATES TRADE WITH THE CARIBBEAN

DEVELOPMENTS in Caribbean trade during the past generation have not failed to draw the attention of citizens of the United States to its rapidly changing economic conditions. Nevertheless, few realize that for the United States the growth of its imports and exports to this part of the world tends to bring the importance of this trade back toward a standard reached a century and a quarter ago. Before the American Revolution, the coast towns of the British North American colonies had a lively interest in the trade to the West Indies and in the policies which the home government and other European states adopted which bore upon the development of that commerce. This interest in Caribbean trade continued when the thirteen colonies became independent.

Of the total merchandise exported from the United States in 1801, 58.3 per cent went southward—apparently all of it to the Caribbean—to the British West Indies, 21 per cent, to the Spanish West Indies other than Honduras and Campeche, 19 per cent, and to the French West Indies, 15 per cent. Only in the next year is the first small shipment to South America, to Brazil, mentioned.[1] Later, developments such as the westward expansion of the United States, the increase in the export of foodstuffs and raw materials to more advanced countries of Europe, and the political and economic difficulties of the Caribbean region during the nineteenth century, lessened the relative impor-

---

[1] Charles Lyon Chandler, *Inter-American Acquaintances* (Sewanee, Tenn., 1917), p. 23.

tance of the north and south exchanges even though their absolute totals increased. By 1830, about a fifth of the exports of the United States and about a sixth of its imports went in the Caribbean trade. Even this proportion was not kept up. The tendency was downward and in the eighties and nineties the proportion of the exports sank to about a twentieth. Imports had a more rapid growth, but they also fell in relation to the total and at the end of the century were less than 10 per cent.

Foreign trade of the United States had, of course, in the century that was coming to an end, grown by leaps and bounds, and even these low percentages were not inconsistent with steadily rising totals in dollar values and in quantities. The exports to the Caribbean, worth less than $10,000,000 in 1821, had risen to a value of $56,500,000 in 1900, and the imports had increased from a similar amount to a value of $76,300,000.

New conditions which affected the trade of the Caribbean as a whole, after the turn of the century, gave a special impulse to the trade of the United States. Industrial development to the northward gave Americans greater interest in the region because its nearness made it one of the easiest to reach among foreign markets and sources of supplies. Its long coastline made it easily accessible in ocean commerce and to a degree lessened the influence of the inadequate internal communication facilities. A gradual improvement in public order helped to increase production by the local populations and the development of enterprises supported by foreign capital. In later years, too, the change of the United States from a debtor to a creditor position among the nations of the world increased the amount of American capital seeking employment both in local production and in international commerce. As a result the amounts of trade going north and south not only greatly increased but increased so much that they came to be a greater proportion of the total in spite of the very rapid expansion of American foreign trade.

The advance made since the beginning of the century is summarized in the following table:

THE CARIBBEAN IN THE FOREIGN TRADE OF THE UNITED STATES [2]

Years	Exports			Imports		
	Total	To Caribbean	Percentage to Caribbean	Total	From Caribbean	Percentage from Caribbean
	Millions of Dollars		bean	Millions of Dollars		bean
1900	1,394	56	4.0	849	76	9.0
1910-14 average	2,165	141	6.5	1,688	180	10.7
1928	5,128	380	7.4	4,091	461	11.3
1929	5,241	395	7.5	4,400	506	11.5

The Caribbean came to take roughly half of the rapidly increasing exports to Latin America. Formerly, largely routed out of New York, this trade spread to other ports, especially those of the gulf coast.

The markets increased their demands for both animal and vegetable food products raised on American farms, and as their economic development progressed they took larger amounts of the textiles, machinery and vehicles, chemicals, and specialties which were the product of American factories.

In the opposite direction, the region became a shipper to the United States of its great staples to even greater value. It became the great supplier of tropical fruit to the American market, shipping all but an insignificant portion of such imports; it became the second most important source

---

[2] For 1900, compiled from *Commerce and Navigation of the United States, 1900* (Washington, 1900), Vol. I, pp. 56-59; for 1910-4 and 1928, *Statistical Abstract of the United States, 1929* (Washington, 1929), p. 486; for 1929, *Foreign Trade of the United States in the Calendar Year 1929*, U. S. Department of Commerce, Bureau of Foreign and Domestic Commerce, Trade Information Bulletin No. 684 (Washington, 1930), p. 46.

IMPORT TRADE OF THE UNITED STATES FROM THE CARIBBEAN [3]

(In millions of dollars)

Region	1900	1910-14 Average	1921-25 Average	1929
The Islands				
Total	52.0	181.7	411.8	381.0
Bermudas	.4	.6	1.1	.8
Jamaica		6.1	6.8	7.5
Trinidad and Tobago	11.8	5.4	5.1	10.8
Other British		1.7	2.2	2.9
Cuba	31.3	122.0	299.6	207.4
Dominican Republic	3.6	3.6	8.1	8.5
Netherlands West Indies	.3	.4	4.3	64.6
French West Indies	.0	.0	.1	.1
Haiti	1.1	.8	1.6	1.4
Virgin Islands	.5	.2	.6	.6
Porto Rico	3.0	40.9	82.3	76.4
Central America and Panama				
Total	8.8	17.3	36.4	44.8
British	.2	1.4	2.4	3.3
Costa Rica	2.9	3.7	5.1	5.2
Guatemala	2.4	2.8	10.0	8.5
Honduras	.9	2.7	6.0	12.8
Nicaragua	1.5	1.4	6.0	5.7
Panama	...	3.7	4.6	5.4
Salvador	.7	1.3	3.3	3.8
Northern South America				
Total	14.8	22.5	65.8	156.9
Colombia	4.3	11.9	49.4	103.5
Guianas				
British	3.7	.4	.7	.8
Netherlands	1.2	.9	.7	1.2
French	.0	.0	.1	.1
Venezuela	5.5	9.1	23.3	51.2
Summary of Imports				
The Islands	52.0	181.7	411.8	381.0
Central America and Panama..	8.8	17.3	36.4	44.8
Northern South America	14.8	22.5	65.8	156.9
TOTAL, Caribbean	75.6	221.5	514.0	582.7

[3] Compiled from *Commerce and Navigation of the United States, 1900,* Vol. I; *Statistical Abstract of the United States, 1929,* pp. 486-487; *Foreign Trade of the United States in the Calendar Year 1929,* pp. 46-47; and *Twenty-ninth Annual Report of the Governor of Porto Rico, Honorable Horace M. Towner* (San Juan, 1929), p. 17.

EXPORT TRADE OF THE UNITED STATES TO THE CARIBBEAN [4]

(In millions of dollars)

Region	1900	1910-14 Average	1921-25 Average	1929
The Islands				
Total	48.1	248.0	315.9	294.0
Bermudas	1.1	1.4	3.6	4.0
Jamaica	} 8.8 {	4.9	8.5	9.1
Trinidad and Tobago		3.3	5.2	6.7
Other British		4.4	7.0	7.4
Cuba	26.5	63.0	181.3	128.9
Dominican Republic	1.3	4.4	15.3	14.2
Netherlands West Indies	.5	.8	3.1	24.2
French West Indies	1.8	1.6	2.6	3.4
Haiti	2.9	5.8	10.9	8.8
Virgin Islands	.6	.8	1.9	2.3
Porto Rico	4.6	33.1	76.5	85.0
Central America and Panama				
Total	6.5	37.5	58.7	90.8
British Honduras	.6	1.4	1.9	1.9
Costa Rica	1.4	3.4	5.1	8.3
Guatemala	.7	2.8	7.2	11.5
Honduras	1.1	2.8	10.3	12.8
Nicaragua	1.1	2.4	5.3	7.0
Panama	...	22.4	22.8	41.1
Salvador	.6	2.0	6.1	8.1
Northern South America				
Total	7.7	13.0	44.0	96.5
Colombia	2.7	5.7	25.9	49.0
Guianas				
British	1.9	1.8	2.1	1.1
Netherlands	.5	.7	1.0	.9
French	.2	.3	.5	.2
Venezuela	2.4	4.4	14.6	45.3
Summary of Exports				
The Islands	48.1	248.0	315.9	294.0
Central America and Panama	6.5	37.5	58.7	90.8
Northern South America	7.7	13.0	44.0	96.5
TOTAL, Caribbean	62.3	78.5	418.6	481.3

of coffee supplies, the greatest source of crude petroleum imports, and practically the only source of imported sugar.

The economic significance of the advance in the various

---

[4] For sources of information see footnote 3.

areas in the foreign trade of the United States since 1900 is shown in the tables on pages 224 and 225 in which the prewar rise in the leading units of both import and export trade and the marked increase since the World War are well brought out.

The totals of this trade do not fully reflect its importance, for it is to a high degree commerce which supplies raw materials for unfilled American needs. The Caribbean furnishes to the United States, in the main, goods which the latter does not produce or produces in quantities insufficient for the supply of the domestic market. These are chiefly unmanufactured foodstuffs and industrial materials. On the other hand, the American exports to the Caribbean are distinctively manufactured goods. The export of these means that there are sold abroad goods the value of which represents in high degree the wages of labor and the profits of industry. For these reasons the import of a million dollars' worth of goods from a highly industrialized region like Europe—goods made up in greater part of manufactured articles—and exports of a similar value to Europe made up largely of raw materials have less interest for the American manufacturers and workmen than an equal value of trade with the Caribbean in which the characteristics of the merchandise are reversed.[5]

If the trade of these areas has become of increasing significance to the United States, it is equally or more true that the trade with the United States has taken on new significance for them. The proportion of the total imports and exports drawn from and destined to the United States has shown a tendency to rise.

In each of the larger groups, the United States has come to be the greatest individual supplier and in many instances the greatest individual buyer. In some cases, the United

---

[5] Detailed charts and tables showing this contrast are found in *Commerce Reports,* June 9, 1930.

States accounts for more than half of the total trade inward and outward.

SHARE OF THE UNITED STATES IN THE FOREIGN TRADE OF THE CHIEF CARIBBEAN AREAS [6]

Region	General Imports into Country Named		Domestic Exports from Country Named	
	1913, Per Cent	1928, Per Cent	1913, Per Cent	1928, Per Cent
The Islands				
Cuba	53.7	60.8	80.0	72.8 [1]
Dominican Republic	62.9	61.3	53.8	27.9 [1]
Haiti	76.2 [4]	77.3	4.5 [7]	8.2 [2]
Central America and Panama				
Costa Rica	12.7 [4]	45.2	9.3 [4]	27.0 [3]
Guatemala	50.6	57.9	38.2	54.3
Honduras	67.3 [4]	79.8 [5]	86.9 [4]	76.3 [5]
Panama [8]	...	...	...	...
Nicaragua	56.2	55.2	35.3	47.3
Salvador	39.2 [4]	39.9	14.6 [4]	13.1
Northern South America				
Colombia	26.7	48.4	44.5	83.0
Venezuela	38.5	52.3 [6]	28.7	23.6 [6]

[1] Decline due largely to growth of sugar exports to countries other than the United States.
[2] Coffee exports go largely to Europe, especially France.
[3] The United Kingdom is the chief purchaser of coffee from Costa Rica.
[4] 1912–13.
[5] 1927–28.
[6] 1927.
[7] Average, June 30, 1909, to June 30, 1913.
[8] Statistics do not satisfactorily distinguish between trade of Panama and of the Panama Canal Zone.

Out of these detailed figures of trade rises an inescapable conclusion as to the relation which the United States bears to its economically weaker neighbors to the southward. However diverse their climates, resources, populations, and

[6] Compiled from *Commerce Yearbook, 1926, 1929; Statistical Abstract of the United States, 1929*, pp. 486-487, and *Foreign Commerce and Navigation of the United States* in the calendar years 1914, 1915 and 1928, U. S. Department of Commerce, Bureau of Foreign and Domestic Commerce (Washington).

governmental organizations, they are bound to the United States by economic interests stronger than any divergent influences which may from time to time affect their public policies. Under the influence of nationalistic programs and international jealousies, the various governments have, in some periods in the past, disturbed and checked the commercial interchange which neighborhood and the contrasting character of national needs encourage. They may do so in the future, but those who have in their hands the formulation of public policy will do a great service for the people they represent when they emphasize the importance of maintaining and strengthening the important economic factors which work for unity of interest among the American nations.

The general exports from individual countries show some curious shifts since the beginning of the century reflecting in many cases the gradual increase in the importance of the United States as a buyer and the decline of European purchases. The relative international positions in Cuban trade in 1900, 1913, and in current years show no important changes. One such change may be in the course of development, for the great increase in the Cuban production of sugar under the stimulation of conditions created by the World War has pushed the crop up beyond the capacity of the American market. This market is now open to the Cuban product only under higher tariff payments than were formerly exacted and under competition with increasing amounts of tariff-free sugars from Porto Rico, Hawaii, and the Philippine Islands. As a result Cuba has been forced to send increasing amounts of her sugar exports to markets other than the United States and to turn her attention to the possibility of diversifying her national production, thus to broaden her international economic outlook. Haitian sales continue to be made to almost half of their value in France where the coffee of the island enjoys a market established in the colonial period. Germany, which was a strong competitor in 1913, in later years has fallen back sharply, but the markets in a number of countries formerly unimportant for Haiti now take almost a third of the exports.

Over half of Dominican products were sold in the United States at the beginning of the century, but the American share of the total now shows a tendency to decline. British areas, on the other hand, have advanced their purchases with the growth of the Dominican sugar industry and in some years now buy half of the total exports.

The destinations of Central American exports furnish a number of interesting contrasts reflecting not difference in sorts of crops raised so much as established trade preferences. Honduras, in which the fruit trade holds so dominant a position, sells important quantities only to Great Britain and the United States, the proportion going to each varying sharply with the trade policy adopted by the producing interests. The relatively small trade of Nicaragua goes to the United States chiefly, with lesser amounts to France, Germany, and Great Britain, all of which formerly took larger shares than at present. Costa Rica ships its bananas chiefly to the United States and its coffee to the United Kingdom which in recent years absorbs more than half of all exports. The distinctively coffee republics of Central America, Guatemala, and Salvador furnish interesting illustrations of trade preferences. The former ships its bananas and in recent years increasing quantities of coffee to the United States, but the greatest market for its coffee continues to be Germany, as has been the case in normal times for a generation. Salvador, the only one of the Central American states which has no banana export industry, also finds its coffee market in the United States in recent years less attractive than that in Germany which now takes about one-third of the total shipments.

The rapid advance of Colombian exports accompanying better water communications, the rise of coffee production, and the growth of the oil trade have involved greatly increased shipments to the United States. In 1903, slightly over half of the exports went to the northern republic which now absorbs more than four-fifths of the total. All other competitors showed marked losses. On the other hand, Venezuela shows a sharply contrasted development. In the period before the war, the United States took about a third of the goods sent abroad and Germany was rapidly increasing her purchases. In later years, both of these countries show a relative decline. The United States now takes less than a fourth of the total, and nominally the Netherlands absorbs over half of the exports. These figures, however, are deceptive, for in the great development of Venezuelan oil, the Dutch Colonies off the coast have become an *entrepôt* in the foreign trade, and for this reason the real destination of the shipments passing to Curaçao and Aruba is obscured.

The general advance of exports to the United States, as has already been indicated, is partly due to its geographical position and to its increased industrial and financial strength. Another important influence is the American commercial policy adopted toward the staple Caribbean products as reflected in tariff charges. In marked contrast to European countries, which as a rule levy relatively high duties on articles which on the Continent are characterized as "colonial products," the United States, except as to sugar, has followed the policy of admitting them duty-free or on payment of low customs rates. All but one of the chief Caribbean exports enter the United States free of duties. As a result, less than 12 per cent of the exports from Central America entering the United States pay any duty at all. On goods from the West Indies other than Cuba, less than 8 per cent pay duties, while from Colombia and Venezuela only about 0.3 per cent of the value of all shipments is subject to any charge whatever. Under these conditions, the Caribbean has found the United States, for the greater portion of its products, a great free market of rapidly growing consuming capacity unequaled anywhere else in the world.[7]

Analysis of the imports into the Caribbean also shows interesting changes in the origin and character of the goods purchased. The nearness of the United States to the market, the fact that its trade enjoys in all the markets "most favored nation" treatment, and in Cuba special concessions given to the trade of no other nation, the development of better steamship services from American ports, the growth of American experience in exporting, and the heavy local investment of American capital drawing after it purchases of American goods for enterprises controlled by Americans, all tend to give to American shipments to the region an even greater share than is usually taken of its exports.

Over three-fifths of Cuban purchases continue to come in recent years from the United States and no other supplier furnishes 5 per cent of the total. The Dominican Republic is to about the same degree dependent on American supplies with the United Kingdom and Germany disputing about evenly for some 12 per cent of the trade.

Central America is increasingly an American export market. In none of the republics do American goods make up much less than two-fifths of the total and in Honduras they are almost four-fifths. In Costa Rica, Germany and the United Kingdom divide a trade about half as great as that of the United States. In Guatemala, Germany sells roughly a fourth as much. The United Kingdom sells about 10 per cent of Nicaraguan purchases, and 6 per

---

[7] Based on the returns for 1928. *Statistical Abstract of the United States, 1929*, p. 485.

cent of the imports into Honduras. American sales are six times as great in the first case and twelve times as great in the second. In Salvador, German sales are second to American but total only about 8 per cent.

Imports into the republics of northern South America also show the growing preponderance of American shipments. Colombian purchases from the United States which were slightly less than a quarter in 1913 are now about half of its total imports. The United Kingdom has fallen in importance. It supplied a fifth of Colombian demands in 1913 but a steadily decreasing proportion in later years. Germany and France have seen the position of their exports to the republic fall off in even more marked degree in the past few years.

Venezuelan imports before the World War were less than two-fifths from the United States. Over one-half now has that origin. The United Kingdom and Germany, which together had an outlet in Venezuela almost equal to that of the United States in 1913, have seen their shipments decline in relative importance, so that in some recent years they have had a value less than half as great.

The trade of the European colonial areas in the Caribbean, taken as a whole, has advanced fairly steadily in value since the beginning of the century, though when changes in the value of money are taken into consideration the position of some of the weaker units has not improved. In none of the units, except certain of the British West Indies, has a marked development occurred on the basis of local resources.

The trade of the British West Indies, taking the figures of value for that varied collection of communities as a whole, shows a satisfactory advance. In 1900, imports and exports together totaled $58,690,000. In 1928, they totaled $168,000,000. Though the advance was marked it was not equal to that of a number of other groups. Central American trade, for example, was only about two-thirds that of the British West Indies in 1900, but in 1928 it reached a third more than that of the islands. American trade plays in most of the British island units a less important part than in neighboring regions. In 1927, about 30 per cent of the imports came from the United States and slightly more of the exports had that destination. In Jamaica, however, export trade of the United States accounted in 1927 for almost half of the total of that island.

In spite of the increase in the export and import values indicated, the economic position of the islands is not satisfactory, and the possibility of its improvement has been given repeated examination by the local authorities and by the governments of Canada and the United Kingdom. A number of commissions have studied possible adjustments of trade policy which might stimulate local economic activity, and the Canadian–West Indies agreements have sought by tariff arrangements and the establishment of steamship services to increase the export and import trade between these sections of the British Empire. The latest of these agreements, that of 1927 establishing a direct fortnightly service with Canada, and the preferential tariff arrangements with Great Britain appear to have increased commercial interchanges, but are too new and too temporary in their foundations to allow judgment as to the degree to which they will improve conditions which have long been a subject of complaint.[9]

---

[8] The comparisons in the above paragraphs are based on statistics in *Commerce Yearbook, 1929*, Vol. II.

[9] Detailed presentations of the conditions to be met are found in *Report of the West Indian Sugar Commission*, Cmd. 3517 (London, 1930); *Report of the First West Indies Conference Held in Barbados, January-February, 1929* (London, 1929), and *Canada, The Customs Tariff and Amendments with Index to September 15, 1928* (Ottawa, 1928). For the earlier period of decline in British West Indian sugar planting see Lowell Joseph Ragatz, *The Fall of the Planter Class in the British Caribbean, 1763-1833* (New York, 1928).

Though the dependence of this area upon trade with the United States is less marked than in some others, the maintenance of good commercial relations with the northern republic is here also one of the essentials for economic advance. So important, in fact, are these relations that they place limitations about the special concessions which otherwise might be granted to other countries to develop intercourse with them. As one of the representatives to the First West Indies Conference, held in Barbados in 1929, declared, "We are so close to the American continent and we do so much trade with that continent . . . that we have to be particularly careful in passing any rule or regulation which will interfere with our business." [10]

The French and Netherlands holdings are small in area and of very restricted local resources. The former are of comparatively small importance for the United States. Their trade, increasingly in rum, has in recent years shown encouraging advance under the stimulus of a trade agreement with France. Though their commerce is primarily with the mother country, the imports from the United States show a tendency to increase. Their exports to the United States, because of small resources, do not have large proportions.[11]

In current years, the Netherlands West Indies lying off the coast of Venezuela occupy an exceptional position among the smaller Caribbean communities and an exceptional position in the trade with the United States. Long a practically valueless colony, they have become, through the development of Venezuelan oil resources, one of the most active areas in the Caribbean. Though their commerce is in all but small percentage transit trade, it has shown a remarkable development. As late as 1911-3, the

---

[10] *Report of the First West Indies Conference Held in Barbados, January-February, 1929*, p. 29.
[11] *Commerce Reports*, April 7, 1930, p. 9.

exports were less than a million dollars in value and the imports less than two million. The great advance has occurred in the years following 1923. In 1927 the exports were worth over $54,000,000 and the imports over $57,000,-000. The exports to the United States in 1927 totaled $29,933,000, and in 1929 rose to $64,588,975. American exports to the islands were $6,431,000, in the first year and $24,166,575 in the second.[12]

Since the opening of the century, all of the groups into which the trade units of the Caribbean fall have had great increases in the value of their commerce, and two of them have changed in relative commercial importance for the United States. In United States imports and exports, the islands, due to the commerce with Cuba, were in the leading position in 1900 and they continue to be so in spite of the difficulties of the Cuban sugar industry. They shipped 70 per cent of the imports into the United States in 1900 and in recent years have maintained about the same position. They bought 77 per cent of the exports in 1900 and only a little less in current years, though the share in 1929 was only 61 per cent.

The other divisions, Central America and the north coast of South America, have had greater changes in relative importance. In 1900, Central America and Panama accounted for 11 per cent of the imports and 10 per cent of the exports. In 1929, imports were only 7 per cent of the total in spite of heavy fruit shipments, but the exports had risen to almost 19 per cent of the total due to the exceptionally advantageous position of the United States as a source of supply.

Northern South America in 1900 supplied about 20 per cent of the imports from the Caribbean but had increased its share in 1929 to 27 per cent, a result reflecting the heavy purchases of Colombian coffee and Venezuelan oil. The

12 *Ibid.*

values of the shipments meanwhile had increased tenfold.[13] The north coast purchases from the United States also showed a good gain, rising from 12 per cent of those in the Caribbean region in 1900 to 20 per cent in 1929.

[13] PERCENTAGES OF UNITED STATES TRADE WITH CARIBBEAN COUNTRIES

Region	Imports into United States		Exports from United States	
	1900	1929	1900	1929
The Islands	70	65	77	61
Central America	11	7	10	19
Northern South America	20	27	12	20

CHAPTER XIII

PUBLIC LOANS

FEW factors in the economic development of Latin America involve such widespread popular misconceptions as the public loans which the republics have contracted in foreign countries. Many believe, for example, that the high standard of public honor which should assure the strict fulfillment of all contracts involving the public credit goes unobserved in Latin America while other countries have held themselves to it from time immemorial. On the other hand even speeches by presidential candidates have spread the impression that loans have been by some legerdemain forced upon the unwilling governments of the weaker states by those who became their creditors. It is a common belief that the rates of return on the loans currently made are extortionate, that the nation representing the lender is active in inducing the acceptance of the loan and its restrictive terms, and that once made the military forces—generally in popular discussion "the marines"—are employed to force the borrower to meet his contract. Such beliefs have contributed greatly to popular misapprehensions as to the problems of the Caribbean republics and the steps which their governments have taken for their solution.

Default on the public debts of Latin-American states or on obligations which they have guaranteed has played a large part in the discussion of international obligations. Many have as a result come to believe that elsewhere the scrupulous payment of interest and amortization charges takes place and has always taken place as a matter of course.

The facts run quite to the contrary. The history of

public debts shows a surprisingly long list of failures by
governments to meet their financial pledges. They run
through all sorts of forms, from payment of obligations in
debased or in fiat money to open repudiation of loans contracted with citizens and foreigners. Nor is the irregular
escape from pecuniary liability a practice long outgrown
by even the "more advanced" states. The payment of
"gold" obligations to their own citizens with depreciated
paper by the countries of continental Europe after the
World War is a recent and painful example. The readjustment of the war debts owed to foreign countries
involved a modification of the terms of the original loan contracts not willingly accepted by the creditors.

These are "extreme cases" but so are, from the debtor's
point of view, all the adjustments of public obligations which
force the creditor to accept less than that for which he had
contracted. A review of the practice of the better developed
nations even under less unusual circumstances shows that
standards of honor which demand the meticulous observance
by a government of the terms of its contract are of surprisingly brief history and that few if any governments can
boast a clean slate. The more or less willingly granted
"loans" which, for example, increased again and again the
public debt of France in the old régime, only made possible
a better showing than would have been brought by default.
The state was bankrupt, in fact, long before it confessed it.

Even in Great Britain the duty of the government faith-
fully to discharge its obligations is one of much later recognition, at least in practice, than is generally supposed.
Charles II borrowed from the goldsmiths of London the
equivalent of $6,000,000 at 8 per cent—a large amount for
that time. In 1672 the debt was repudiated. Later, an
agreement was made to pay interest at 6 per cent, but
repayment of the principal was refused. A new default
soon followed. And "only in 1745, after the British Revolu-

tion, did the government compound with the creditors by agreeing to pay 3 per cent interest with the option of discharging the debt on payment of one-half of the principal sum." [1] Thus even the traditional standards of British commercial ethics have not always been reflected in the practice of the government.

The history of certain of the states of the American Union also furnishes illustrations of the fact that the duty of governments to keep their contracts has not been measured only by their abilities. Eight of the southern states are reported as having securities in default approximating $75,200,000, not including interest which in most cases was at 6 per cent. The defaults have continued for periods ranging from about fifty-five to eighty-five years. It is a popular misconception that the bonds in question rose out of the Civil War or the carpet bag governments or were irregular or speculative issues. This appears not to have been the case. Portions of the issues by seven of the states found their way into trust funds held by the Federal Government. No question appears to have been raised concerning their binding character. Suit by the United States against the defaulting states has been considered but because of the political questions it would raise has not been instituted, though settlement of certain of the bonds held by the Federal Government, those involving North Carolina, was made in May, 1928. No means has been found by which private owners can secure payment, in fact, in one state at least, Mississippi, the constitution now contains a special provision repudiating the securities involved. The existence of these unpaid obligations of American states may well be borne in mind by those who criticize the failure of certain "weak foreign governments" to meet payments guaranteed by their "plighted faith." [2]

[1] A. E. Davies, *Investments Abroad* (Chicago, 1927), p. 4.

[2] The detail of these commitments so far as they affect British interests may be found in the various issues of the *Annual Report of the Council*

All in all, the importance of the "honor of governments" in financial matters cannot be too much emphasized for the benefit of both the governments and those who loan to them, but it is a mistake to believe that practice and theory have long coincided even among the best established of nations.

The popular belief that loans by foreigners to the weaker states frequently, if not generally, involve outside political pressure to force them to assume financial burdens, is as difficult to overcome as it is unfounded. That such abuses have never occurred, it is not necessary to prove. In the average case and particularly in our own day, international loan contracts are ones entered into willingly by the borrower for the accomplishment of some purpose which the local government has determined to be demanded by public policy. The decisions to borrow are not always wise, and the alleged need may become clearer because agents of the lenders may declare themselves willing to advance the money and even outline the terms on which the loan will be granted, but such loans are not "forced" upon the borrower by the lender.

As a matter of fact, weak governments, especially if their control may be strengthened by the fresh resources, may be active bidders for loans which an impartial critic might consider unnecessary or which would compromise public credit. Under such circumstances, not infrequently the representatives of the borrowers have on occasion stooped to the grossest misrepresentation to secure the outside financial assistance. Some of the worst abuses which have ever occurred in international loans have arisen in cases of this nature, and no effective means of checking them has yet been devised.

Outstanding examples of contracts of this sort involving, in fact, sharp practices by both borrowers and lenders are

of the Corporation of Foreign Bondholders, especially the *Fifty-fifth Annual Report . . . for the Year 1928* (London, 1929), and its supplement.

certain loans to Caribbean countries most of which were negotiated in the period 1869-72, involving chiefly British and French interests. A Select Committee of the British Parliament, reporting on the loans, found that the agents of the borrowing countries had seriously exaggerated and misrepresented the resources of their countries, their development and the status of the governments. The brokers who presented the loans to the public, too, were guilty of gross dishonesty in their representations, in their use of the funds which came into their hands to manipulate the market, and in their dealings with the borrowers. In certain of these loans, so extreme were the terms agreed upon that the interest and amortization charges stipulated in the contracts were greater than the current national income.[3]

In other cases loans may be made to "strong" governments such as those controlled by firmly established dictators. Of these there have been not a few in Caribbean history. The yield of loans may be misappropriated or frittered away. From the point of view of succeeding administrations such borrowings are indefensible. The dictatorship never truly "represented" the people. Those who overthrow such governments not infrequently show that they would gladly escape the consequences of the contracts made in the nation's name.

Finally, governments, whether of insecure tenure, unrepresentative of the people, or merely ones which support ill-advised projects, may with the best of intent obligate their peoples by loans contracted for projects good in themselves but which are not crowned with success. Lack of judgment may bring losses quite as real as those arising

---

[3] The committee's report is found in Great Britain, *Report from the Select Committee on Loans to Foreign States,* July 29, 1875, Parliamentary Papers, House of Commons, 1875, Vol. 11. The loans in question included the 6 per cent Federal States of Central America Loan of 1825, the Honduras Loans of 1867 and 1870, the Honduras Paris Loan of 1869, the proposed Honduras Ship Railway Loan, the Santo Domingo Loan of 1869, and the Costa Rica Loans of 1871 and 1872.

from less excusable causes. Here also the feeling may develop that since the end sought was not secured there should be no obligation to pay.

Whatever the government which made the loan may have been, weak, strong, or mistaken, and whatever the purpose and actual use made of the loan, the obligation ultimately finds reflection in the tax rate. The burden thus put upon the public is often the cause, or at least the occasion, for movements for repudiation of national liability, especially if the tax burden was already heavy before the levies due to the new loan or if the benefit sought is not obtained or is slow of realization.

For circumstances such as these, no effective remedy has developed. If the government making the loan is in effective control and is recognized by foreign powers, its people cannot under the rules regulating international relations feel itself unbound by the terms of the contracts entered. The government may lead its people into better or worse position, it may be guilty of "abuses" in handling their international affairs of financial and other sorts, but so long as it is in recognized control, its acts are those of the population for which it is presumed to act.

Legislation cannot be effective against all abuses, but the circumstances which surround the making of loan contracts have changed and have to a great extent eliminated irregularities. The borrower no longer has the same temptation to stoop to misrepresentation; in fact, with the better information at the disposal of the public, any misrepresentation is now easier to discover and when discovered destroys its own purpose. The responsible lender, on his side, is hedged around by law but even more by custom and the desire to protect his own good name. He cannot adopt practices tolerated in an earlier day and continue in business. It is still, of course, true that borrower and lender may both think it to their advantage to present the conditions of the contract to the public in a more favorable light than others might think justified, but the possibility of abuse by either side or by both in collusion is much less than it was formerly and cannot be, in the long run, to the advantage of either.

The interest rates charged Caribbean countries have also been a subject of frequent adverse criticism, both in the United States and the borrowing republics. In the past, they have in certain cases been extraordinarily high, particularly in the case of small loans advanced to revolutionary leaders or to governments tottering to their fall. Instances are reported from Haiti in which gourdes nominally worth twenty cents were advanced on condition than an equal number of dollars should be paid in satisfaction of the loans. Other loans are reported as demanding interest payments as high as 35 per cent. Publicly floated issues have in some cases, due to their low issue price, involved payments ranging up to 16 or 17 per cent, though the nominal rate was much lower. Such loans are gamblers' risks and probably never justified. They rise out of peculiar circumstances and are not properly cited as examples of normal practice.

In normal circumstances, international like other loans are ones in which the actual interest rates are determined by the probability that the payments agreed upon will be met. The risk is calculated after consideration of the stability of the government, its record of performance in paying its debts in the past, the country's natural resources and their development, actual and expected, the special guarantees of payment, and many other factors which enter into the determination of the credit of a nation in much the same way as they determine the credit of an individual.

The actual rate charged Caribbean states by lenders after all these elements are considered is, it is asserted, as a rule higher than in comparable domestic loans and higher than in loans to other countries. This has been true and continues, with some exceptions later discussed, to be true at the present time. It is not, however, as is often believed, the result of an unjustified discrimination. These republics, like other states, borrow in the open market in which they can present their needs to all lenders. Even when, as was formerly the case, British interests were the chief lenders or when, as at present, American firms are active in making the loans, there is competition among the firms seeking the loans which gives the borrower the advantage of securing the lowest rates which any responsible group thinks the risk justifies.

The argument is often made in the borrowing countries that nevertheless the rates are unjustifiably high in comparison with domestic loans and especially in view of the fact that special guarantees are given "to assure that there shall be no risk." But such arguments do not bear close analysis. The lender grants better rates in domestic loans because these are to enterprises the operation of which he can easily follow and his rights against which he can protect under local legislation with which he is familiar, in which he has confidence, and the terms of which he can have enforced in the local courts. He feels he assumes a greater risk in lending in a country where these factors are, at least in his belief, less certain.

The special guarantees which the contract may contain are also in his mind elements which reduce his risk, but do not eliminate it. In the long run his reliance must be on the good faith of the borrowing state and its willingness to do its utmost to protect its credit. To be sure, there is still theoretically the possibility that force may be used for the collection of public debts. But he knows that in practice such a right does not exist. If the lender is a European he knows, if a loan in the new world is involved, that his government whatever might otherwise be its impulse would hesitate to try to force payment, because doing so might bring about action which would involve the opposition of the United States to occupation of American territory by non-American powers. If he is an American he knows that he cannot call on his government for the use of its armed forces to collect from his debtors.

The attempt by certain European powers to collect public debts and other claims from Venezuela by force at the beginning of the century aroused widespread ill feeling, was highly expensive, and seriously damaged the prestige of those involved. It seems highly unlikely that the incident will be repeated.[4] In the last analysis, therefore, the lender justifiably feels that even the special guarantee which may be given his loan does not eliminate the risk that attaches to loans to independent states which by their position cannot be forced to live up to their contracts. This risk he feels is especially to be taken into account in states in which disturbance of public order, or failure of key crops may make prompt payment impossible.[5] The special guarantee is not without value since it makes the engagement of the borrowing state more explicit than it otherwise would be, but it by no means assures that there will be no default nor guarantees that payment will be exacted by military forces.

The records as to the service of their public debts which

[4] The resolution of the Second Hague Conference whereby the contracting powers agreed not to have recourse to armed force to recover debts due their nationals unless the debtor nation refuses arbitration, or, having accepted arbitration fails to give the award effect, puts the creditor nominally in a stronger position than is here indicated, but actually the forcible collection of public debts in the Caribbean region seems very unlikely to be undertaken by any power.

[5] The position of the bondholders of the Mexican debt at the present time is an example illustrating that in which lenders stand when the borrowing state declares itself unable to meet its obligations. What the "capacity to pay" may be, naturally will be differently estimated by borrowers and lenders particularly when the former feel that a rehabilitation program necessitates undertaking far-reaching social reforms of expensive character. The Mexican loans of 1903 and 1910 were covered by special guarantees but went into default with the other federal obligations in July, 1914. Certain payments were made in 1926 and 1927 under an adjustment of 1925 but the debt service then again went into default.

the Caribbean states have made should be judged only with the conditions they have had to meet in mind. They became borrowers at the time when international loans of the sorts with which we are familiar were a new development. There were no established practices regulating the information submitted to justify the contracts, the terms of the contracts themselves, or the manner in which the loans were offered to the public. It is not to be wondered at if the early loans often had characteristics which would make similar engagements at the present time highly irregular.

The period following the independence of the countries which were once the Spanish mainland colonies was one in which European countries expected a rapid economic development to follow the abolition of the restrictive economic policy of Spain. Optimism induced investments in private enterprise and in loans to governments. The new nations shared the enthusiasm of the lenders. But the economic boom did not occur. The future had been discounted too heavily. Investors in private enterprises suffered heavy losses, and those who had bought public securities could not collect the amounts due on the debt services.

In addition, many of the early loans, particularly in Central America, were comparatively small in amount and floated under circumstances which gave rise to long drawn out disputes as to whether they were binding. Some were undoubtedly of such shady character that any government would hesitate to urge payment of what was "nominated in the bond." In not a few cases, the governments of the states against which the obligations ran were, through long periods, of such uncertain tenure that no policy looking toward protecting the public credit was given serious attention. It is to be remembered, too, that the records available for the earlier loans are very largely the records of claims urged by the creditors and hence often do not state or do not consider, as a judicial body would, the counter claims or extenuating circumstances which might be urged by the debtor. On the whole, therefore, a summary review of the debt record from a present day point of view is apt to err by painting the picture too darkly.

The record of defaults by countries, counting as full years all years of partial default, is as follows:

NUMBER OF YEARS OF DEFAULT OF INTEREST ON THE EXTERNAL
DEBTS OF CARIBBEAN COUNTRIES

Countries	Number of Years Considered	Number of Years Default Occurred	Per Cent of Years in Default
West Indies			
Cuba (1898-1928)	31	1	3
Dominican Republic (1869-1928)[1]	60	26	43
Haiti (1804-1928)	125	5	4
Central America and Panama			
Costa Rica (1827-1928)[2]	102	23	23
Guatemala (1827-1928)[2]	102	66	65
Honduras (1827-1928)[2]	102	93	92
Nicaragua (1827-1928)[2]	102	53	52
Salvador (1827-1928)[2]	102	36	36
Panama (1904-1928)[2]	25	0	0
Northern South America			
Colombia (1821-1928)	108	56	51
Venezuela (1834-1928)	95	44	46
TOTAL	946	403	42

[1] No data are available for the earlier period of Dominican independence.
[2] The short period of the existence of the Central American Federation is not included. If included it would show two more years of default.

There are some cases where the debt record might have been worse if the new states had been stronger, for in the cases of Haiti, the Dominican Republic, and Honduras, at least, the loans floated even under the influence of the optimism which prevailed were unimportant and borrowing was slow to develop because of the notorious weakness of their governments. The record would probably have been less favorable than it is, also, but for the fact that two of the states, Cuba and Panama, have only recently come into existence and now along with certain of the older states borrow under circumstances which minimize the danger of default.

A general summary tends to obscure the fact that the Caribbean states vary greatly among themselves as to the character of their debt records. Honduras, for example, from 1828 to 1925, a period of 98 years, was in default in 93 years while Costa Rica, in 102 years, has been in default only in three periods covering 23 years.

Even when due emphasis is given to factors such as these, the debt record of the group of eleven Caribbean republics has not been a favorable one. Taking one state with another, they have been in default during 403 years of a total of 955 years of independent existence, or about 42 per cent of the time.

This would indeed be a discouraging record if present performance were no better than the past average but fortunately a fairly steady improvement is evident. If the percentage of default be reviewed by periods the result is as follows:

PERCENTAGE OF TIME IN WHICH CARIBBEAN DEBTS WERE IN
DEFAULT IN CERTAIN PERIODS

Years	Percentage	Years	Percentage
1821-30	55	1881-90	40
1831-40	73	1891-1900	33
1841-50	64	1901-10	42
1851-60	66	1911-20	19
1861-70	38	1921-28	8
1871-80	55		

An examination of the record since 1910 is especially encouraging. In that period, except for defaults caused by special circumstances arising out of the World War, in Cuba, Nicaragua, and Salvador, and out of the revolution in Haiti, the only instances of failure to keep up foreign loan service have been in Guatemala and Honduras. The former resumed its debt service in 1913 and the latter in 1926. Since that time no Caribbean state has defaulted.[6]

This steady improvement is due to a number of influences—some arising within the republics themselves, others affecting their prosperity and economic positions because of changes in world markets on which they have but little influence.

The governments of the states themselves have, in some cases at least, become stronger. Public order has been better maintained, public income has increased, and a greater sense of responsibility has been felt by those in power. As a result of the latter, consideration is given not only to circumstances which would enable the country to secure a loan, but also to its probable effect on the treasury and on public credit.[7] The stronger states have thus become

---

[6] The summary statements above are based on a tabulation of the interest payments on the external debts for each year of their existence. A mathematically accurate compilation cannot be made with the information available, but the table indicates fairly the general course of development. Defaults on internal debts and sinking funds are not considered but their inclusion would not greatly modify the result. Partial defaults were considered as total defaults and defaults for part of a year only were listed as defaults for the year. Disregarding partial defaults and defaults for parts of years would not have changed the result materially. The chief sources used in the compilation were:

Balch, Emily Greene, *Occupied Haiti* (New York, 1927).

Camp, Thorne and Company, Inc., *Latin America Service* (New York, various issues 1928-1929).

Chapman, Charles Edward, *A History of the Cuban Republic* (New York, 1927).

Davis, H. P., *Black Democracy* (New York, 1929).

Fifty-fifth Annual Report of the Council of the Corporation of Foreign Bondholders for the Year 1928 (London, 1929).

Robertson, William Spence, *History of the Latin American Nations* (New York, 1922).

Statesman's Yearbook (London, annual).

Sweet, William Warren, *A History of Latin America* (New York, 1919).

Great Britain, *Report from the Select Committee on Loans to Foreign States,* July 29, 1875, Parliamentary Papers, House of Commons, 1875, Vol. 11.

[7] See as a recent example the message of the President of Costa Rica, May 1, 1928, summarized in the *Fifty-fifth Annual Report of the Council of the Corporation of Foreign Bondholders for the Year 1928.*

more discriminating in the making of loans at the same time as they have become better able to pay the loan services.

Joint action by groups of creditors has also had an indirect but important influence on the debt record through the pressure they have been able to exert upon the governments to keep up their debt services. They have also, by pooling their information, been able to give those floating new issues and the public better information as to whether conditions are such as to justify the floating of new securities.

Some of the most indefensible contracts were made before the activities of such organizations got under way and they inherited the unwelcome task of making such adjustment as was possible of the claims of a public which bought "in profound ignorance of what they were getting." [8]

The most important of the bondholders' protective associations is that now known as the Corporation of Foreign Bondholders, a British organization founded in 1868 and incorporated under license of the Board of Trade, as an association without profits on August 1, 1873. At the time of its founding, British citizens were already heavy holders of foreign securities, many governments issuing them were bankrupt, and the helplessness of the individual bondholder over against the foreign government which had taken his money emphasized the need of joint action for the protection of common interests. In practice, the corporation has acted in various cases for other foreign bondholders as well as the British group. In its present form the corporation rests on a Special Act of Parliament of 1898.

Organizations similar to the Corporation of Foreign Bondholders have arisen in a number of countries whose citizens hold lesser amounts of foreign public securities. Among these are the Association Nationale des Porteurs

---

[8] Great Britain, *Report from the Select Committee on Loans to Foreign States,* July 29, 1875, Parliamentary Papers, House of Commons, 1875, Vol. 11.

Français de Valeurs Mobilières of Paris and the Association Belge pour la Défence des Détenteurs de Fonds Publics of Antwerp. Efforts to create a similar organization in the United States have not yet materialized, doubtless due to the fact that citizens of the United States have only recently become important investors abroad and the need of a protective organization has not made itself felt.

The primary interest of organizations of these sorts is properly the protection of the interests of those who are already holders of foreign securities. Incidentally or collaterally their representatives may be drawn into discussions of intended loans where the security proposed for these might affect the service of debts already contracted. It may occur and indeed has occurred that their advice will be sought by governments which find themselves embarrassed as to what measures should be adopted in local public finance better to assure the service of bonds already issued. Their advice may be directly sought on the best means for arranging new loans, but in the average case, from the nature of things, the main functions of such organizations lie in the defense of the interests of holders of securities already issued, who are a definite body, rather than consideration of the interests of foreign borrowers or of the holders of a possible future issue of securities.

While no private organization has arisen in the United States comparable to the bondholders' protective organizations of Europe, a practice has developed in the Department of State which does have an influence on the floating of foreign loans in the United States. It is not a practice which, like the bondholders' organizations, is based on an interest in collections nor indeed directly concerned with the economic soundness of the proposed transactions. These are outside its intent and matters of private arrangement. Nevertheless, since foreign loan contracts may affect the relations between countries, the government has felt that it can properly ask to be informed by American bankers concerning proposed loans prior to their consummation. The statement issued concerning this practice is a very guarded one and shows that the object is to put the Department of State in a position to survey the national interests which may be affected while not assuming any engagement in connection with the loan contract or its enforcement.

The essential part of the statement, issued March 8, 1922, reads:

> The Department of State cannot, of course, require American bankers to consult it. It will not pass upon the merits of foreign loans as business propositions, nor assume any responsibility whatever in connection with loan transactions. . . . The Department believes that in view of the possible national interests involved it should have the opportunity of saying to the underwriters concerned, should it appear advisable to do so, that there is or is not objection to any particular issue.

Neither the private organizations which have been set up nor the practices followed by the United States came into being with Latin-American or Caribbean conditions exclusively in mind, but both have had an influence on the loans which countries in these regions have made. The prevalence of default in the earlier history of Latin-American public finance has made cases arising in that part of the world ones which have made loans there of particular interest to the European groups, and the circumstances arising after the World War involving very heavy draft of capital from the United States into Latin-American countries have had the same result for the United States. Further, the particular importance of Caribbean countries to the United States, because of both its economic and political relations to them, make all developments in public finance there a matter of more than usual concern.

Since 1922, scores of Latin-American loans have been proposed, reported to the Department of State, and floated.

Almost all of these issues have been ones in which consideration of their bearing on American relations has not presented any ground of policy for raising objection. Where what have been considered to be unfair conditions have appeared, especially ones in which advantage was being taken of the inexperience of the borrowing country, the Department of State has objected. In such cases the issues have been dropped or modified.[9]

Besides the extra-national influences on the making and service of the loans of the Caribbean countries exercised by bondholders' protective associations and by the practice of the Department of State of the United States, there exist other more specific factors which have increased the stability of the Caribbean debt services. These fall into a number of classes:

1. Special guarantees may be given the lender by the pledging of certain revenues for the service of the loan. Particularly when such pledges are only engagements between the parties, it may be said that they have no binding character beyond that of the contract itself. Nevertheless, their statement gives an added solemnity to the engagement. A pledge to turn over certain revenues at stated intervals, if disregarded, visualizes the default and makes it possible for the creditor to urge his rights in a more specific manner than when his claim rests only on a general undertaking to pay interest and amortization charges. Though there are many instances where such agreements have been disregarded they are not without influence. Use of such expedients in wide variety in Latin America and elsewhere is far more general and of much longer standing than is popularly supposed.

2. Special guarantees of the sort above mentioned may be given greater weight by provisions for the filing of

---

[9] See an article by Arthur N. Young, *Ingenieria internacional*, November, 1927.

copies of the contract in some public office such as the legation or embassy of the country of the creditor, or the contract may require that its terms be given the tacit or express approval of a government official of the country of the creditor. Provision may be made that any dispute as to the meaning of the contract shall be arbitrated by named authorities.

3. By general treaty one government may agree not to increase its debts beyond its capacity to pay—the latter to be ascertained in agreement with a foreign government.

4. Engagements may be made by which the actual collection of certain of the revenues is put in the hands of nonnational officers, nominated by a foreign government, by the lenders or the borrowers. These officials may enter on their functions from the beginning of the loan or only in case of default. They may be given the duty to pay the amounts falling due on the loans directly to the creditors, or to a trustee for them, only the balance above that needed for the debt service being turned over to the national treasury.

A wide range of agreements of these sorts is found in the practice of nations. Though they are usually political in origin they have economic consequences which may and often do go beyond the immediate political object sought and bring a general stabilizing influence affecting not only the debt service the guarantee of which was the original object.

The debt arrangements in the Caribbean have come to involve in increasing measure the attention of citizens of the United States, both because of the special political and commercial interest which the United States has in Caribbean developments and because in recent years American capitalists have played a growing rôle as lenders to foreign countries generally. These arrangements are one of the most important influences in the recent improvement of the record of the republics in their foreign debt payments.

No general policy followed by lenders or by the United States government is indicated in the various contracts. They have arisen in response to the circumstances of each case and range from agreements in which there is no participation by the United States to ones in which it exercises an explicit and far-reaching responsibility. In the pages following, the various economic engagements are reviewed with reference to their content rather than their dates, beginning with those in which the functions assumed by the United States government have been of more extensive character.

Political developments arising out of disturbed order and threatened intervention by European powers in the two republics of the island of Haiti have brought about engagements by which the United States has assumed unusual functions in connection with the administration of their public finance.

The arrangement with the Republic of Haiti of September 16, 1915, is the more far-reaching. Under its terms the United States undertakes to aid Haiti in developing its resources and in the firm establishment of its finances. The President of the United States nominates and the President of Haiti appoints a Receiver-General and a Financial Adviser—in practice the same person. This officer as Receiver-General is to "collect, receive and apply" all customs duties. As Financial Adviser he also has functions in the spending of all the national income for he is "an officer attached to the Ministry of Finance, to give effect to whose proposals and labors the Minister will lend efficient aid." Customs revenues are applied first to the expenses of the customs receivership, then to the Haitian public debt, then to the maintenance of the constabulary which acts as an army-police force, and finally to the current expenses of the government. Monthly reports are made to the two governments. The national debt cannot be increased nor the customs duties lowered without the consent of the United States.[10]

At the time of the establishment of the American control Haitian finance was in a deplorable condition. The government accounts were confused and the administration of public funds was characterized by irregularity and dishonesty. The payments on the public debt were in questionable position. The changes which were introduced in public finance were far-reaching and have been frankly recognized as beneficial by even the greatest critics of the making of the treaty.

Revenues and expenditures are now under an efficient system of accounting. Better control of collection has increased the yield of customs and internal revenues, the Haitian government having authorized the American officials to take over the latter in 1924. Better expenditure has allowed the undertaking of public works on a scale never before approached.

Since the national income depends largely on levies on agricultural exports which fluctuate with crop and market conditions, an unobligated cash balance to be used in emergencies has been built up amounting in 1928 to more than $3,870,000. It reached a new high record in the year ending September 30, 1929. The currency has been stabilized, the floating debt has been retired and foreign claims have been liquidated, liens upon customs duties have been removed, and the foreign debt reduced. Trade has shown an encouraging increase.

Contemporaneously with these developments, public rev-

[10] Only the financial developments under the treaty are here discussed. A general review of developments is found in Raymond Leslie Buell, *The American Occupation of Haiti,* Foreign Policy Association Information Service, Vol. V, Nos. 19-20 (New York, 1929). The official point of view is set out in the annual reports of the American High Commissioner and of the Financial Adviser–General Receiver. See also S. De La Rue, *Review of the Finances of the Republic of Haiti, 1924-1930* (New York, 1930).

enues have steadily risen from $3,786,936 in 1916-7 to $10,084,203 in 1928.[11] The gross public debt was reduced from $33,794,000 in 1916-7 to $18,279,000 in 1920-1. Thereafter, new loans for refunding operations and other purposes were made which extended the provisions of the customs receivership during their period which was set at thirty years. Subsequent reductions of the debt brought its total to $17,735,400 on September 30, 1929.

Provisions in the loan contracts require that when the income rises above $7,000,000 certain amounts in addition to those regularly devoted thereto shall be applied to the sinking fund. If the income is sufficiently high to require regularly the maximum payments the last of the new loans will be paid off in 1943 instead of 1952. Haiti may devote additional moneys to the retirement of bonds purchased at or below par and thus hasten still further the cancellation of the debt. From the financial point of view the American administration of Haiti has been an undoubted success.

The arrangements in the Dominican Republic, like those in Haiti, arose out of conditions which threatened to make control of the customs income a matter of international disagreement. Economic development in the republic before 1905 was as irregular and unsatisfactory as its political and social progress. Dominicans, individual foreigners, and at least the representatives of foreign governments, European and American, had been involved in numerous transactions which, looked at in retrospect, are no cause for pride.[12]

---

[11] *Seventh Annual Report of the American High Commissioner at Port au Prince, Haiti, 1928* (Washington, 1929), *Commerce Reports,* May 14, 1928, and *Republic of Haiti, Port au Prince Monthly Bulletin,* Vol. VI, No. 9, September, 1929, and *Financial Developments in Latin America during 1929,* U. S. Department of Commerce, Bureau of Foreign and Domestic Commerce, Trade Information Bulletin No. 707 (Washington, 1930), p. 16. Hereafter cited as "Trade Information Bulletin No. 707." Revenues in 1929 were 42,521,528 gourdes (par 20 cents gold).

[12] The detail is available in Sumner Welles, *Naboth's Vineyard: The Dominican Republic* (New York, 1928), and in Melvin M. Knight, *The*

The result of bad government and ill-advised loan contracts giving foreigners far-reaching and sometimes overlapping degrees of control over Dominican finance was that in the early years of this century the republic was confronted by conditions which threatened its independence. Pressure for settlements by European and American claimants was incessant, and a number of European governments were considering action to take over the administration of the customhouses to secure payment of the claims of their citizens. To avoid the possible development of what would practically be an indefinite occupation of American territory by non-American political interests, the United States inquired as to the disposition of the government to accept American coöperation.

It has often been charged that the resulting arrangement, the adjustments in which were not completed until 1907, was not a "free will" engagement. In one sense it was not. But it was one forced on the Dominican Republic by circumstances rather than by an imperialistic program of the United States. The American government and the American people took over the responsibilities assumed in the treaty, only with general misgiving in the development of a Carribbean policy new and to all concerned unclear in details. Acceptance came only after a two-year delay and modification of the original proposal which cut down the functions to be carried out by the authorities nominated by the United States government.

When negotiation of a treaty was started, the government found itself confronted by a public debt and claims which had arisen under regular and revolutionary governments to an amount which it could not pay. Review of the various items to determine their justice was arranged, and a loan was sought to refund the obligations found to be

---

Americans in Santo Domingo (New York, 1928). The latter volume is highly critical of American policy.

proper and to provide for certain public improvements. The plan for the loan was dependent upon assistance from the United States in collecting the customs revenues and in their application to the service of the proposed bond issue.

The original proposal of 1905, by which the United States was to coöperate to this end, met opposition in the Senate of the United States, and a modus vivendi was put into operation until a new arrangement was made which was approved two years later.

This treaty of February 8, 1907, provided that the President of the United States should appoint a General Receiver and staff who should collect the customs dues until the bonds should be paid. After payment of administrative expenses each month, $100,000 was to be turned over to the representative of the creditors for the debt service and the balance of the collection was to be turned back to the government. If in any year the customs revenues exceeded $3,000,000, half of the surplus was to be used for redemption of the bonds. Until the issue was retired the Dominican Republic was not to increase its debt or modify its customs duties without a previous agreement with the United States. The similarity of many of these terms to ones appearing in the later Haitian agreement discussed above indicates that the experience under this treaty was made the basis of the more extensive one negotiated in 1915 with the neighboring republic.

The years following 1908 showed both the advantages and limitations of the system set up. For a time, peace was maintained, and the economic position of the country showed steady improvement. Then followed less satisfactory maintenance of public order and an increase of the public debt by at least $7,000,000 without prior agreement with the United States. An acrimonious dispute arose as to whether the Dominican Republic had not violated Article III of the treaty of 1908 concerning the increase of the public debt and modification of the import duties. The Dominicans alleged that the increase in the debt was due to expenses incurred in putting down revolutions. To avoid recurrence of such problems the United States urged the acceptance of a Financial Adviser with functions similar to those already described as exercised by the similar officer in Haiti.

Inability to come to an agreement resulted in the establishment of a military government by the United States under a proclamation issued November 29, 1916. American control lasted until 1924 when on July 12 a new President was inaugurated. The last of the American marines left on September 18. No provision for the extension of American control through arrangement for a Financial Adviser had been made.

On December 27, 1924, a new convention was signed to replace that of 1907 though on the same general lines. The rise in public income which had occurred under the customs receivership had forced the government to devote more of the yield to debt payments than was considered necessary. It was therefore agreed that the receivership should continue but should apply to the sinking fund, in addition to the annual requirements, only 10 per cent of the customs income, if any, in excess of $4,000,000 per year. The other provisions were similar to those of the convention of 1907, except for the addition of a clause providing that any dispute arising concerning the convention should be settled by arbitration. This clause, if loyally supported, may prevent the rise of such controversies as resulted in the intervention of 1916-24.

As in the case of Haiti, the economic effects of the customs receivership in the Dominican Republic have been favorable. The advance has had many causes but the greater efficiency in collecting the customs, the regular service guaranteed the foreign debts, the lower interest rates obtained, and the greater amounts of money made available for the expenses of government have all been important factors in the improvement which has occurred. Greater advance would doubtless have occurred if peace had not been subject to interruptions.

Exports, in all nonindustrial countries such as this, are subject to the irregularities that always are found in trade dependent on crop yields, but they have shown a steady rise from $6,896,098 in 1905 to $28,755,000 in 1928. Imports in the same period increased from $2,736,828 to $26,788,-000.[13] The balance of trade has been uniformly favorable except in the postwar slump of 1921. Internal improvements have been marked. The government is now making a serious effort to encourage production in secondary agricultural lines to cut down the dependence on the sugar industry which is largely controlled by foreign capital. Railway services have been extended and even more important advance has been made in the building of highways, which have increased from 78 miles in 1915 to 557 in 1927.

Public income has shown encouraging advance, reaching $15,319,000 in 1927. The receipts from customs have been adequate to handle the foreign debt service with regularity and to make it possible to turn increasing amounts back to the local treasury. The amounts thus paid over were $1,346,246 in 1905 and $3,477,845 in 1929. Dominican credit has been improved and the public securities enjoy a high rating in world markets.

The showing in the public debt has also been satisfactory. At the establishment of the customs control the nominal debt was readjusted from a total of $33,833,510 to about $17,000,000. The original loan agreement was for $20,-000,000, but by 1920 the external debt had been reduced to $9,322,000. Thereafter, it rose through a loan of

---

[13] Both imports and exports declined sharply in 1929 due to the depression in world markets. *Report of the 23d Fiscal Period, Dominican Customs Receivership, Calendar Year, 1929* (Washington, 1930), p. 15.

$10,000,000 in 1922 and by refunding, following the treaty of 1924, was again increased. Repayments brought it down at the beginning of 1928 to about $15,000,000, but it increased during the year through a new loan to $20,000,000. It stood at $19,684,000 at the end of 1929.[14] Due to the provisions in both Customs Conventions that portions of the revenue, above stated amounts, be used to retire the bond issues, they have been paid off at greater than the normal rate. Under the treaty of 1907, special reductions of the debt were made in fourteen out of the seventeen years for which it ran, and similar payments have been made annually under the convention of 1924.[15]

In two other Caribbean republics, Cuba and Panama, the position in public finance is influenced by treaties with the United States. The control in the first case rests primarily on the second paragraph of the so-called Platt Amendment, now incorporated in the permanent treaty. It provides that the Cuban government "shall not assume or contract any public debt, to pay the interest upon which, and to make reasonable sinking fund provision for the ultimate discharge of which, the ordinary revenues of the island, after defraying the current expenses of government, shall be inadequate."

Of all the much discussed provisions of the agreement this has been least criticized. In practice it has been accepted to mean that Cuba is under obligation before negotiating a foreign loan to consult the United States. President Machado apparently has argued that consent of the United States is not necessary, but the generally accepted opinion is to the contrary.[16]

Though this provision may have and probably does have

---

[14] Trade Information Bulletin No. 707, p. 13.

[15] The figures quoted are summarized from the annual reports of the Dominican Customs Receivership, the *Commerce Yearbook, 1929* (Washington, 1929), Vol. II, and *Commerce Reports*, May 28, 1928.

[16] See Chapman, *op. cit.*, p. 641.

a very real importance it cannot be said to have brought about satisfactory conditions in Cuban finance. Cuba started her independent history under exceptionally favorable circumstances. The American commissioners, in negotiating the treaty of peace with Spain, refused to allow the mother country to transfer to Cuba any portion of the so-called Cuban debt which had been incurred largely by expenditures to put down revolutions in the island. Cuba started with no foreign debt.

The first few years of independent history were financially promising. Subsequently, the island has at various times had recourse to foreign loans under circumstances which show that however effective the provision above cited may be in preventing borrowing beyond the capacity of the island to pay, it has not been one which has assured that borrowing shall occur only when money is needed nor that it shall be wisely spent. The debts of Cuba are in the main the result of irregular economic and political conditions and of extravagant expenditures which a better organized government at least in large part could have avoided.

When the American occupation of the island came to an end, there was $689,000 in the treasury. At the end of the first president's term, some $26,000,000 were in the vaults, though there were outstanding obligations of an amount about as great. Meanwhile, a bonus law passed in 1903 and modified the next year resulted, in February, 1905, in a loan contract for $35,000,000. Its advisability was questionable and the distribution of the money to the veterans of the revolution was attended by flagrant abuses.

In the presidency of Gomez, another loan of $16,500,000 was made to put through much needed sanitation and paving works which had been previously planned. The money was extravagantly spent. To complete the work and for other purposes, another foreign loan was found "necessary" in 1914 for $10,000,000 by the first Menocal administration, in spite of a remarkable rise in current treasury receipts. In the same period, the domestic debt rose to fifteen or sixteen millions.

Then came the war period with greatly increased income but even greater increase in expenditures. Two new loans for $7,000,000 and $30,000,000 were made in 1917, the latter a war loan spent in greater part for purposes having remote, if any, relation to the war. A portion was employed for purchasing an elaborate presidential mansion at "more than double the cost of the White House in Washington." [17] By the end of the Menocal administration the domestic debt had reached new heights.

Cuba defaulted on the bonded debt, domestic and foreign, in 1921, but was shortly enabled to resume payment through an emergency loan of $5,000,000 arranged through the good offices of the United States. The period of the Zayas administration was financially disastrous. The sugar industry was struggling under the effects of postwar deflation, business generally was disorganized, the financial interests with few exceptions were bankrupt, and the government faced an extraordinary and much padded floating debt.

These circumstances brought a far-reaching economic "intervention," though officially the acts are not so characterized. The government was in urgent need of money, but consent to borrow was not forthcoming until the administration had deflated the claims in the floating debt, seriously cut the current budget, reformed the personnel of the cabinet, and in various other ways modified its internal organization. The "clean up" being assured, a contract for a $50,000,000 loan was signed in 1923, including specific provisions as to the purposes for which the money should be used. Once the money was in hand, however, the "reforms" in large degree were forgotten.

The control of Cuban finances by the United States pro-

---

[17] *Ibid.*, pp. 393-394.

vided in the permanent treaty is not one which prevents unwise debts.[18] It gives no power to check the building up of a floating debt. A weak Cuban administration can create a situation in which the United States is forced to grant permission for an increase of the debt which it may believe could have been avoided or to refuse permission and thereby induce a general business depression. The arrangement gives no power to control the actual expenditure of a loan, once the money has passed into the hands of the local administration. Indeed no far-reaching control of this sort was contemplated when the provisions of the treaty were drafted.

The debt actually borne by Cuba is not unusual. An impartial observer regrets not the burden which it places on the population, but the very limited benefits which contracting the obligations has brought. In total amount, the funded debt has varied as amortization has occurred and as new loans have been made. In 1914, it reached $67,828,000. In 1923, it touched its peak at $114,694,-000, since which time it has fallen to $83,061,400 on December 31, 1929.[19] Since 1914, the foreign trade and public revenues have both more than doubled in value. In spite of the current depression in the sugar industry, the debt service, so far as this item indicates the situation of the country, is now in better position than before the World War.

---

[18] There have been instances, however, in which the United States has felt justified in making its opinion known when certain proposed actions alone or in connection with other circumstances might justify intervention or put an objectionable strain on the Cuban treasury. See the discussion of the Zapata Swamp project in Chapman, *op. cit.*, and in *Foreign Relations of the United States* (Washington, annually), for 1912 and 1913. See also the Nuevitas Carbarien Railway incident described in Benjamin H. Williams, *Economic Foreign Policy of the United States* (New York, 1929), p. 202.

[19] Not including "public works serial certificates." These from 1927 to the end of 1929 are reported to have totaled $60,000,000. The debt at the end of 1929, excluding these certificates and the floating debt was $83,061,-400. Trade Information Bulletin No. 707, p. 12.

No specific treaty provisions have been made for the supervision of the public debts of Panama. As interpreted, however, the treaty of November 18, 1903, places this country as to its public debts in a position comparable to that of Cuba. "The United States guarantees and will maintain the independence of Panama," and the detail of the treaty creates for American interests so dominant a position in the affairs of the republic that Panama is not in fact free to borrow at will or even to pledge certain funds which have arisen out of the treaty.

Of these two are of importance. The United States agreed to pay Panama $10,000,000 as compensation for special privileges which Panama granted and in addition $250,000 per year beginning nine years after the ratification of the convention. The Department of State of the United States has exercised a certain supervision over the use made of these funds on the ground that the treaty payments were intended to insure income which would facilitate the maintenance of a stable government. An attempt by Panama to pledge $6,000,000 of the first fund and the annuity to promote the building of railways was abandoned after objection by the United States. A later proposal of a similar sort was approved on the acceptance by Panama of certain items as to the loan and the location of the railway.

Five major foreign loans have been floated and there exists a small internal funded debt. The service of the first of the foreign loans, that of 1914, was met from the annual annuity payments. That of the loan of 1926 was met from income from the $6,000,000 so-called constitutional fund which was invested in New York. If the income was not sufficient, the unpledged balance of the annuity payments was to be drawn upon. For the two loans of 1926, for various purposes including railway extensions and national highways, income from the Chiriqui railroad and certain enumerated taxes were pledged. An external consolidation loan of $12,000,000 was floated with American bankers in 1928, and the national bank floated an issue of $1,000,000 in mortage certificates with Canadian interests. In 1929, a commission of American experts made recommendations for improving financial administration, resulting in a decree to improve accounting and the adoption of an economy program.[20]

Under the conditions outlined, Panama has made an excellent record in its foreign debt service. There have been no defaults. The public debt, of which about seven-eighths is external, amounted to $18,686,000 in September of 1928. It has recently shown a tendency to increase in a period of expanding government functions.

The arrangements made by the government of Nicaragua concerning its debt services stand in a peculiar position. They were undertaken in the belief that a treaty was to be entered with the United States under which an American loan was to be arranged. But neither the treaty nor the loan came into existence and the chief debt benefiting from the arrangements has been a British issue dating from 1909.

Out of the political disturbances of 1909, there arose in October of that year engagements accepted by the party leaders looking toward the economic and political regeneration of the country. These were the "Dawson Agreements," so named after the American minister at Panama who at the instance of the Department of State had been instrumental in drawing them up.[21] There followed the negotiation of the Knox-Castrillo convention providing that Nicaragua was to seek a loan subject to the approval of the United States for the purpose mentioned above. As security for the loan, the customs receipts were pledged and it was

---

[20] *Ibid.*, p. 19.
[21] *Foreign Relations of the United States* (1911), p. 652.

agreed that they should be collected by an officer nominated by the bankers, approved by the United States, and appointed by the President of Nicaragua. The convention was accepted by the Nicaragua Congress on June 14, 1910, by a vote of 30 to 6, but after long delay failed in the United States Senate on May 9, 1912.

Meanwhile, New York bankers had agreed to make a loan of $15,000,000, believing that the treaty would be ratified, and Clifford D. Ham, an American citizen, was designated as Collector of Customs by the bankers, approved by the Secretary of State of the United States, and appointed by the Nicaraguan government.

Nicaragua was now in dire financial straits. The debased currency was a drag on business. British creditors were pressing for payment on the so-called Ethelburga loan, the service of which defaulted. A provisional loan was negotiated with New York interests for $1,500,000 followed by another in 1912 for $755,000. In connection with these emergency accounts arrangements similar to those which had been planned under the treaty for the collection of customs were worked out, as well as one creating a High Commission of one Nicaraguan and one American, the latter appointed by the Secretary of State of the United States.

The failure of the loan project due to the defeat of the convention and the continuance of domestic disturbances led to further adjustments of a financial nature and the pledging at subsequent times of various of the resources of the republic as security for the moneys advanced. At last, conditions took a turn for the better, the financial position of the republic improved, and in June, 1924, the New York bankers ended all connection with Nicaraguan international finance. Later domestic difficulties have brought renewed borrowing, but the receivership has continued to function in collecting the customs revenue and in payment of the debt service. Mr. Ham whose designation was approved by the

Secretary of State of the United States on November 7, 1911, served as Collector-General until June, 1928, when he was succeeded by Irving A. Lindberg, who had been appointed Deputy Collector in 1912.[22] The customs receivership will continue to exist until the bonds outstanding are paid.

From the Nicaraguan, as from the Dominican experience, it is clear that the establishment of a customs control does not of itself guarantee public order. It may bring better service of the public debts and make possible lower interest rates on loans and more liberal terms of amortization. It appears to have done so in Nicaragua. It has been honestly and efficiently administered. The customs collections have risen since 1912 from 1,172,482 cordobas, practically equivalent to dollars, to 3,917,553 cordobas in 1929.[23] Internal revenue not under the customs control makes a much less favorable showing and in recent years totals appreciably less than a decade ago. Serious irregularities in its collection still exist.

Due to the success of the customs administration, the service of the foreign debt has been reasonably met, though the upset caused by the European War caused temporary irregularity. The funded debt, early in 1930, consisted of but two items, the sterling bonds of 1909, known as the Ethelburga loan, and the customs guaranteed bonds of 1918. The former mature in 1943. They were originally issued to an amount equivalent to $6,083,125 but as of March 31, 1930, only $2,823,674 were outstanding. Of the

---

[22] The detail of the financial arrangements is given in W. W. Cumberland, *Nicaragua, an Economic and Financial Survey* (Washington, 1928); in a pamphlet published by the Department of State of the United States under the title *A Brief History of the Relations between the United States and Nicaragua, 1909-28* (Washington, 1928) and in *Foreign Relations of the United States*.

[23] Based on *Report of the Collector-General of Customs for the Period of January 1, 1929, to December 31, 1929,* pp. 4, 15, and *Statistics of the Commerce of 1927* (Managua, 1928).

customs guaranteed bonds of 1918, $3,744,150 were issued but they were reduced to $1,646,700 as of the same date. The total funded debt, therefore, was only $4,470,374 which, granted favorable conditions, is not a formidable amount. Estimates have been made that it may be possible to retire the customs guaranteed bonds in six or seven years and the loan of 1909 in not over thirteen years.

Salvador is the smallest and most thickly settled of the Central American republics and one whose government has made marked advance in recent years. Like that of Costa Rica, the government of Salvador has sought and markedly profited by the aid of foreign capital in the development of the national resources. Its financial history involving foreign debts presents strong contrasts. In 1827, it assumed a sixth of the debt of the old Central American Federation, but allowed the service to go promptly into default, a condition continuing until 1860 when the obligation was paid off in cash at 90 per cent under a compromise arrangement.

Thereafter no entries appear until 1889 when a series of borrowings was begun, one of the objects of which was, as a rule, to supply the country with a rail transportation system. As a result, Salvador has now more miles of railways per thousand square miles than any other Central American country. As they developed, these projects came to involve various undertakings by which portions of the customs dues, both import and export, were mortgaged for the service of the debts and various adjustments were introduced affecting the rights of the government in the railroads. During these years, the current expenditures were regularly greater than the receipts, and the deficits were met by borrowing money. This budget practice, taken with the public improvements program, greatly increased the debt burden, but the debt record after the adjustment of 1860, except for one brief period, was kept free from defaults until 1920. Since 1860, Salvador has the best record of any Central American state.

The years following the European War, however, brought the government into financial difficulties, and in 1921-2 the debts went into default. To meet the situation, a general reform of public finances was undertaken late in 1921 and brought into operation in 1923. It involved one of the most interesting debt arrangements in Central America and one which has thus far been highly successful. A settlement of all the debts of the republic, internal and external, was made including the payment with accumulated interest of the obligations to the Salvador Railway Company. The detail of the arrangement shows an elaboration of the expedients adopted earlier in Costa Rica and is a good example of what may be done through loan contracts and the cooperation of governments to assure regularity in collection of revenues and the creation of conditions which favor their application to the purposes to which they have been pledged.[24]

The three issues contracted for in September, 1923, totaled about $21,500,000. The service of each of the loans in their order was made a claim on 70 per cent of the national customs returns. It was agreed that if this income did not prove sufficient then the lien was to be extended, if necessary, over the total customs revenue.

The percentage specified was arrived at by review of the actual customs receipts for the years 1910-20, the latter date being the latest for which figures were available when the negotiations were begun. It was found that 70 per cent of the actual yield in this period was nearly twice the interest and sinking fund charges for the three loans and therefore, it appeared, an ample guarantee. The customs are not to

---

[24] In making these loans Minor C. Keith, mentioned below, was a party to the negotiations. The full statement of the agreements is found in *Diario oficial*, San Salvador, viernes, 21 de julio de 1922, num. 163.

be changed so as to reduce their gross return while any of the bonds remain outstanding and unpaid.

The fiscal agent, representing the lenders, agreed to set up its own agency in the republic for the direct supervision of customs collection during the life of the bonds. The head of this office, the Fiscal Representative residing in Salvador and his employees have the right to take part in inspections of merchandise and to inspect the customhouse accounts. Customs revenues reserved for the loan are paid directly to the representative of the lenders to be sent to New York monthly.

If a delay of thirty days occurs in the debt service, the first lien, upon the demand of the fiscal agent, extends over all the customs revenues and the customs administration is to be turned over to a Collector-General appointed by Salvador from two persons selected by the fiscal agent with the concurrence of the Secretary of State of the United States. While the government of the United States is not a party to the loan contract, it has taken cognizance of its existence and to a degree given assent to its terms. An exchange of notes with Salvador has taken place by which Salvador has assured the United States that it will coöperate with the United States and the bankers in carrying out the loan, and the United States, on its part, states that the Secretary of State is prepared to carry out certain stipulations of the agreement referring to him. These latter involve three articles in the contract.

In case "any disagreement, question or difference of any nature whatever" concerning the contract arises between the parties thereto, the matter is to be referred through the Secretary of State to the Chief Justice of the Supreme Court of the United States or if he does not act to some other member of the federal judiciary for decision. Both parties agree to accept and abide by the decision given as "final and conclusive."

If the republic defaults for thirty days the fiscal agent selects with the concurrence of the Secretary of State two persons one of whom Salvador agrees to name as Collector-General of Customs.

The Collector-General, if appointed, is to report promptly all rules for the collection of the customs which he may make, one copy being sent to the Department of State. He is to send there also copies of his monthly and annual reports of the sums received and disbursed.

The test of all agreements of this sort is in their actual working. Thus far the operation of this one has been uniformly favorable. W. W. Renwick, a man with extended experience in Central and South America, was appointed Fiscal Representative. Revenue collection improved in efficiency and in yield—the latter contributed to, also, until 1929, by the high current prices of coffee which increased local buying power and therefore import of foreign goods. Debt service has been promptly met. The 70 per cent of the customs pledged for the loan service has been more than sufficient to meet the charges. In 1928, it was necessary to take only the 70 per cent of the receipts up to June to satisfy the debt claims and in 1929 only the 70 per cent up to May.

The moneys made available to the government since the loan contract have enabled it to push through a program for the sanitation and paving of the capital and the building of a system of trunk-line highways which is the best in Central America. The external debt, which rose to 47,-279,000 colones after the loans of 1923, had been reduced to 43,194,000 colones at the beginning of 1930.

The history of Honduras shows the worst default record of any American country and the greatest abuses practiced by lenders upon a weak government. In 102 years of national life up to 1929, the republic was in default 93 years. On the break-up of the Central American

Federation, Honduras assumed one-sixth of the debt but paid no interest upon it. By 1867, principal plus interest amounted to over three times the original debt. Then began a series of efforts, well intentioned but very badly managed, by which the government sought to clear its old debt and to get funds for an "interoceanic" railroad. This latter undertaking was too great for a state as undeveloped economically and politically as Honduras, and both the representatives of the Republic and of the lenders were guilty of irregularities in the management of the bond issues which made the result much worse than might otherwise have been the case.

Four loans were marketed between 1867 and 1870 of a face value of over £6,000,000. The money raised by sale of bonds was used to manipulate the market, the representatives of Honduras itself were guilty, it appears, of acting beyond their powers and of questionable practices in the use of the funds which came into their hands. Finally what money did reach Honduras was poorly spent, largely on a stub railroad from the Atlantic. In 1872-3, all the loans went into default, "the interest having been paid out of the money borrowed." [25] A British Parliamentary inquiry later, in 1875, roundly criticized the circumstances under which the obligations came into existence.

At the end of these ventures in high finance, Honduras had pledged the customs dues at the port of Amapala, then its only port of importance, its "interoceanic" railway and its revenues, the produce of the mahogany forests and other state domains. The interest and amortization payments undertaken became greater than the entire public income.

Default continued as a matter of course. Various proposals for adjustment followed each other during the half century following, most of them involving the railroad

---

[25] *Fifty-fifth Annual Report of the Council of the Corporation of Foreign Bondholders for the Year 1928*, p. 225.

dream. Meanwhile the "debt" grew apace with accumulating interest charges to reach a fantastic total of about $154,000,000. In 1909, the British Minister entered an agreement with the President of Honduras looking toward an adjustment which met American opposition as beyond the capacity of the republic. Subsequent negotiations resulted in an agreement approved by the bondholders in May, 1923, and finally ratified by the Congress of Honduras in February, 1927, by which the principal of the external debt amounting to £5,398,570 and accumulated interest of some £25,000,000 were to be retired on payment of sixty half yearly installments of £20,000. The total payments were thus to be cut to a capital sum of about $6,000,000 with no interest.[26] The external sterling debt had been reduced at the end of July, 1929, to the equivalent of $5,400,000.[27]

The collection of this debt service is peculiar. The government of Honduras allocates for this purpose the proceeds of a 3 per cent tax on the value of consular invoices of imports. The tax is collected outside the country by a non-national agency, the National City Bank of New York, through special stamps obtainable only through the bank. A portion of the tax yield is set aside monthly for the half yearly installment, and any insufficiency is met from the proceeds of the first revenues of the following half year. Other consular revenues are pledged if needed. Disputes as to the loan are to be settled by arbitration. Up to date, the yield of the pledged revenues has been ample to meet the payments and assuming that peace is maintained the debt should be easily carried.

The financial condition of Honduras is still not prosperous. In 1928 steps were taken to liquidate debts of the

<hr>

[26] The full text of the arrangement is found in *Fifty-third Annual Report of the Council of the Corporation of Foreign Bondholders for the Year 1926* (London, 1927), pp. 246-249.

[27] Trade Information Bulletin No. 707, p. 17.

government with local banks by floating a loan of $1,500,-000 under an arrangement involving New York banks, the loan to be amortized by payments falling due to the government from certain fruit company interests of the north coast. Efforts are under way also to amortize the internal debt and to improve the budget practice which in the past has built up the internal debt through recurring deficits. Government finances showed favorable balances in 1927-8 and 1928-9.

Costa Rica has had a varied and interesting experience with foreign loans, none of which has involved a power of supervision or control by foreign governmental agencies nor by private agencies outside the republic. On the breaking up of the Central American Federation in 1827, Costa Rica assumed its share of the debt, some $65,000, and in 1840 paid it off at about 85 per cent in cash. Thereafter, no foreign loans were negotiated until 1871, when a loan was taken from Bischoffsheim and Goldschmidt, then active in Central American finance. Another loan followed the next year.

The time of the first of these loans marks also the beginning of the connection of Minor C. Keith with Costa Rica affairs. He became justly the most prominent figure in the public finance of Costa Rica and a great and still unappreciated unofficial proconsul in the expansion of American interests in Central America as a whole. Keith became interested in the railroad projects of Costa Rica, but in 1874 the money from the loans by which they were being built was exhausted and the payments thereon went into default. He continued to push construction of the railway, becoming himself heavily involved in the enterprise, and acted as the agent of Costa Rica to secure an adjustment of the debt and fresh money for the project which was crowned with success in 1885.

For ten years, payments were regular, then a new default occurred to be followed two years later by another adjustment with the bondholders negotiated by Keith. Still another adjustment was put through by his coöperation after the default of 1901-11. During this long period of connection with Central American affairs, Keith had expanded his interests to include the large-scale production of bananas which came to contribute an important part of the freight carried over the railroad.

The loan arising out of the adjustment of 1911, the oldest now running in Costa Rica, is interesting because it is an outstanding example of trust placed in an American citizen who had identified himself with Central American interests and won the confidence of the local authorities.[28] It is interesting also as an illustration of the special guarantees which may be offered by states not financially strong, involving the delegation of a comprehensive but unofficial control over local public finance to foreign interests.

The loan of 1911 was made a first and preferential charge on all the customs duties of Costa Rica, the monthly proportion to be paid to a designated agent. At the end of each half year, at least five-sixths of the amount for the service of the next half year was to be kept in hand. If payments were defaulted for thirty days the government was bound to consent to the appointment by Keith of a customs agency having the sole right to collect the customs.

Subsequent loans have contained additional items of guarantee. A loan of 1916 was secured on a first mortgage on the alcohol and liquor monopoly under terms similar to those described above, but providing that the amount due be turned over weekly. The Costa Rican loan of 1926 adopted the same general plan of guarantees and created a special trustee to carry out the duties which are frequently per-

---

[28] An interesting popular account of the work of Minor C. Keith is found in Samuel Crowther, *The Romance and Rise of the American Tropics* (New York, 1929), pp. 143 *et seq.*

formed by fiscal agents. It provided that after meeting the demand of prior claims all the yield from the pledged revenues should be turned over daily to the trustee's representative until the amount due for the month be paid. The amounts so collected are forthwith forwarded to New York. If default occurs, the trustee may appoint a Special Collections Agency which shall, subject to the prior right of other bondholders, have the right to collect all the import and export duties, the revenue of the alcohol and liquor monopolies and all other revenues at the time pledged to the service of the bonds. If any dispute arises concerning the rights of the bondholders, either party may submit the question to the Chief Justice of the Supreme Court of the United States or, if he cannot act, to the Associate Justice next in seniority of rank. "The decision of the arbiter, given in writing, shall be final and binding upon all parties to the dispute." [29]

The history of the external debts of Guatemala shows substantially the same features as that of the other Central American republics. In period of defaults the republic is outranked only by Honduras though payments have been made regularly since 1912, which constitutes a better recent record than that of any other Central American state except Costa Rica.

In the various contracts which have been entered, pledges of specific revenue occur as early as 1856 but their terms were at various times disregarded. Grants of the same security have at times been made to different lenders resulting in conflicts of interest between British and German and British and American capitalists. Some of the contracts with American firms have provided for deposit of signed copies in the legation of the United States in Guatemala

---

[29] The text of the contract is found in La Republica de Costa Rica and Central Union Trust Company of New York as Trustee . . . , Trust Agreement, dated November 1, 1926 (n. p., n. d.).

and have stipulated that the holders of the bonds shall have the right to ask the protection of the United States if the agreements are violated.

The demoralization of publc finance during the régime of the dictator, Estrada Cabrera, lasting from 1898 to 1920, brought the government into financial difficulties from which it has recovered in recent years through the influence of more conservative presidents and under the high prices which have obtained for coffee. A new currency system has been established on a gold basis, government budgets have been balanced, and government receipts have markedly increased.[30] The administrations have not been willing to accept bonds for much needed improvements in terms involving "guarantees" of the more extensive sorts outlined above, but American advisers have twice been called in to assist in planning financial reforms, and an American, Findley B. Howard, has been employed to work in the customs service. In July, 1929, a new tariff, drawn under his supervision, went into effect which is expected materially to increase the public revenue.

British capitalists have been the chief lenders to Guatemala, and three British loans of 1895, 1913, and 1928, are still partially outstanding. These totaled £1,-667,400 in 1929. The chief other items are an issue of 1927, of which $2,436,000 were outstanding in 1929, and two issues of Los Altos Railway Bonds of 1924 and 1927, amounting at the same date to $3,137,000. The public debt at the end of 1929 was officially reported as $15,556,018 of which the greater part was external.[31]

Like Guatemala, Colombia has had an irregular debt record, but has avoided making agreements which delegate

---

[30] *Commerce Reports,* April 29, 1929, p. 307.

[31] Trade Information Bulletin No. 707, p. 15; for previous years see *Fifty-fifth Annual Report of the Council of Foreign Bondholders for the Year 1928,* pp. 211 *et seq.; Ibid.,* 1929, p. 222; and *Commerce Yearbook, 1929,* Vol. II, p. 322.

to foreign governments or to foreign capitalists any direct control over branches of the public income. Revolutionary debts beginning as early as 1820 promptly went into default, and the record of the country under the five changes of names under which it has at various times gone shows a wide variety of loan agreements under which various pledges of property and income have featured, including the yield of the customs, of the customs at designated ports, of the tobacco monopoly, of the salt mines, rights in the Panama Railway, public lands, and the general revenues. These pledges have not prevented defaults. In fact, for about half of its history, the republic has not been able to meet its debt payments though the record since 1904 is clear.

The economic advance during the past quarter century has been extraordinary but the development of the natural resources has even now hardly begun and the internal communications system is still far from satisfactory. Exports were worth $11,986,000 in 1905 but reached $113,909,000 in 1928—an increase of almost tenfold. Public revenue has showed rapid increase and the flow of foreign capital into enterprises in the country has been much greater than at any previous time in the country's history.[32]

In the years of prosperity following the recovery from the postwar slump, speculative activity was high and government borrowings for the developmental program heavy. The currency conditions and budgetary practice in Colombia in spite of its general economic advance were not, however, satisfactory in the first part of this period,

---

[32] The ordinary revenue rose from $14,145,817 in 1912 to $63,267,000 in 1927. *Republica de Colombia, memoria que presenta el ministro de hacienda y credito publico al congreso nacional en las sesiones ordinarias de 1925* (Bogotá, n. d.), p. 14, and *Commerce Yearbook, 1929,* Vol. II, p. 180. The estimated ordinary revenue in 1930 was $62,068,880. Trade Information Bulletin No. 707, p. 10. Investments of British and American citizens in Colombia in 1913 totaled $36,470,000 and in 1929, $298,402,500. Compiled from statistical tables in Winkler, *Investments of United States Capital in Latin America* (Boston, 1928).

and in the years following the European War they became steadily worse. The government decided to ask the assistance of foreign economists in working out plans for reform. A group of American experts headed by Dr. Edwin W. Kemmerer was employed, and in 1923 a new system of fiscal legislation and procedure was adopted. The banking system was reformed, an elastic currency on the gold standard was established, and modern budgetary methods were introduced.[33]

These improvements have been followed by important loan transactions which have simplified the list of outstanding obligations and furnished large sums of money for development. The only important outstanding foreign commitments are now the balances from a loan of 1927 amounting to $25,000,000 and one of 1928 of $35,000,000. The total funded debt as of December 31, 1928, was 82,194,070 pesos.[34] At the end of 1929, the outstanding foreign loans of the national government, the departments, the municipalities, and the Agricultural Mortgage Bank totaled 181,701,-738 pesos.[35]

Colombia in 1930 was going through a period of depression. The heavy borrowings have not yet been reflected in a general strengthening of the economic position and the decline in coffee prices has affected business conditions adversely. There seems to be reason to believe that a fairly long period of adjustment is in prospect though, providing that the government adheres to the fiscal program which has been adopted, public finances should be sound.

The financial position of Venezuela is unique among those of the Caribbean states. The country has not been without

---

[33] The position of the debts and the reforms undertaken are detailed in the *Memoria* above cited.

[34] The exchange rate of the peso in December, 1928, was $.9709. The statistics above are from *Commerce Yearbook, 1929*, Vol. II, and the Camp, Thorne *Latin America Service*, December 26, 1929.

[35] Trade Information Bulletin No. 707, p. 10.

long disturbed periods and long drawn out economic crises. In the first part of this century its treatment of foreign interests brought its policy in public finance into the limelight and gave rise to a heated discussion of the principles involved in forcible collection of public debts by American and European nations, a number of declarations of national policy as to such collection, and the formulation of a general international convention on the subject. But the financial difficulties other than those involving public debt into which the other American republics have at different times fallen, Venezuela has avoided to a surprising degree.

After an unfortunate experience with paper money issued in 1811 at the very beginning of her history, Venezuela abjured the attempt to create value through the printing press. No government since that time has dared to run counter to the established practice. The banks which now issue paper bills are allowed to do so only by keeping a heavy gold cover and maintaining the convertibility of paper and gold.

Unfortunately, the default record of the republic is not so favorable, though since 1879 payments on foreign debts have been regularly made except in 1892 and in the troubled period of 1898-1904 when the difficulties with European powers again brought a break. Taken as a whole, the last half century of Venezuelan financial history makes a record which compares favorably with that of other Caribbean republics. For this there are a number of reasons. Venezuela was able in the first half of her history to secure adjustments with her creditors which materially cut down her obligations. Through the greater part of the last fifty years, the country has been under the control of dictators who have been able to maintain domestic peace, at least in those portions of the republic contributing in an important way to public revenue. In recent years, the direct and indirect returns from the development of the oil industry have greatly strengthened the financial position of the government.

As a result, there is now only a small external debt outstanding, the unredeemed remainder of the 3 per cent Diplomatic Debt of 1905, resulting from the adjustments made following the forward action by European powers in 1902-3. On this debt, originally amounting to £5,223,100, payments have been made regularly. In June, 1928, the government began remitting twice the amount required under the contract. The debt would doubtless be retired even more rapidly but for the fact that it bears so low an interest rate. On December 31, 1929, the outstanding external debt amounted, in dollar equivalent, to only some $5,689,077. The internal debt of Venezuela was a somewhat smaller amount.[36]

The position of the national treasury is no less extraordinary. In a message to Congress on April 21, 1928, President Gomez announced that after meeting all current expenditures the government had in hand on the thirty-first of March cash sufficient to pay off the entire national debt, internal and external, and leave a balance of over $5,000,000, United States gold. At the end of 1929, the balance of the account of the government in the Bank of Venezuela payable at sight was more than twice the amount of the public debt and in May, 1930, the Venezuelan Congress recommended that the next budget include an item to pay off the entire foreign debt.[37] In current years, in fact, the financial position of Venezuela in relation to its public debt has become not only unique among the republics of the Caribbean but probably unmatched among the states of the world.[38]

---

[36] *Commerce Reports,* June 9, 1930.

[37] Trade Information Bulletin No. 707, p. 24.

[38] See annual reports of the Council of the Corporation of Foreign Bondholders, especially for the year 1928, and *Commerce Yearbook,* Vol. II, 1926-9. In 1930, a recommendation of General Gomez to the Venezuelan

A review of the financial arrangements of the independent Caribbean states shows that in the entire list there is only one which has not undertaken special engagements involving coöperation with American interests, either actively by agreements between the governments or through contract with private interests necessitating approval by the government, or through the establishment of special fiscal arrangements by which American financial groups discharge functions usually performed directly by the government or by coöperation with American advisers.

Study of the financial arrangements cannot fail to impress upon the student their far-reaching political and economic importance. For both the United States and the Caribbean states, they are important primarily to the degree that they promote public order. Without its maintenance, growth of stability in social and political institutions is hindered, economic advance is checked, and international relations both commercial and political are disturbed. On the other hand, to the degree that financial coöperation of the sorts above reviewed can contribute to peace, and the development of responsible governments it may become an active element in the laying of the groundwork for full development of natural resources, for the increase of national wealth, for greater resources for the local government, for greater international exchange, material and cultural. In addition to these general considerations, the coöperation in financial matters has for the Caribbean states and the United States a peculiar political importance. If it can be made to serve the ends outlined it will make possible the gradual elimination of possibilities that the control of their territories by American states may be questioned. Action to avoid such contingencies has been the policy of the

---

Congress was approved looking toward retirement of all the public debt. This would leave Venezuela at its centenary as the only large country of the world without a public debt. See *Commerce Reports,* June 9, 1930.

United States but fundamentally their avoidance is of equal concern to all the American commonwealths.

How far the improvement which has come in the financial position of the various states has been due to the special arrangements above discussed it is impossible to state. The stronger units probably would have improved their positions; in any case, the weaker ones almost certainly would have had a much less favorable record than they have made in recent years had they relied upon their own efforts. In few, if any, of these countries has the time yet come when they can borrow on as favorable terms without "guarantees" as with them and the administration of public finance is, in far the majority of them, still so weak that it is not to be presumed that assistance and advice, official or unofficial, may not for a considerable period be sought with profit beyond their borders.

Great as the advantages may be which come from the stabilization measures outlined it is clear that they are in the long view exceptional. They may be unavoidable, but they are unwelcome. They are expedients, means to an end the accomplishment of which will lead to their abolition. It is not to be expected that their utility will be of as short duration as is usually contemplated by the public or perhaps even by those directly engaged in the making of the agreements, for the conditions which they are planned to remedy are ones which change but slowly.

The special obligations undertaken by the United States are ones assumed by the government and by the public without enthusiasm as the best solution of tangled situations. Both will welcome the development of conditions which will make them no longer necessary. Where they will meet the case, arrangements much to be preferred are those which involve the least possible participation by one government in the financial affairs of another. Far-reaching measures for the control of the fiscal affairs of one government by officials chosen by another can hardly fail to be productive of friction and international misunderstanding even when undertaken with the best of intent.

NOTE ON CERTAIN FEATURES OF CARIBBEAN LOANS

The conditions under which international loans are made are by no means uniform and from the nature of the case cannot become so. There are given below comments on certain points on which there continues to be difference of opinion as to what are the facts and what is good practice.

1. It is often declared that the issue prices at which loans to Carribean states are offered to the public make them an indefensible burden to those who are to pay off the loans at par. As a rule, however, the issue prices show no marked contrast to those involving loans to other states, in which the risk is equally great. In the table below are found a number of examples of the rates offered.

2. The price of the loans to the bankers often has no close relation to the price at which the loans are offered to the public. In a small issue or one for a government not well known to the market, the costs of floating the securities may be relatively high. The risk is increased, also, if the political and economic position of the government may be subject to brusque changes. Circumstances such as these may justify charges which would otherwise be indefensible. In some minor Caribbean issues, for example, the difference between the price to the bankers and the price to the public has run as high as eleven or twelve dollars per hundred dollars of face value of the bond.

3. The price of the loans to the bankers is usually not announced, but is considered "confidential" between the borrower and lender. Whether this is a defensible practice has been questioned. As is indicated above, the lender, in agreeing to float a loan at a certain price, assumes financial risk for which he is entitled to compensation. On the other

hand, it is questionable whether those who float a loan stand toward the public in the position of a dealer in common merchandise, who by accepted practice is not under obligation to disclose the cost of his merchandise to him.

Those who offer the securities representing the loans accompany them with statements they believe to be accurate but do not guarantee. In their offering of the securities, they act, in fact at least, toward the public, also in a confidential rôle. When the bankers set forth to the possible buyer the credit of the borrowing country, it may well be questioned whether the price which the borrower has agreed upon with the bankers is not in itself an indicator of the borrower's credit which should be disclosed to the purchaser of the securities.

4. The character of many prospectuses announcing bond issues is still undoubtedly subject to criticism. Misstatements are infrequent but one familiar with local conditions in the countries to which the prospectuses refer is often struck with the fact that the whole picture is not presented. Half statements which may literally be true may deceive the unwary or uninformed investor more easily than misstatements. The declaration that those offering the bonds have investigated them and believe them to be true adds to the chance that the buyer of the bond may be misled by those from whom he looks for trustworthy advice.

5. Whether after a bond issue has been offered to the public it is permissible for those floating the loan to support it in the market is still, it appears, an open question. The practice is frequent in the American market. It is not looked upon as favorably in the United Kingdom. Flagrant abuses occurred from this practice in London in the third quarter of the nineteenth century.

Examples of the conditions surrounding certain Caribbean loans are given below.

An often cited illustration of the abuses which occurred

in loans to weak governments in an earlier day is the Hartmont loan negotiated with Santo Domingo in 1869. Hartmont was given authority to fix the nominal amount of the loan himself. It was to yield £420,000 and he was to retain £100,000 as compensation. Six per cent bonds were issued at 70 in London, totaling £757,700, but the public did not support them and they were sold at from 50 to 55 per cent "to Bischoffsheim and Goldsmith and others and later on by them to the public." It appears that the cash which was actually paid to Santo Domingo was £38,095, though Hartmont asserted that he tendered £211,110 "and that negotiations for annexation to the United States prevented acceptance." [39]

The following table gives an indication of the conditions under which certain recent loans to Caribbean countries have been floated. Information for most of the earlier loans is fragmentary and in not a few cases, due to the circumstances surrounding their issue, probably no longer obtainable. The nominal interest rates in many of the earlier loans stood in strong contrast to the actual proposed yield to maturity due to the fact that the issues were offered to the public at less than par. In many cases, the borrowing government did not actually pay the proposed interest to the maturity of the loans, nor repay the principal when due. Frequently investors had to accept "revisions" and "adjustments" of their claims so that the actual yield often fell far below that contemplated. On the other hand, of course, in the international bond market as in others, there were many cases when high returns were obtainable by taking advantage of market fluctuations. The later loans cited below offer fewer contrasts with those granted the stabler countries of the

---

[39] Charles P. Howland, *Survey of American Foreign Relations, 1929* (New Haven, 1929), p. 76; *Fifty-sixth Annual Report of the Council of the Corporation of Foreign Bondholders for the Year 1929* (London, n. d.), pp. 322-323; and J. H. Hollander, "The Readjustment of San Domingo's Finances," *Quarterly Journal of Economics,* Vol. 21, p. 405.

world. The prices to the bankers floating the loans are indicated in the few cases where they have been ascertainable.

CONDITIONS OF ISSUE OF CERTAIN CARIBBEAN LOANS

Issue	Amount	Interest per Cent	Price to the Public	Yield to Maturity	Price to Bankers
Colombia	$25,000,000				
External s. f. g. b.	($20,000,000				
(Sept., 1927)	in U. S.)	6	92.50	6.55	91.18 1
External s. f. g. b.	$35,000,000				
(March, 1928) ...	($26,083,000				
	in U. S.)	6	95.00	6.35	91.30 1
Costa Rica					
External 5 per cent					
Gold Loan, 1911 ..	£1,389,500	5	...	...	80.00 2
7 per cent Loan, 1926	$8,000,000	7	95.00	7.40	88.00 3
7½ per cent Gold Loan (Pacific Ry.), 1927	$1,800,000	7½	100.00	7.50	90.00 4
Cuba					
5 per cent Loan of 1904	$35,000,000	5	97.00	5.18	...
External Sinking Fund Loan of 1923	$50,000,000	5½	99.25	5.55	...
Dominican Republic Loan of 1912	$1,500,000	6	...	...	97.50 5
Guatemala					
8 per cent External Secured Gold Bond, 1928	$2,515,000	8	101.00	7.96	...
Haiti					
30-Year Dollar Loan, 1922	$16,000,000 ($40,000,000 authorized)	6	96.50	6.61	92.137 6
Nicaragua					
6 per cent Sterling Loan of 1909	£1,250,000	6	92.00– 93.50	6.48– 6.57	...
Panama					
5½ per cent Gold Loan of 1923	$4,500,000	5½	97.50	5.69	...
5 per cent Gold External Secured Sinking Fund Loan	$1,200,000	5	96.75	5.20	...
Salvador					
A.B.C. Bonds, 1922-3	$6,000,000 A Bonds	8	100	8.00	88.00 7

1 Thus reported in Esteban Jaramillo, *Tratado de ciencia de la hacienda publica*, Segunda edicion (Bogotá 1930), p. 520.
2 *Fifty-sixth Annual Report of the Council of the Corporation of Foreign Bondholders for the Year 1929*, p. 126.
3 *Gaceta*, December 25, 1926.
4 *Gaceta*, March 31, 1928.
5 *Survey of American Foreign Relations, 1929*, p. 105.
6 *A Review of the Finances of the Republic of Haiti, 1924–30* (n. p., 1930), and *Haiti, Annual Report of the Financial Adviser-General Receiver for the Fiscal Year, October, 1926–September, 1927*, p. 91.
7 Only the A Series is above listed. The three issues authorized reached a total of about $21,500,000. Price to bankers is given in *Diario*, July 21, 1922.

CHAPTER XIV

FOREIGN INVESTMENTS

INVESTMENTS outside the national boundaries before the nineteenth century were exceptional and relatively small in amount. Colonial policies discouraged crossing of the lines of national control and even in the more advanced countries of western Europe industry and finance had no broad international basis. As the century progressed colonial holdings came to depend increasingly for their development on capital from outside their own borders. The industrial states of the world offered more opportunities for the investment of foreign capital in their public securities and in the development of their natural resources. The new states relied upon the citizens of other nations to finance their issues of public securities and welcomed them to invest their capital in private enterprises within their borders. There thus came to exist financial interdependence among nations far more intimate than had before been known.

The reliance on foreigners for capital supplies has been most marked in the newer countries. All the states of America have drawn heavily upon the old world for financing both public and private enterprises. As they have developed local resources, the relative importance of foreign capital has tended to decrease even though its actual total may not have diminished or may even have continued to increase, but without the assistance of foreign funds in their earlier years the advance of such areas, for example, as the United States, Canada, and Argentina would undoubtedly have been retarded.

The country whose citizens have been leaders in lending

money abroad has been Great Britain. France and Germany also have developed large investments in foreign countries. The citizens of all these nations continue to have large holdings outside their homelands, but the leading place in making new capital advances is now held by lenders in the United States, a country which since 1914 has passed from the ranks of "debtor" nations to that of a creditor and now has investments abroad estimated as of January 1, 1930, to total possibly $15,366,000,000, not including short term loans and war debts due to the United States treasury. Of this amount well over one-third is invested in Latin America.[1]

Though it is common practice to speak of foreign investments as being held by named nations, what is regularly meant is that citizens of the nations mentioned have investments abroad of the amount indicated. Loans by one government to another such as were involved in the transfers rising out of the World War are exceptional and when foreign investments are spoken of such loans are not as a rule in mind.

Investments abroad by American citizens were, of course, made even before the United States became on balance a creditor nation. They were not large in amount and totaled, it is estimated, even as late as the beginning of this century only some $455,000,000, of which almost two-thirds was in Latin America, chiefly in Mexico and Cuba.[2] This capital was in far greater part in private or direct investments rather than in foreign government securities or in those of foreign corporations not branches of American companies. Such investments continued to grow in the Caribbean and in Latin America generally in the period before the World

---

[1] Ray Hall, *The Balance of International Payments of the United States in 1929,* U. S. Department of Commerce, Bureau of Foreign and Domestic Commerce, Trade Information Bulletin No. 698 (Washington, 1930), p. 31.

[2] Harry T. Collings, *Die Kapitalexpansion der Vereinigten Staaten in Lateinamerika* (Jena, 1927), p. 7.

War. In the former region American interests increased most markedly in the sugar and tropical fruit industries. The capital was largely raised by the investing companies out of their own resources or on their own credit rather than by offering securities to the general public.[3] This practice has continued after the war, extending to new lines, particularly the oil developments on the north coast of South America. But the financing carried through in the post-war period brought experience with a wider variety of securities, and increased American interest in shares in foreign subsidiaries and obligations of foreign governments.

In the Caribbean region, however, American capital has continued to be invested for the greater part in private ventures and bonds of private enterprises rather than in government securities. A complete list of the lines which have relied upon American financing would include almost all of the major economic developments.[4]

What the exact amount of foreign investments held by American citizens or those of any other country is at any period, it is always impossible to state. Issues floated on the American market are not necessarily all bought by Americans, or if bought by them may be subsequently sold. Americans may buy foreign issues. Americans may make direct investments in foreign countries without any obligation to report the amount of the capital involved or the losses or reinvestment of earnings that may subsequently occur. Any statement is therefore one which is only an estimate

[3] Wendell E. Thorne, "American Investments in Corporate Securities," *Commerce Reports*, Oct. 1, 1928, p. 3.

[4] The varied activities in which American capital entered in the Caribbean area in 1929 is set out in Max Winkler, *Prosperity and Foreign Investments*, Foreign Policy Association Information Service, Vol. VI, No. 1, May, 1930. See also his *The Ascendancy of the Dollar, A Summary of American Foreign Investments in 1927*, Foreign Policy Association Information Service, Vol. IV, Special Supplement No. 1, 1928; the annual reports on the international balance of payments, by Ray Hall, published by the U. S. Department of Commerce; and *Commerce Reports*, October 1, 1928, January 21, 1929, January 28, 1929.

and always contains a certain percentage of error. The table which follows shows the total estimated investments at various periods in the Caribbean region.

ESTIMATES OF AMERICAN INVESTMENTS IN THE CARIBBEAN [5]
(*In millions of dollars*)

Region	1912	1916	1920	December 31, 1928		
				Van Norman	Winkler	Various Sources
The Islands						
British West Indies	....	25.0 [1]	30.0	....	....	....
Cuba	220.0	400.0	525.0	1,324.0	1,525.9	1,300.0
Dominican Republic	7.5 [2]	..	..	55.0 [2]	23.9	90.0
Haiti	[2]	..	..	[2]	30.7	36.0
Central America and Panama						
Costa Rica	7.0	20.0	25.0	....	35.7	42.0
Guatemala	20.0	12.0	15.0	....	38.2	67.0
Honduras	3.0	10.0	18.0	....	12.9	60.0
Nicaragua	2.5	5.0	5.0	....	24.0	17.0
Panama	5.0	20.0	30.0	....	36.3	40.0
Salvador	2.5	..	..	....	15.3	31.0
Central America and Panama	..	..	..	225.0	....	....
Northern South America						
Colombia	2.0	..	30.0	212.0	260.5	305.0
Guiana	5.0	5.0	5.0	7.5	....	7.0
Venezuela	3.0	10.0	40.0	125.0	161.5	190.0
TOTAL	277.5	507.0	723.0	1,948.5	2,164.9	2,185.0

1 Jamaica only.
2 Haiti and Dominican Republic together: 7.5.

5 The estimates are chiefly compiled from the following sources:

Dunn, R. W.—*American Foreign Investments* (New York, 1926).

Fisk, H. E.—*Inter-ally Debts* (Bankers' Trust Co., New York, 1924).

Halsey, F. M.—*Investments in Latin America and the British West Indies*, U. S. Department of Commerce, Bureau of Foreign and Domestic Commerce, Special Agents Series, No. 169 (Washington, 1918).

Ingalls, W. R.—*Wealth and Income of the American People* (York, Pa., 1922).

Osborne, J. B.—"Protection of American Commerce and Capital Abroad," *North American Review*, Vol. 195, 1912.

As the American investments in this part of the world have increased, the relative importance of those held by citizens of other countries has declined. British citizens formerly held first place here as in other sections of Latin America, but in financial undertakings as in the international trade of the region they are in current years less prominent. An estimate as of the end of 1928 indicates that while American capital in the Caribbean then amounted to well over $2,000,000,000,[6] the British holdings had a value between four hundred fifty and five hundred million dollars and all other foreign investors accounted for probably little more than a third of that amount.

The American preponderance is most marked in the island republics, especially Cuba, the premier foreign investment area of the entire region. In the smaller foreign investments in the island of Haiti, however, the relative position of American holdings appears to be even stronger than in Cuba. In northern South America, European investments are of greater importance. British holdings in Venezuela reached a value of some $125,000,000 at the end of 1928, as compared to $190,000,000 for the United States. Other

---

Van Norman, L. E.—"Problems of American Investments Abroad," *Current History*, April, 1929.

Winkler, Max—Estimates of December 31, 1928 (letter).

Many of the estimates are qualified by such words as "around," "over," "upwards of," and "not more than." Some are based on detailed summaries but generally this is not the case.

No attempt is made to explain differences in the estimates cited.

[6] This figure would be markedly increased if the value of properties in Porto Rico and the Canal Zone were added. These represent American holdings in the Caribbean, but are not strictly foreign investments of sorts above discussed. There are no figures available on investments in Porto Rico by different nationalities. An estimate of "foreign and mainland holdings in Porto Rico" as of 1928 in Victor S. Clark, *Porto Rico and Its Problems* (Washington, 1930), p. 417, puts them at $176,294,000. Securities of corporations and investments in public securities, both chiefly American, are the main items. Real estate and mortgage holdings by Spaniards are also a factor. The general balance sheet of the Panama Canal on June 30, 1929, showed assets of $516,899,886. *Annual Report of the Governor of the Panama Canal, 1929* (Washington, 1929), p. 107.

foreign investments are estimated at $90,000,000. In Colombia, the heavy American investments in public securities in recent years make the total of American interests in the country now stand next after those in Cuba. They are almost four times as great as those of European countries.

FOREIGN INVESTMENTS IN THE CHIEF CARIBBEAN AREAS AS OF DECEMBER 31, 1928 [7]

(*In millions of dollars*)

Region	American Investments	British Investments	All Other Foreign Investments
The Islands			
Cuba	1,300	200	..
Dominican Republic	90	2	6
Haiti	36	..	2
Central America and Panama			
Costa Rica	42	25	10
Guatemala	67	15	15
Honduras	60	6	1
Nicaragua	17	6	1
Panama	40	4	..
Salvador	31	15	2
Northern South America			
Colombia	305	50	30
Guianas	7	20	10
Venezuela	190	125	90

In the Guianas, American investments are relatively small, totaling about $7,000,000 as compared to $30,000,-000 by Europeans. In the island colonial areas, also, American capital plays a relatively less important rôle, though large investments have been made by American interests in various enterprises in Jamaica and the Netherlands West Indies.

The sum of all foreign holdings in Central America is

[7] This table does not include investments in Porto Rico and the Canal Zone. The figures allow for drop in value of American sugar investments of $200,000,000 during recent years.

much less than is popularly supposed. It represents only about an eighth of the total foreign investment in the Caribbean. About a third of foreign investments in Central America as a whole are in European hands, but those in Honduras and Nicaragua are in much less proportion so held, while in Costa Rica foreign holdings, chiefly British, are 40 per cent of the total.

The greatest of Caribbean foreign investment areas, a favorite since the beginning of the century and the one in which American capital has played an increasingly important rôle, is Cuba. In 1896, the American holdings were estimated by Secretary of State Olney at $50,000,000.[8] An estimate of 1909 placed them at $141,000,000.[9] After the World War, they reached $525,000,000,[10] and the Cuban Chamber of Commerce estimated them as $1,505,000,000 in 1928.[11]

The total of American interests has not in recent years kept up the earlier rate of advance due to the general depression in Cuba and, allowing for a drop of $200,000,000 in the value of sugar properties in recent years, American investments were estimated to be about $1,300,000,000 at the end of 1928.

Properties involving the sugar industry are far the most important single item in the American investments in Cuba and in the region as a whole. In 1924, their value was estimated at $417,568,000 by the United States Tariff Commission.[12] Estimates of their current value, including holdings other than lands and equipment directly used in

---

8 *Foreign Relations of the United States* (Washington, 1896), p. lxxxv.
9 Dunn, *op. cit.*, p. 120.
10 Ingalls, *op. cit.*, p. 60.
11 Quoted by the New York *Times*, January 18, 1928.
12 Quoted in Leland Hamilton Jenks, *Our Cuban Colony* (New York, 1928), p. 285. The author presents a table giving the holdings by various interests in the period 1925-7. The total in all lines he estimates as $1,140,000,000 in 1928, a figure lower than that given by most other students of Cuban conditions.

sugar manufacture, run from $600,000,000 [13] to $800,-000,000.[14]

Other lines in which American capital holds a prominent and in most cases dominant position are banking, railways, public utilities, and mining. Practically all of the public debt is also held in the United States.

Since Porto Rico is an American island, all the economic developments in the island by Porto Rican and United States interests may be considered American, but no satisfactory estimates of their total value are available.[15] Foreign holdings are relatively unimportant. All the public securities floated outside the island, now amounting to about $35,000,000, have been issued in the United States. The sugar factories owned by other than local capital represent predominantly American holders and the tobacco industry depends on American capital.

American investments in the other West Indian units are all small compared to those in Cuba. In the Dominican Republic, they date back to 1892, when the San Domingo Improvement Company took over responsibilities formerly in the hands of Netherlands interests. These totaled public security values of about $10,000,000 face. They were the beginning of obligations which later played a prominent part in bringing about the financial arrangements of 1905 and 1907 establishing the American control of customs. A number of subsequent issues of public securities have marked the development of the financial relations of American interests to the government of the country.[16]

---

[13] *Ibid.*, p. 285.

[14] Winkler, *Investments of United States Capital in Latin America* (Boston, 1928), p. 183. This volume contains a detailed discussion of investments by American companies in Cuba and other Latin-American areas.

[15] Victor S. Clark, *Porto Rico and Its Problems* (Washington, 1930), p. 418, estimates the wealth of Porto Rico at "something like 650 million dollars."

[16] These are discussed in detail in the annual reports of the Customs Receivership and in Sumner Welles, *Naboth's Vineyard: The Dominican Republic, 1844-1924* (New York, 1928), *passim.*

Investments in private enterprises, now more important than those in public obligations, involve important banking activities, the greater part of the productive capacity of the local sugar industry, steamship lines, public utilities, and certain mining enterprises. In 1912, the American investments, all told, were estimated to total $4,000,000 but at the end of 1928 had greatly increased, standing at about $90,000,000.

Foreign investments in Haiti are much less important. They are in all but small part now held by American interests. American participation in the public debt, the external portion of which reached $15,828,894 on September 30, 1928, became an important factor only after the agreements establishing American control over the local finances. Private enterprises financed by American capital are most important in the public utilities of the more important towns, railways, and sugar developments. Before the World War all American interests totaled about $4,000,-000, as compared to $36,000,000 at the end of 1928.

Among the colonial areas those under British control are far the more important American investment fields. The earlier ventures were in the fruit trade, which continues to be the greatest local American interest, especially in Jamaica. Railways and mining activities have also attracted American capital. The total investment in Jamaica alone is estimated to reach $25,000,000.[17] In Trinidad, American interests are in control of the famous asphalt lake and a number of American companies are active in petroleum developments. An American aluminum company has extensive bauxite operations in British Guiana. A large number of enterprises of lesser importance are found in the smaller British possessions.

The French possessions have not proved attractive fields for American investors. In the Dutch West Indies, the

---

[17] Winkler, *op. cit.,* p. 222.

only important American properties are those connected with the refining of petroleum on the island of Aruba.

Contrary to popular impression the American investments in Central America are relatively small. In all the five republics, though they have increased rapidly in recent years, especially in the portion represented by public securities, they were at the end of 1928 still less than a sixth as great as those in Cuba, only about two-thirds as great as those in Colombia, and little more than those in Venezuela. These Central-American interests represent about one-tenth of the financial stake of American citizens in the Caribbean region.

Contrary to the usual belief, too, these investments are not in large share in the regions in which American political action has been most prominent. Guatemala and Honduras lead among the investment areas, but have figured practically not at all in international political difficulties, while Nicaragua, where international relations have been most disturbed, stands at the bottom of the list.

Before the World War American investments in Guatemala were estimated at $20,000,000, chiefly in railroads and public loans, the first American participation in which dates from 1908. Subsequently investments have increased in a number of lines including railroads, still the most important item, the fruit industry, now the second after coffee production in contributions to export trade, electrical companies, mining and petroleum enterprises. The total American holdings in Guatemala are now given as worth $67,-000,000. In Honduras, in which American properties have a value of some $60,000,000, the investments in the fruit industry on the north coast far outrank all other items. Minor holdings are chiefly in mines.

In Salvador American investments have grown markedly in the period following the World War. In 1913, they were reported as worth $3,000,000, as compared to $31,-

000,000 at the end of 1928.[18] In contrast to its neighbor, Honduras, Salvador has no export fruit trade, and American capital is primarily invested in a railroad system, which is connected with the American controlled railroads of Guatemala, and in the public debt. Before 1921, Salvadorean loans were floated in the British market; thereafter, New York has furnished all the major loans amounting, between 1923 and 1928, to over $21,000,000. Minor American investments are in mining companies and banking.

Though American commercial interests have long been active in Costa Rica, the financial position of citizens of the United States has been, until recently, relatively weaker than that of nationals of European countries. Public finance has involved chiefly British lenders, though since 1926 about half of the public debt is American. American investments of all sorts prior to 1914 totaled only $7,000,-000, of which the greater part represented one mining company which had entered the country in 1907. Activities in mining, fruit production, and a number of enterprises of lesser importance in scattered lines make up the total of $42,000,000 of American investment.

Least attractive to Americans have been, in Central America, the opportunities offered in Nicaragua. In spite of the fact that the collection of customs has been since 1912 subject to control set up with the coöperation of American interests, and in spite of the fact that these latter have frequently advanced money to the government, the greater part of the foreign obligations has been and continues to be British. Former American holdings of controlling interests in the National Bank and the Pacific Railroads of Nicaragua have been repurchased by the government. The $17,000,000 of American investments in the country include customs bonds, fruit producing enterprises, mines, lumber operations, sugar plantations, and

---

18 *Ibid.*, p. 270. Winkler estimates them as $43,000,000 in 1928.

public utilities, none of which occupies a dominant position in the total.[19]

After Cuba the investment areas of the Caribbean which have proved most attractive to Americans in late years have come to be the republics of the north coast of South America. This flow of capital has been a part of the movement to acquire greater holdings in all Latin-American states which has been so outstanding a feature of the period since 1914, but it has been accentuated by political and special economic factors.

Both Colombia and Venezuela have had since the beginning of the century relative freedom from civil disturbances, a fact which has encouraged investors in the belief that these republics have joined the ranks of the stabler Latin countries. Neither has yet developed a government founded on a wide popular suffrage freely exercised, and especially in Venezuela the maintenance of public order has been dependent upon a centering of governmental functions in the hands of a single man of advanced age, but the maintenance of peace has furnished opportunity for orderly economic development and thus encouraged the development of economic resources by both natives and foreigners. In each of these republics, foreign investments now run to about $400,000,000.

Colombia has a wide variety of climates and natural resources which make possible a diversified economic life, the development of which has been retarded largely by lack of modern facilities of communication. Until recently, no large amounts of foreign capital found investment within its borders. Those which did so entered chiefly as public loans which were floated almost entirely in Europe. Since 1920, practically all the new public loans have been floated in the

[19] W. W. Cumberland, *Nicaragua, An Economic and Financial Survey* (Washington, 1928), estimates the public debt and claims at $8,350,000 and private holdings by foreigners in agricultural, industrial, and commercial enterprises at $10,000,000.

United States. In the eight-year period following, $171,-
074,557 were invested by Americans in the public securities
of the republic. Of these obligations slightly more than one-
third each were taken by the Central Government and by
the departments. The rest represented agricultural mortgage bank bonds guaranteed by the government and loans
to municipalities.[20] These investments are far the greatest
American investments in public securities found in the
Caribbean. The moneys were borrowed in greater part to
refund previous obligations and to furnish funds for public
improvements, particularly railways and roads. The public
securities investments represent here a proportion of the
total American holdings larger than in any other of the
leading Caribbean areas.

Next after public securities the chief American properties in Colombia are in petroleum developments. The companies hold extensive concessions but actual production has
occurred only by interests controlled by the Standard Oil
Company of New Jersey which is said to have spent $25,-
000,000 in development.[21] Two American fruit companies
have properties approaching a value of $10,000,000.
Minor amounts of capital are represented by activities in
production of gold, platinum, emeralds, coffee, sugar, and
by public utilities.

All told, American investments which were estimated at
$2,000,000 in 1912 now reach a value of over $300,000,000.

The American investments in Venezuela are about two-
thirds as great as in Colombia, but among them public
securities are conspicuous by their absence; in fact, the
foreign obligations of the country are very low and are

[20] Summarized from a circular by the Finance Division of the Bureau
of Foreign and Domestic Commerce, Grosvenor M. Jones, Chief, U. S.
Department of Commerce, Washington.

[21] Winkler gives a list of the companies holding concessions and a
sketch of their financial organization, p. 118. See also Halsey, op. cit.,
p. 243, and Dunn, op. cit., p. 75.

being rapidly paid off. Foreign investments are therefore almost exclusively in private enterprises among which far the most important are the petroleum companies.

As in Colombia, the rise of American interest in Venezuela is spectacular and has occurred practically since the World War. Before the conflict the total was put at $3,000,000, by 1920 at $20,000,000, by 1924 at $75,000,000, of which one half was in oil developments. At the end of 1928, the valuation stood at $190,000,000. The petroleum properties are still far the most important factor. Of lesser value are American interests in mines and in public utilities. British investments, chiefly in petroleum, were valued in 1916 at $40,000,000 but were said to be worth $125,000,000 at the end of 1928. Other foreign holdings are estimated at $90,000,000.

The steady inflow of foreign capital into all the relatively undeveloped Caribbean areas has a significance as yet imperfectly appreciated. It has been intended both by the governments making loans and by investors in private enterprises that out of the new resources shall come a stimulation of local life and production. The degree to which each will occur cannot yet be measured. It seems fairly clear that the government loans have in a number of cases been spent in ways which will give only a delayed if not problematical return, at least until what has already been spent is supplemented by still greater sums.[22]

There are many examples elsewhere showing that the development of resources often lags after the creation of facilities for marketing. Of this fact the history of not a few of the American railroads furnishes striking examples. Public treasuries not infrequently find on this account that the expense of public improvements is not as easy to carry

---

[22] The railway expenditures in Colombia are perhaps the best example. They have not been made in a manner which has created a national system of communications, nor indeed a system serving effectively any of the major economic districts.

as the expected increase in taxable wealth led those who counseled the expenditures to believe. To probably a lesser degree the same may prove to be true of the investments in private enterprises which have been made in the Caribbean in recent years, though many among these have already proved their soundness. Others will meet disappointment because local conditions prove less favorable than has been anticipated, because the public policy of the local governments may be or become illiberal, or because of unforeseen conditions in world markets. All these risks, however, are ones which investors everywhere face.

The rapid rise of economic holdings in the hands of foreigners, like the rise of the import and export trade of the region, will emphasize their interest and that of their governments in the maintenance and the development of better standards of public service. The total holdings of foreign interests in the Caribbean now approach a value of $3,000,000,000, an amount greater than the value of all real property and improvements in Alabama and Mississippi in 1922.[23] This is wealth in the Caribbean but owned outside it, all but a small proportion of which has come into existence in the last quarter century. It cannot fail to make its owners and their governments solicitous about Caribbean conditions to a far greater degree than formerly.

The figures cited above are from estimates of the amounts of investments in foreign securities and direct investments. Until 1930, no serious attempt had been made to value the commercial and industrial properties held abroad and belonging to residents of the United States and its territories, apart from the total holdings. In coöperation with the interests holding such properties, a government survey was then undertaken to estimate in general the value of these

---

[23] These items were then worth for Alabama $1,419,872,000 and for Mississippi $1,138,959,000. *Statistical Abstract of the United States, 1929* (Washington, 1929), p. 294.

"direct investments" as distinguished from "portfolio investments" acquired "through purchase of foreign securities publicly offered and through the international securities movement." The information collected was based on confidential statements by the investors to government officials. The results for the Caribbean area are given below. It is to be noted that some of the figures vary from those arrived at in other estimates elsewhere cited.

AMERICAN DIRECT INVESTMENTS IN THE CARIBBEAN [24]

Cuba and the West Indies
Cuba	$ 918,957,000
Dominican Republic	69,322,000
Haiti	14,191,000
Jamaica	21,941,000
All other West Indies	29,340,000
TOTAL	1,053,751,000

Central America and Panama
Costa Rica	22,166,000
Guatemala	69,979,000
Honduras (including British Honduras)	71,485,000
Nicaragua	13,002,000
Panama	28,459,000
Salvador	29,466,000
TOTAL	234,557,000

Northern South America
Colombia	123,994,000
Guianas	5,688,000
Venezuela	232,538,000
TOTAL	362,220,000
GRAND TOTAL	$1,650,528,000

[24] Compiled from *American Direct Investments in Foreign Countries*, U. S. Department of Commerce, Bureau of Foreign and Domestic Commerce, Trade Information Bulletin No. 731 (Washington, 1930), pp. 18 *et seq.*

Investment developments are discussed above primarily from the standpont of the foreign lenders. From the point of view of the local populations and their governments the "foreign invasion" involves other elements of importance.

Liquid local capital in most of these areas is small in amount. The local investments, chiefly in agricultural industries, are usually ones which yield a low return on the value of the properties and do not represent "active" capital. Local enterprise in industrial undertakings is not marked. Even the efforts which have been made to encourage the development of small manufactures through high tariffs have often resulted in the establishment of plants financed by foreign rather than local capital. As a result, if resources are to be developed only by the cumulative earnings of the local population, advance will be discouragingly slow.

Under these circumstances it is natural that those in control of the governments should be anxious to hasten national progress by encouraging the entry of foreign capital and initiative. Though many individuals both within and outside this and other tropical areas feel that these influences tend to become agencies of objectionable exploitation, the governments of the Caribbean states and the local groups most actively interested in development of local resources are in all but very exceptional cases anxious to encourage the further entrance of foreigners into their countries.

There is little doubt that it will continue probably to a degree which will make developments which are extraordinary at the present day seem insignificant. It is probable that in the future as in the past the enthusiasm of the local governments may lead them, in the desire to promote development, to grant terms in some cases so generous as to be against the public interest. Tax programs also may not be effective in securing from "extractive industries" and others a fair contribution to the public treasuries. Mistakes of this sort are not confined to Caribbean countries and they can be guarded against there as elsewhere only by the development of better standards in the local government.

It is at this point that many critics of current developments believe that the danger of capitalistic development for the Caribbean and other weak nations with undeveloped resources becomes greatest. It is argued that the enthusiasm of the local governments for advance such as has occurred in the industrial nations and their inexperience may lead to their bartering away to the foreigner the control of the more easily exploitable national resources, especially when these can be worked by large-scale operations. Thus the absentee investor may ultimately become the only one to profit greatly from the resources exploited, while the local population is kept in the position of economic serfs and the weak local government becomes the servant of powerful foreign financial groups. For these reasons, it is concluded, these states should indulge sparingly in the luxury of foreign capital and look upon its entry always with anxiety, if not apprehension.

Abuses of the sorts mentioned are no doubt theoretically possible, and incidents in the history of the United States and other countries are not lacking which demonstrate that powerful economic groups can, under special circumstances, influence if not control the action of governments. Estimate of the degree to which such conditions actually exist is always difficult and is especially so in the Caribbean countries in which the relative inactivity of local capital makes that of foreign origin appear of unusual influence. The local population there tends to regard the foreign investor as one who "loans" his money but has no interest in the country as such. In addition, "creditors" are never popular and "foreign creditors" are apt to be even less so than others. As a result "nationalistic" criticism often becomes florid, acrid, and not infrequently divorced from facts and practical considerations.[25]

There can be no doubt that the great economic development of the last quarter century in the Caribbean is due in large degree to the entry of foreign capital and to the encouragement which it has been given by the governments. There can be no doubt either that the entry of foreign capital has greatly increased public income and made possible a higher standard of life for the better favored classes among the population. It has also greatly influenced the life of the common people, though they still live, as compared to those in the more advanced nations, on a very low standard of life. This is the circumstance which makes criticism of the foreigner who "is absorbing the country's wealth" and "taking his profits abroad" a popular theme for the local politician and the well-meaning foreign critic. Both are prone to overlook the fact that changes in national living conditions come slowly and are influenced not only by present-day opportunities but by long established custom. They are apt to forget the conditions existing before the foreign enterprises were established, and make their comparisons not on the circumstances of, say, thirty years ago, but on what has been achieved in more advanced countries—and there only as a result of slow advance through many generations.

How far foreign and local economic interests do succeed in controlling the action of the various local governments it is impossible to say. That they do seek to influence governmental decisions in matters touching them may be assumed. If they did not, they would stand in strong contrast to those in other parts of the world. That they exercise a continuing control over political action is certainly not the case, as is shown by the frequent adoption of measures of restrictive character in spite of their opposition. In many

[25] See, for examples, Jenks, *op. cit.*, pp. 278-280.

cases, it seems clear the foreign and the local business enterprises are in matters of this sort too often both sinned
against and sinning.

The degree to which "foreign interests" have actually
"absorbed" the natural resources of the Caribbean countries
is equally difficult to ascertain. There are no satisfactory
figures of national wealth, in fact it would be impossible to
compile ones which over a period of years would be acceptable in most of these areas because the "true value" of properties varies so greatly with the position of their chief products in world markets. In any case, however, it is certain
that foreigners own a much smaller proportion of local resources than critics usually assume.

In Cuba, where foreign investments have reached figures
far greater than anywhere else in the Caribbean, one Cuban
estimate indicates that some 15 per cent of the national
wealth represents American investments.[26]

A careful study of Nicaraguan finances indicates that
about 10 per cent of the national wealth in addition to the
public debt is there in the hands of foreigners.[27] On this
basis perhaps foreign investments would amount to 17 or 18
per cent of the total. This would make the holdings by
foreigners about proportionate to that in Cuba. About 20
per cent of the public wealth of Porto Rico is estimated to
be held by nonresidents of the island, chiefly Americans.[28]
Estimates for other units are not available but it seems clear
that in few if any cases would the percentage be as high as
in these cases.

This "dependence" on the foreigner which is general
throughout the Caribbean is real and is very properly a
matter of public concern, especially since these foreign capital holdings represent the most active portion of that within

[26] This estimate and others are given in Chapman, *A History of the
Cuban Republic* (New York, 1927), p. 620.

[27] Cumberland, *op. cit.*, p. 16.

[28] Clark, *op. cit.*, pp. 416 *et seq.*

these countries, but it is a relation neither without precedent nor necessarily alarming. Other countries have in course of their development faced similar conditions and have found in the coöperation with foreign capital a means of winning their economic independence.

Whether a similar outcome can be counted upon in the Caribbean republics depends primarily upon their people. If the local population responds to the new conditions which the borrowed capital itself helps to create as those of temperate regions have done, presumably the result will be similar. Economic independence, like political independence, will be theirs for the winning.

CHAPTER XV

TOWARD INDEPENDENCE

INDEPENDENCE, equality, self-sufficiency, these are ideals precious to all states, and the first two have long been recognized in international law as characteristics of all full sovereign nations. The facts of everyday life show that none of these concepts is absolute.

Time was when the organization of the life of the world was simpler, when exchanges, material and cultural, with foreign countries were exceptional and negligible. Then it could be argued to better effect that states were units unto themselves, sovereign internally and externally and economically self-sufficient. A nation might then develop its own civilization and its own natural resources with little if any coöperation from outside its borders and exercise little influence on what occurred elsewhere.

But those days are gone, and every nation, great or small, now finds itself in the development of all branches of its life adopting the experience of others, profiting from the culture of others, dependent upon others for foodstuffs, raw materials, and manufactured goods and in turn contributing to the progress of other nations with which its relations assume importance. The fundamental characteristic of the century in which we live has been the growth of interdependence, cultural, political, economic. The older concepts of equality and self-sufficiency continue basic, but in practice they are modified by the development of an interdependence which puts very real limitations about the freedom of action of all nations.

The influence which individual states can exercise under

the conditions which in our own day emphasize the internationalization of world activities still depends, however, on the same elements which gave them power in the days when association was less characteristic of the world's affairs.

The strength of any state is determined by the elements, human and material, which it has and can develop within its own borders. Climate, population, natural resources, contact with the outside world, the character and virility of the national culture, all help to determine its power and its relations with its neighbors. They are the measure of the degree to which a nation can maintain its independence, cultural, political, and economic, and influence the developments in states with the civilization of which it comes into contact.

Prominent among these factors are those directly or indirectly of economic character. Conditions promotive of internal peace and favorable to accumulation of national wealth, assuring its equitable distribution, raising the standards of education and living conditions, encouraging the development and diversification of industry, setting up economical means of communication, and fostering international exchange, these are items which, though not all economic, have economic bearings which make them contribute to make a nation strong internally and externally.

Perhaps no country in the world has developed such influences to the degree which its endowment makes possible. Certainly few parts of the world have in the past had greater lack of economic independence than the Caribbean region.

Since the period of discovery this area has been in high degree controlled by conditions and policies determined outside its own boundaries. During the colonial period legislation adopted in the mother countries influenced the character of its population, fostered certain industries and limited others and regulated the course of international trade.

Political independence was won by the greater part of the

region in the early part of the nineteenth century but it brought with it no corresponding economic independence. In part, this continues true, due to the fact that, though trade legislation in other countries no longer directly controls the development of industry, in many cases it does so in effect since the markets for typical Caribbean products are few and tariff policies adopted in foreign markets limit the possibility of their sale.

But in major part the failure to develop greater economic strength is a consequence of local circumstances, some permanent and some modifiable, but thus far only slightly modified by the endeavors of the local populations.

A review of the economic circumstances which have limited the advance of the Caribbean nations and of the changes which have in recent years occurred in them is essential to any appreciation of what they may expect of themselves and of what the world may expect of them.

No impartial student can fail to consider at times whether there is a "Caribbean region" distinguishable from others in more than a superficial way. It is a unit in the narrower geographical sense: it is that section of the new world lying roughly between the fifth and twenty-fifth degrees north of the equator and between the fifty-fifth and ninetieth degrees west of Greenwich. But it often seems that in almost no other way is it a unit. Included are divergent climates, diverse products, various races, within which exist classes of inhabitants strongly contrasted in the scale of social development, in economic strength, and in political experience. Old world and American governments, dictatorships and régimes professing popular institutions, crown colonies and territories with almost complete self-government, regions of varied and of limited resources, go to make up this complex of contrasts. French, Spanish, Dutch, English, and aboriginal tongues are spoken. These among other factors which make Caribbean problems diverse determine what the Caribbean is and will influence what it can become, but they seem to emphasize its diversity rather than its unity.

But, in spite of the interplay of this variety of influences, there are some common factors of fundamental character which allow conclusions as to the advance achieved, the progress which may reasonably be expected, and the public policies, national and international, which give promise of success. Such conclusions do not uniformly support hopes that the Caribbean region is soon to work its way out of the difficulties with which it has had to deal and still deals. They are not all of them such as justify the enthusiasm of those who, generally from a distance, consider the Caribbean region a paradise of retarded development. They do not on the other hand confirm the conviction of those who think it to have obtained, at least so far as the human factors are concerned, the greatest advance possible in tropical areas.

At the outset, in any forecast of future developments, a grouping of the smaller and the larger units is necessary, for the former, through their limited areas, meager resources, and populations already crowding the food supply, are politically and economically a problem by themselves. These colonial areas, except in the case of the Dutch islands off the Venezuelan coast, which profit by the development of the oil trade and to a lesser extent certain others which will have a limited importance because of their port facilities, are politically and economically highly dependent areas, often meeting the expenses of local government with difficulty, dependent on imports for all but the simple foodstuffs locally raised, and without natural resources which can be made the basis of diversified industry or unused lands which can be counted upon greatly to increase their present contribution to foreign trade. Foreign trade, in fact, in not a few cases, has shown a tendency to decline through competition in world markets by better favored Caribbean and other areas.

The politically independent areas stand in a more favorable position though they vary greatly in outlook among themselves on almost every point. The factors which control the degree to which they may expect to secure independence are overlapping in influence and not of the same importance in different areas. Among them are the following:

1. *Resources.* In few ways do Caribbean republics furnish greater contrasts than in their natural resources, though this is true to a much greater extent of the resources which may be made to contribute commercial products than of those which now enter world commerce in large amounts. Colombia, with its varied endowment, stands in this respect in sharpest contrast with less well favored areas such as Honduras, Panama, and the Dominican Republic.

In all of these units, present conditions are much less encouraging than they may become because of the emphasis which is regularly placed on one or a few products. These are staples and enjoy the advantages and suffer the limitations which attend the marketing of staples. Sugar, coffee, oil, and fruit will all have large markets at all times but at least the first three are products in which production beyond the capacity of the world to consume may occur and has occurred. All are lines in which investment is necessarily one running over long periods and therefore difficult to adjust to rapidly changing market conditions.

Better use of natural resources by production of a greater diversity of products is fundamental for economic stability in the Caribbean areas and the efforts of both foreign and domestic capital to that end are ones the importance of which for healthy national development it is difficult to overemphasize.

Broadening of the basis of national economic activities is not necessarily limited to production for export. The creation of locally produced supplies for domestic consumption may also greatly increase the degree of economic self-sufficiency and improve the national balance of payments. The current developments in this direction in Cuba are eloquent of what may be attempted by other areas to their lasting advantage. Heavy imports of foodstuffs such as corn, rice, wheat, meats, eggs, and vegetable and animal fats are, at least in the better endowed areas, hard to defend and in a large number of the simpler manufactures local production should grow as fiscal policies and conditions of public order come to encourage initiative and the building up of enterprises through the investment of domestic and foreign capital.

2. *Climate.* It is not clear how far climatic influences limit the advance of Caribbean nations. All of them lie within the tropics, a fact which from our present outlook does not promise a brilliant future for their populations if what they can be is to be judged from conditions of life which have come to exist locally or from what has proved possible in other parts of the world where circumstances have been substantially similar.

If, on a globe of the world, the thumb and finger be placed on the northern and southern boundaries of the Caribbean region and the sphere be then turned on its axis it will be seen that in none of the territory passing beneath the hand has a civilization of advanced character for the common people been attained. This is not a conclusive test, but the case is not materially modified if isothermal lines and rainfall areas be made the basis of review. Great nations have not risen in the warm, moist areas of the torrid zone. Here "the blessings of adversity" have been denied to the local populations. They have been handicapped by the abundant yields of the tropics and have contented themselves with a standard of life unacceptable to peoples of regions of more rigorous climates. The progress which science makes in the elimination of disease, and in otherwise making the tropic regions ones in which European stocks can establish themselves, may do much to change the civilization. The influence of increasing world commerce on local conditions may stimulate new wants in the local populations and increase the economic competition among them.

In a number of the republics, further, there are large areas in which temperature is modified by altitude and in which, therefore, a civilization based on European or native stocks may develop free from some of the handicaps that affect the low-lying coast regions.

3. *Population.* Taken as a whole the populations of Caribbean republics have not, at least up to the present, shown great economic aptitudes. Though, as has been indicated, this may be at least in part explained in the lowland areas by the character of the climate, the fact is that elsewhere also economic activity has not shown steady and encouraging advance. The most active elements of the populations have been those which are of European ancestry or which have shared European ancestry. Where aboriginal and African stocks have predominated economic activity has been to a greater degree that of a static civilization and characterized by a low standard of life.

Most of the independent Caribbean areas have populations far smaller than their resources can easily support. In some cases, this circumstance itself may have slowed down development because lack of competition has made so small the effort needed to secure what the local standard of life demands. Greater population pressure alone, however, will not necessarily give greater incentive to production. Dense settlement is found in Haiti and some of the smaller islands with a Negro population, in Guatemala in sections of practically pure Indian stocks, in Salvador with people of mixed Indian and Spanish ancestry, and in Porto Rico with a population among which the reported percentage of people of European ancestry is about the same as in the South Atlantic states of the United States.

The less thickly populated republics may well seek to encourage selected immigration and most of them would welcome it. Conditions of public order and the necessity of competing with the local labor supply at low wage rates have been discouraging influences. Up to the present, except in Cuba in favorable years, additions through immigration of European stocks have been negligible. If a stream of immigration should develop, especially one from the Latin countries of southern Europe which would by general culture, language, and religion be easily adaptable to the Spanish background of the local civilization, the economic outlook of the Caribbean republics might be greatly strengthened.

4. *Education.* Closely bound up with the standard of life which the populations feel spurred to attain is their general standard of education, not of a literary sort only but of a character to make them useful agents in industrial development and in the conduct of public affairs. Here the showing thus far made in Caribbean communities is beyond question not one of encouraging character. So long as educational conditions comparable to those of the present continue or so long as economic or other conditions continue to make better popular education impossible, marked improvement in industrial organization and in government is not to be expected.

When the great mass of the workers are unable to read the printed page and to help fit themselves through its aid for the tasks of modern industry and commerce, high differentiation of the national life is impossible and in government the best that can be hoped for is government by the small class of the élite. Backward and in some cases almost primitive social conditions among the common people are one of the greatest handicaps of the Caribbean states. Improvement has occurred over the past generation, but only in favored spots has it been sufficiently marked to create the presumption that the population is firmly on the way to the establishment of more satisfactory standards.

5. *Communications.* Improvements of means of travel from place to place continue to be one of the great needs of most Caribbean countries. Highways contribute to the maintenance of public order, help to open up natural resources otherwise inaccessible, and promote production by cutting down marketing costs. But the Caribbean republics among regions in close commercial contact with the outside world continue to be one of the least well supplied with roads and railroads. In area, they are equal to over 46 per cent of the continental United States, but their railway mileage is less than that of a state like Iowa or Kansas. Their highways of all kinds total about half those in service in either of these states. Even this comparison understates the case, for the railroads are often of varying gauges, not joined in national systems, and carry a low average freight per mile. The roads, except for short stretches near the chief cities, are seldom usable for vehicles the year around and are often little more than ones on which bullock carts may pass. Highway construction is now being fostered in practically all the republics but an adequate system of communications is still found in none of them.

6. *Commerce and Industry.* Much more encouraging, at least on the surface, has been the commercial and indus-trial advance since the opening of the twentieth century. In certain lines, it has been so remarkable as to create the presumption that the traditional social conditions must be in process of rapid transformation. Production of crops, even of those which enter local consumption, has in some areas greatly increased. The movement of economic goods has reached higher and higher levels. Foreign trade has advanced so rapidly in the last generation that the yields which were formerly the cause of intense rivalries on the part of the European consuming nations seem petty in com-

parison. Domestic capital has reached higher totals and large amounts of foreign money have sought investment in local industries.

There is no doubt that economic advance, especially in goods produced for export, has outrun that in any other line. It has helped to improve also the general social status of the population and to strengthen the local governments. The amounts and character of the merchandise of domestic and foreign production carried by merchants in even remote interior towns is conclusive evidence that the commercial flow has come to affect not only the lives of resident foreigners and the local well-to-do class but of those who formerly lived nearer to the margin of subsistence.

But the satisfaction to be taken on this account is limited. Though the great increase of commercial and industrial activity has beyond doubt been a beneficent influence, the most marked advance has been in lines the number of which is discouragingly small. It has been, as a rule, in too restricted areas and too largely the result of foreign initiative and capital to justify the hope that it is soon to broaden to affect the lives of the people at large as similar developments have done in more advanced areas. Much more remains to be done before the economic life of the region assumes that rounded character which can help to guarantee economic and political stability. The economic flowering of the Caribbean in a way which will greatly broaden the horizon of the average citizen is still to come.

Development of a wide diversity of products, especially of manufactures, which figure in international trade or even in the local life does not now seem to be in prospect for any of the republics. Substantial increase of major crops and the development of manufactures for greater supply of local wants may be. Dependence on relatively few products need not mean either instability or lack of healthy national development. The pioneers of the United States, the pioneers of every country, have lived under circumstances which have limited what initiative could accomplish and confined their economic effort to few activities. Such limitations have not made impossible the creation of stable communities nor reaching out after higher standards of life. They should not do so in the Caribbean.

7. *Public Order.* Maintenance of the peace is primarily a political function but it has also a close relation to economic advance. It is commonplace that political and economic influences interact as cause and effect. Public order creates opportunity for economic advance and economic advance makes easier the maintenance of public order. Lack of protection from disturbance of the peace has been until our own generation one of the serious handicaps of the independent areas. In some of these, indeed, public order continues to our own day to be but imperfectly assured.

Students of Latin-American politics frequently emphasize the fact that the "revolutions," which in many units have marked the shifts of political power from one group to another, are not marked by heavy casualties or great destruction of property. This is true, but it is easy to underestimate the influence which the conditions which lie back of the "revolutions" have upon economic life. The heavy expenditures for military purposes by administrations which realize that their control depends on force cuts down what might otherwise be spent in developmental services, the uncertainty of protection of property disheartens citizens who would launch new private enterprises supported by domestic and foreign capital and tends to encourage the investment of savings abroad. Foreign capital is turned away by any unusual political risk.

Disturbance of public order, however, now seems clearly becoming less a factor. The progress made varies greatly from country to country but in the large there can be no doubt that the advance accomplished in other lines has been accompanied and to a degree caused by better assurance of the peace.

Review of the handicaps overcome and to be overcome in the Caribbean shows them still to be many and of major character but when present-day conditions are compared with those of a generation ago there can be do doubt that substantial progress has been made. Compared with Europe and the United States the Caribbean is still a backward area but the Caribbean of to-day compared to that of 1900 shows changes which are highly encouraging.

It is no longer the socially backward, economically insignificant, politically disturbed section of the American tropics which our fathers knew. It has been drawn into the current of world affairs as never before. Its international trade has become active and of large volume, local industry, though still small, is increasing, the internal problems of its communities are receiving greater attention. Public services are being improved, irregularly, it is true, but there is no doubt that advance is made. Budgetary practice is still in a number of cases unsatisfactory, but it is beyond doubt far better than a generation ago. The debt service is better maintained than at any previous time. The Caribbean republics are no longer a group characterized by chronic default on their foreign obligations. The wider contact in all lines with the outside world is making the discharge of international duties of its members both greater in importance and easier of accomplishment.

Survey of the problems to be faced emphasizes also the degree to which they are domestic, not international, and economic rather than political. Resources, climate, population, education, communication, local commerce and industry, and public order—these are all things which international policies adopted by the local governments or by foreign states can affect but little or not at all. Some, indeed, are even beyond the reach of domestic policy. Action by the local government may, however, in most of them favor or discourage the coöperation of domestic and non-domestic interests in the national development and advance may be greatly hindered or helped by the standards adopted. Health measures, laws on immigration, educational enterprises, the opening up of undeveloped resources, land policies, tax policies affecting industry, encouragement of diversification of products, budgetary practice, programs for foreign borrowing, road building, and a great variety of similar factors contribute to determine what the local development will be. In all such activities, the problems to be solved are characteristically domestic. The greater problems of the Caribbean states, like the greater problems of others, are internal problems and must be solved by their own peoples.

The economic development which has occurred during the past generation does not seem at first sight to confirm this conclusion, for three of the great staples the increase in the production of which accounts for a large part of the increase in economic activity have been developed chiefly by foreign initiative, in the main for export to foreign countries and with relatively little dependence upon the local public authorities. Even in these cases, however, the creation of conditions favorable to production has depended upon the policies adopted by the local authorities. Further advance will also do so especially upon success in shaping conditions to encourage the rise of new lines of production, broaden the range of economic activity, quicken local initiative, and raise the national standard of life.

The advance made during the past generation in many lines is not, however, indication that social, political, and economic conditions have become comparable with those in the more advanced industrialized regions of the temperate zones nor that they will soon become so. That standard, indeed, Caribbean nations may never reach but what has been done is promise of what continuance of wise domestic policies may accomplish. It is also to be remembered that diversification of production, which is perhaps the greatest need of the republics, always comes slowly. It depends upon long sustained experiments to determine what lines are economically profitable, on the adoption of legislation favoring the new lines of activity, and on gradual modification of well established habits of the agricultural population.

Though advance in the new lines, particularly in new lines affecting export trade, may be less spectacular than has been that in the great staples in the past generation, its effect on the life of the local population may be of greater moment. It may do more than the development of production of sugar, coffee, fruit, and oil has done to stimulate within the people desire for the standards of civilization reached by more advanced nations. Such standards are now neither reached nor approached by the common people of any Caribbean community. Whether, under the handicaps which surround all human activities in the tropical regions and in areas of limited natural resources, they can be reached or even approximated is still not evident but it is also not disproven.

Whatever time may demonstrate in this field, it is beyond doubt that great social and political advance in the Caribbean states is possible, indeed it is already occurring, though not uniformly even in areas apparently comparable in physical and racial endowment. The advance is slow; it will continue to be so. The time when the Caribbean was with show of reason characterizable as a region of "disorder, disease, and distrust" is passing, and for the more advanced areas has passed, but the time when the average citizen will enjoy a standard of life comparable to that of his brethren in Europe or in the United States, if it is to come, is still beyond the vision of the present generation.

As national wealth grows, as natural resources reach

greater development, as public services improve and the standard of life rises, the Caribbean states should reach out toward that economic independence which is essential if their political independence is to bring them the blessings which it may. Even though the circumstances under which they live may keep them, in economic relations, less self-sufficient than are states with varied resources and emphasize the fact that their independence increases only as their interdependence with other members of a family of nations grows, their greater stability should make solution of their domestic problems easier at the same time that it emphasizes the fact that the greatest of their national problems are ones they themselves must solve.

To the degree that stability and orderly progress come to be characteristic of the Caribbean, indeed, not only its domestic affairs but its international problems, to which so much attention has been given, will become easier of solution. So long as public order is insecure, domestic disturbance may always bring foreign complications through violation of the rights and property of resident foreigners. But if order be well assured, the possibility of international difficulties narrows and the coöperation of foreign and domestic interests for the development of national resources, to the general advantage, is increased.

Thus the influence of the growth of a broader, sounder economic basis for the national life of the Caribbean states may reach beyond their purely domestic concerns to their relations with the outside world. Their political independence in international relations they may guarantee by winning greater economic and political independence and stability in their domestic concerns.

As these standards come into existence, indeed, not only will the attitude of the governments toward their international affairs be changed. The position of other nations, including that of the United States, more important for most of them than any other factor in their international relations, will be modified. The already great commercial interchanges will reach new heights. The investment of foreign capital for development of local resources will increase. The interest of foreign countries in further development of the Caribbean will grow as the interests of their citizens in the region increase and are given protection and encouragement. As local economic and political stability become better established, the occasions prompting to intervention by countries outside the region will be minimized and its practice will decline. Then it may be argued that the policy of European countries in defense of the rights of their nationals and the policy maintained by the United States have changed, though in reality the change will have been in domestic circumstances within the republics. Then, too, will be laid the foundation for an even broader coöperation, both political and economic, by the American nations, one based on the realization that the greatest strength for all lies in the increased coöperation and interdependence which fuller development of national resources and growing economic and cultural interchange will promote, to the advantage of all the American republics and of the world at large.

BIBLIOGRAPHY

The books and articles listed below include representative works dealing with the development of the Caribbean. Most of them have been published since 1910. They vary widely in character from popular discussions to authoritative studies and government manuals. Economic developments are given greater attention than political relations.

GENERAL

Books

ADAMS, F. U.—*The Conquest of the Tropics* (New York, 1914).

American Sugar Refining Company Annual Reports (New York).

AUSTIN, O. P.—*Trading with Our Neighbors in the Caribbean* (National City Bank, New York, 1920).

BLAKESLEE, G. H.—Ed., *Latin America,* Clark University Addresses, 1913 (New York, 1914).

——*Mexico and the Caribbean* (New York, 1920).

BONSAL, STEPHEN.—*The American Mediterranean* (New York, 1912).

BYNUM, M. L.—*International Trade in Coffee,* U. S. Department of Commerce, Bureau of Foreign and Domestic Commerce Trade Promotion Series, No. 37 (Washington, 1926).

CALDERON, F. GARCIA.—*Latin America: Its Rise and Progress* (New York, 1913).

CHANDLER, CHARLES L.—*Inter-American Acquaintances* (Sewanee, Tenn., 1917).

Commerce Yearbook, Vol. II, U. S. Department of Commerce, Bureau of Foreign and Domestic Commerce (Washington, annually).

COOLIDGE, ARCHIBALD C.—*The United States as a World Power* (New York, 1908).

COOPER, C. S.—*Latin America: Men and Markets* (Boston, 1927).

CORLETT, W. T.—*The American Tropics* (Cleveland, 1908).

CRAKAERT, JACQUES.—*La Méditerranée américaine* (Paris, 1927).

CRICHFIELD, G. W.—*American Supremacy* (New York, 1908).

CROWTHER, SAMUEL.—*The Romance and Rise of the American Tropics* (New York, 1929).

CUTTER, VICTOR M.—*Trade Relations with Latin America* (Boston, 1929).

DAWSON, T. C.—*The South American Republics* (New York, 1903-5).

DUNN, R. W.—*American Foreign Investments* (New York, 1926).

ENOCK, C. R.—*Republics of Central and South America* (New York, 1913).

——*The Tropics; Their Resources, People and Future* (New York, 1915).

FARR AND COMPANY.—*Manual of Sugar Companies* (1929).

FILSINGER, E. B.—*Commercial Travelers' Guide to Latin America*, U. S. Department of Commerce, Bureau of Foreign and Domestic Commerce, Miscellaneous Series, No. 89 (Washington, 1926).

——*Exporting to Latin America* (New York, 1919).

FRANCK, H. A.—*Roaming through the West Indies* (New York, 1920).

FROUDE, J. A.—*The English in the West Indies* (New York, 1888).

Great Britain.—Department of Overseas Trade, *Reports of the British Commercial, Diplomatic and Consular Service.*

HALSEY, FREDERICK M.—*Investments in Latin America and the British West Indies*, U. S. Department of Commerce, Bureau of Foreign and Domestic Commerce, Special Agents' Series, No. 169 (Washington, 1918).

HARING, C. H.—*The Buccaneers in the West Indies in the Seventeenth Century* (London, 1910).

——*South America Looks at the United States* (New York, 1928).

HARRIS, GARRARD.—*The West Indies as an Export Field*, U. S. Department of Commerce, Bureau of Foreign and Domestic Commerce, Special Agents' Series, No. 141 (Washington, 1917).

HART, A. B.—*The Monroe Doctrine: An Interpretation* (Boston, 1917).

HILL, HOWARD C.—*Roosevelt and the Caribbean* (Chicago, 1927).

HOSKINS, H. L.—*Guide to Latin-American History* (Boston, 1922).

HOWLAND, CHARLES P.—*Survey of American Foreign Relations* (New Haven, 1928, 1929; annually).

HUGHES, CHARLES EVANS.—*Our Relations to the Nations of the Western Hemisphere* (New York, 1928).

INMAN, S. G.—*Problems in Pan-Americanism* (New York, 1921).

JAMES, HERMAN G., and MARTIN, PERCY A.—*The Republics of Latin America* (New York, 1923).

JONES, C. F.—*Commerce of South America* (Boston, 1928).

JONES, CHESTER LLOYD.—*Caribbean Interests of the United States* (New York, 1916).

JONES, CHESTER LLOYD, NORTON, H. K., and MOON, P. T.—*The United States and the Caribbean* (Chicago, 1929).

KELLER, A. G.—*Colonization* (Boston, 1908).

KLEIN, JULIUS.—*Frontiers of Trade* (New York, 1929).

KOEBEL, W. H.—*South America: An Industrial and Commercial Field* (London, 1919).

LAHEE, A. W.—*Our Competitors and Markets* (New York, 1924).

LATANÉ, J. H.—*America as a World Power (1897-1907)* (New York, 1907).

———*Diplomatic Relations of the United States and Spanish America* (Baltimore, 1900).

———*A History of American Foreign Policy* (New York, 1927).

———*The United States and Latin America* (New York, 1920).

LONG, RODNEY.—*Railroads of Central America,* U. S. Department of Commerce, Bureau of Foreign and Domestic Commerce, Trade Promotion Series, No. 555 (Washington, 1928).

McQUEEN, C. A.—*Latin American Monetary and Exchange Conditions,* U. S. Department of Commerce, Bureau of Foreign and Domestic Commerce, Trade Information Bulletin No. 430 (Washington, 1926).

MARTIN, P. A.—*Latin America and the War* (Baltimore, 1925).

MASEFIELD, JOHN.—*On the Spanish Main* (New York, 1925).

MEEHAN, M. J.—*The Guianas,* U. S. Department of Commerce, Bureau of Foreign and Domestic Commerce, Trade Information Bulletin No. 516 (Washington, 1927).

MOON, P. T.—*Imperialism and World Politics* (New York, 1926).

NEARING, SCOTT, and FREEMAN, JOSEPH.—*Dollar Diplomacy* (New York, 1925).

O'MALLEY, FRANK.—*Our South American Trade and Its Financing* (New York, 1920).

Pan-American Commercial Conference, Proceedings (Washington, 1911 and 1919).

PAXSON, F. L.—*The Independence of the South American Republics* (Philadelphia, 1916).

PECK, A. S.—*Industrial and Commercial South America* (New York, 1927).

PITMAN, F. W.—*The Development of the British West Indies* (New Haven, 1917).

RAGATZ, LOWELL JOSEPH.—*The Fall of the Planter Class in the British Caribbean, 1763-1833* (New York, 1928).

RIPPY, JAMES F.—*Latin America in World Politics* (New York, 1928).

ROBERTSON, W. S.—*Hispanic-American Relations with the United States* (New York, 1923).

———*History of the Latin American Nations* (New York, 1925).

ROOT, ELIHU.—*Latin America and the United States* (Cambridge, 1917).

———*The Military and Colonial Policy of the United States* (Cambridge, 1916).

RUHL, ARTHUR J.—*The Central Americans* (New York, 1928).

SHANAHAN, E. W.—*South America* (New York, 1927).

SHEPHERD, W. R.—*Latin America* (New York, 1914).

SHERWELL, G. BUTLER.—*Budgets of Latin American Countries,* U. S. Department of Commerce, Bureau of Foreign and Domestic Commerce, Trade Information Bulletin No. 281 (Washington, 1924).

SMITH, J. R.—*Commerce and Industry* (New York, 1925).

South American Handbook (London, 1929).

STUART, GRAHAM H.—*Latin America and the United States* (2nd ed.. New York, 1928).

THOMAS, D. Y.—*One Hundred Years of the Monroe Doctrine* (New York, 1923).

THOMSON, J. E.—*Our Atlantic Possessions* (New York, 1928).

TURNER, JOHN M.—*Trade Development in Latin America,* U. S. Department of Commerce, Bureau of Foreign and Domestic Commerce, Special Agents Series No. 45 (Washington, 1911).

U. S. Department of Commerce, Bureau of Foreign and Domestic

Commerce.—*Foreign Commerce and Navigation of the United States* (Washington, annually).

———*Trade Directory of Central America and the West Indies,* Miscellaneous Series, No. 22 (Washington, 1915).

———*The Cane Sugar Industry,* Miscellaneous Series, No. 53 (Washington, 1917).

———*Caribbean Markets for American Goods,* Trade Information Bulletins Nos. 329, 342, 357, and 402 (Washington, 1925-6).

———*Foreign Trade of the United States, Fiscal Year 1928-29,* Trade Information Bulletin No. 650.

———*International Trade in Petroleum and Its Products,* Trade Promotion Series, No. 80 (Washington, 1929).

———*U. S. Trade with Latin America in 1928,* Trade Promotion Series, No. 88 (Washington, 1929).

———*Financial Developments in Latin American Countries in 1929,* Trade Information Bulletin No. 707 (Washington, 1930).

U. S. Tariff Commission.—*Sugar* (Washington, 1926).

USHER, R. G.—*Pan-Americanism* (New York, 1915).

VERRILL, A. H.—*Getting Together with Latin America* (New York, 1918).

———*South and Central American Trade Conditions of Today* (New York, 1919).

VIVIAN, T. J., and SMITH, R. P.—*Everything about Our New Possessions* (New York, 1899).

WARSHAW, Jacob.—*The New Latin America* (New York, 1922).

WEBSTER, Hutton.—*History of Latin America* (Boston, 1924).

WHELPLEY, J. D.—*The Trade of the World* (New York, 1913).

WHITBECK, R. H.—*Economic Geography of South America* (New York, 1926).

WILLIAMS, BENJAMIN H.—*Economic Foreign Policy of the United States* (New York, 1929).

WINKLER, Max.—*Investments of United States Capital in Latin America* (Boston, 1928).

PERIODICALS

Bulletin of the Pan American Union, Washington, monthly.

"Caribbean Problems," *World's Work,* Vol. 55 (Dec., 1927), pp. 126-127.

CROWTHER, Samuel.—"Are We Imperialists? and What Imperialism

Does in Central America," *World's Work,* Vol. 55 (Feb., 1928), pp. 433-441.

HARDING, G. L.—"Results of American Rule in the Caribbean," *Current History,* Vol. 21 (Mar. 1925), pp. 860-865.

HOARE, Samuel.—"Problems of Crown Colony Government in the Caribbean," *Nineteenth Century,* Vol. 89 (April, 1921), pp. 606-616.

HUGHES, C. E.—"Relations of the United States with Latin America," *American Journal of International Law,* Vol. 19 (April, 1925), pp. 367-369.

MELHAM, M. J.—"Growing Importance of the Caribbean Markets," *Commerce Reports,* Vol. 2 (June 20, 1927), pp. 700-701.

NORTON, H. K.—"Ethics of Imperialism," *World's Work,* Vol. 51 (Jan., 1926), pp. 321-328.

———"Self-determination in the West Indies," *World's Work,* Vol. 51 (Nov., 1925), pp. 77-84; 210-217; 321-327.

"Sugar Crops of the World," *International Sugar Journal,* Vol. 31 (June, 1929), p. 342.

U. S. Department of Commerce, Bureau of Foreign and Domestic Commerce, *Commerce Reports,* Washington, weekly.

CENTRAL AMERICA

BOOKS

CORLISS, James C.—*Latin American Budgets: Central America and Panama,* U. S. Department of Commerce, Bureau of Foreign and Domestic Commerce, Trade Information Bulletin No. 564 (Washington, 1928).

DOMVILLE-FIFE, C. W.—*Guatemala and the States of Central America* (London, 1913).

HARRIS, Garrard.—*Central America as an Export Field,* U. S. Department of Commerce, Bureau of Foreign and Domestic Commerce, Special Agents Series, No. 113 (Washington, 1916).

KOEBEL, W. H.—*Central America: Guatemala, Nicaragua, Costa Rica, Honduras, Panama and Salvador* (New York, 1917).

MUNRO, D. G.—*The Five Republics of Central America* (New York, 1918).

PALMER, Frederick.—*Central America and Its Problems* (New York, 1910).

PUTNAM, G. P.—*The Southland of North America* (New York, 1913).

THOMPSON, Wallace.—*Rainbow Countries of Central America* (New York, 1926).

VILLACORTA, C. J. Antonio.—*Curso de historia de la America central* (Guatemala, 1928).

PERIODICALS

BLACK, H. C.—"Central America Union," *Constitutional Review,* Vol. 5 (Oct. 1921), pp. 223-233.

HALE, W. B.—"With the Knox Mission to Central America," *World's Work,* Vol. 24 (June, 1912), pp. 179-193; (July, 1912), pp. 323-336.

BRITISH WEST INDIES
BOOKS

ASPINALL, A. E.—*The British West Indies* (London, 1912).

CUDNALL, Frank.—*Jamaica in 1928* (London, 1929).

GARDNER, W. J.—*A History of Jamaica* (New York, 1909).

Jamaica, Register-General.—*Census of Jamaica and Its Dependencies Taken on the 25th of April, 1921* (Kingston, Jamaica, 1922).

PITMAN, Frank W.—*The Development of the British West Indies* (New Haven, 1917).

SINCKLER, E. G.—*The Barbados Handbook* (London, 1914).

West Indian Sugar Commission, Report of the (London, 1930).

West Indies Conference Held in Barbados, January-February 1929, Report of the First (London, 1929).

WRIGHT, James M.—*History of the Bahama Islands with a Special Study of the Abolition of Slavery in the Colony* (Baltimore, 1905).

Yearbook of the Bahamas, the Bermudas, British Guiana, British Honduras and the British West Indies (Montreal, annually).

PERIODICALS

COOKE, E. C.—"Sugar Convention and the West Indies," *Economic Journal,* Vol. 17 (Sept., 1907), pp. 315-329.

"Position of the Sugar Industry in the British West Indies," *International Sugar Journal*, Vol. 24 (July, 1922), pp. 344-347.

SHEPHARD, C. Y.—"The Sugar Industry of the British West Indies," *Economic Geography*, Vol. 5 (April. 1929). pp. 149-175.

WATTS, Sir F.—"The Sugar Industry of Trinidad and the British West Indies," *The Planter and Sugar Manufacturer*, Vol. 77 (July 31, 1926), pp. 88-90.

WOOD, E. F. L.—"British West Indies," *Empire Review*, Vol. 36 (Sept.-Oct., 1922), pp. 298-306; 328-341.

COLOMBIA

BOOKS

BELL, P. L.—*Colombia, A Commercial and Industrial Handbook*, U. S. Department of Commerce, Bureau of Foreign and Domestic Commerce, Special Agents' Series, No. 206 (Washington, 1921).

BINGHAM, H.—*The Journal of an Expedition Across Venezuela and Colombia, 1906-7* (New Haven, 1909).

Blue Book of Colombia (New York, 1918).

CUNNINGHAME-GRAHAM, R. G. B.—*Cartagena and the Banks of the Sinu* (London, 1920).

———*The Conquest of New Granada: Being the Life of Gonzalo Jimenez de Quesada* (Boston, 1922).

DU BOIS, J. T.—*Colombia's Claims and Rights* (Washington, 1914).

EDER, P. J.—*Colombia* (London, 1913).

ESCOBAR, Francisco.—*Colombia and Her Commercial Opportunities* (New York, 1915).

FREEHOFF, J. C.—*America and the Canal Title* (New York, 1916).

LEVINE, V.—*Colombia* (New York, 1914).

LOMAZ, J. G.—*Republic of Colombia: Commercial Review and Handbook* (London, 1930).

McQUEEN, C. A.—*Colombian Public Finance*, U. S. Department of Commerce, Bureau of Foreign and Domestic Commerce, Trade Information Bulletin No. 417 (Washington, 1926).

MARTINEZ, Abraham.—*Colombia Yearbook* (New York, 1925-1926, 1927).

NILES, Blair.—*Colombia, Land of Miracles* (New York, 1924).

PEREZ-SARMIENTO, J. M., Ed.—*Colombia 1789-1917: obra de propaganda arreglada y editada* (Cadiz, 1917).

PETRIE, Francis L.—*The Republic of Colombia* (London, 1906).

SCRUGGS, W. L.—*The Colombian and Venezuelan Republics* (Boston, 1900).

TAYLOR, Hannis.—*Why the Pending Treaty with Colombia Should Be Ratified* (Washington, 1914).

THOMSON, Norman.—*Colombia and the United States* (London, 1914).

U. S. Department of Commerce, Bureau of Foreign and Domestic Commerce.—*Colombia: Commerce and Industries, 1922 and 1923,* Trade Information Bulletin No. 223 (Washington, 1924).

URIBE, A. J.—*Colombia los Estados Unidos de America, el canal interoceanico* (Bogotá, 1926).

VEATCH, A. C.—*Quito to Bogotá* (New York, 1917).

PERIODICALS

CHAMBERLAIN, L. T.—"A Chapter of National Dishonor," *North American Review,* Vol. 195 (Feb., 1912), pp. 145-174.

Colombia (monthly), published by the Colombia-American Chamber of Commerce, New York.

DAVIS, George W.—*American Journal of International Law,* Vol. 3 (Oct., 1909), pp. 885-908.

KEIFER, J. W.—"The Fortification of the Panama Canal," *Congressional Record,* Vol. 46, Pt. 2, pp. 1108-1126 (61st Congress, 3rd Session, Jan. 19, 1911).

KNAPP, H. S.—"The Real Status of the Panama Canal as Regards Neutralization," *American Journal of International Law,* Vol. 4 (April, 1910), pp. 314-358.

MAHAN, A. T.—"Was Panama 'A Chapter of National Dishonor'?" *North American Review,* Vol. 196 (Oct., 1912), pp. 549-568.

ROOSEVELT, Theodore.—"How the United States Acquired the Right to Dig the Panama Canal," *Outlook,* Vol. 99 (Oct. 7, 1911), pp. 314-318.

———"Monroe Doctrine and the Panama Canal," *Outlook,* Vol. 105 (Dec. 6, 1913), pp. 745-754.

SCOTT, J. B.—"Treaty Between Colombia and the United States,"

American Journal of International Law, Vol. 15 (July, 1921), pp. 430-439.

THAYER, W. R.—"John Hay and the Panama Republic," *Harper's Magazine,* Vol. 131 (July, 1915), pp. 165-175.

COSTA RICA

BOOKS

CALVO, J. B.—*The Republic of Costa Rica* (Washington, 1894).

FERNÁNDEZ GUARDIA, R.—*History of the Discovery and Conquest of Costa Rica* (New York, 1913).

PERIODICAL

JONES, Chester Lloyd.—"Bananas and Diplomacy," *North American Review,* Vol. 198 (Aug., 1913), pp. 188-194.

CUBA

BOOKS

AIMES, H. H. S.—*A History of Slavery in Cuba, 1511-1868* (New York, 1907).

ATKINS, E. F.—*Sixty Years in Cuba* (Boston, 1926).

BENTON, E. J.—*International Law and Diplomacy of the Spanish-American War* (Baltimore, 1908).

BIGELOW, John.—*American Policy* (New York, 1914).

BUELL, Raymond L.—*Sugar and the Tariff,* Foreign Policy Association Information Service (New York, 1929).

CALLAHAN, James Morton.—*Cuba and International Relations* (Baltimore, 1899).

CHADWICK, F. E.—*The Relations of the United States and Spain* (New York, 1909).

CHAPMAN, C. E.—*A History of the Cuban Republic* (New York, 1927).

DRAPER, Andrew S.—*The Rescue of Cuba* (New York, 1910).

EDWARDS, Paul L.—*Economic Conditions in Cuba,* U. S. Department of Commerce, Bureau of Foreign and Domestic Commerce, Trade Information Bulletin No. 159 (Washington, 1923).

EVERETT, Guerra.—*Trading Under the Laws of Cuba,* U. S. Department of Commerce, Bureau of Foreign and Domestic Commerce, Trade Information Bulletin No. 343 (Washington, 1927).

FORBES-LINDSAY, C. H. A.—*Cuba and Her People of Today* (Boston, 1911).

GONZALEZ, N. G.—*In Darkest Cuba* (Columbia, S. C., 1922).

JENKS, L. H.—*Our Cuban Colony* (New York, 1928).

JOHNSON, W. F.—*The History of Cuba,* 5 vols. (New York, 1920).

MUSGRAVE, G. C.—*Cuba, the Land of Opportunity* (London, 1919).

PORTER, Robert P.—*Industrial Cuba* (New York, 1899).

RENO, George.—*Cuba* (Havana, 1915).

ROBINSON, A. G.—*Cuba and the Intervention* (New York, 1905).

———*Cuba as a Buyer and Seller,* U. S. Department of Commerce, Bureau of Foreign and Domestic Commerce, Special Agents' Series, No. 61 (Washington, 1912).

———*Cuba, Old and New* (New York, 1915).

STUART, G. H.—*Cuba and Its International Relations* (New York, 1923).

TERRY, T. P.—*Guide to Cuba* (Boston, 1927).

U. S. Department of Commerce, Bureau of Foreign and Domestic Commerce.—*Cuba and Other West Indies: A Current Business Analysis,* Trade Information Bulletin No. 15 (Washington, 1922).

———*Cuban Sugar-Crop Financing,* Trade Information Bulletin No. 29 (Washington, 1922).

U. S. Tariff Commission.—*Differences in Costs of Production of Sugar in the United States and Cuba* (Washington, 1926).

———*Reciprocity and Commercial Treaties* (Washington, 1919).

VERRILL, A. H.—*Cuba, Past and Present* (New York, 1914).

WRIGHT, Irene A.—*Cuba* (New York, 1910).

———*Early History of Cuba, 1492-1586* (New York, 1916).

PERIODICALS

BENNETT, Hugh Hammond.—"Sugar Production in Cuba," *Review of Reviews,* Vol. 77 (Jan., 1928), pp. 49-50.

BROOKS, Sydney.—"Some Impressions of Cuba," *North American Review,* Vol. 99 (May, 1914), pp. 734-745.

CAPÓ, Rodriguez.—"The Platt Amendment," *American Journal of International Law,* Vol 17 (Oct., 1923), pp. 761-765.

CLINCH, B. J.—"Spain and Cuba," *American Catholic Quarterly Review,* Vol. 22 (Oct., 1897), pp. 309-319.

DE CORDOVA, Rudolph.—"The 'Virginius' Incident and Cuba," *Nineteenth Century,* Vol. 60 (Dec., 1906), pp. 976-985.

FERRARA, Orestes.—"Cuba Again Asks Justice," *North American Review,* Vol. 227 (June, 1929), pp. 656-660.

FORAKER, J. B.—"Our War with Spain: Its Justice and Necessity," *Forum,* Vol. 25 (June, 1903), pp. 385-395.

HARD, A. B.—"A Century of Cuban Diplomacy: 1795-1895," *Harper's Magazine,* Vol. 96 (June, 1898), pp. 127-134.

KENNEDY, W. M.—"The Revolution in Cuba," *Living Age,* Vol. 276 (Feb., 1923), pp. 463-468.

MOORE, John Basset.—"International Law in the War with Spain," *Review of Reviews,* Vol. 19 (May. 1899), pp. 563-568.

NORTON, H. K.—"Self-Determination in the West Indies," *World Today,* Vol. 47 (Jan., 1926), pp. 147-153.

"Origin and Purpose of the Platt Amendment," *American Journal of International Law,* Vol. 8 (July, 1914), pp. 585-591.

PLATT, Orville H.—"Our Relations to the People of Cuba and Porto Rico," *Annals of the American Academy of Political and Social Science,* Vol. 18 (July, 1901), pp. 145-159.

POOLEY, Howard T.—"Sugar Production in British Tropical America," *International Sugar Journal,* Vol. 29 (Aug., 1927), pp. 411-417.

RODRIGUEZ, J. I.—"Can There Ever Be a Cuban Republic?" *Forum,* Vol. 30 (Dec., 1900), pp. 436-441.

SCOTT, J. B.—"The Attitude of the United States toward Political Disturbances in Cuba," *American Journal of International Law,* Vol. 11 (April, 1917), pp. 419-423.

SPINDEN, H. J.—"Shall the United States Intervene in Cuba?" *World's Work,* Vol. 41 (March, 1921), pp. 465-483.

SYMES, Earl L.—"The Present Status of the Sugar Industry in Cuba," *International Sugar Journal,* Vol. 31 (Aug., 1929), pp. 416-420.

TARAFA, J. M.—"What Sugar Means to Cuba," *Review of Reviews,* Vol. 80 (Oct., 1929), pp. 77-80.

WILLIAMS, B. H.—"Isle of Pines Treaty," *Foreign Affairs,* Vol. 3 (July, 1925), pp. 689-691.

Wood, L.—"Military Government of Cuba," *Annals of the American Academy of Political and Social Science,* Vol. 21 (March, 1903), pp. 153-182.

DOMINICAN REPUBLIC

Books

Albrecht, C. H., and Henry, F. A.—*Development of the Dominican Republic,* U. S. Department of Commerce, Bureau of Foreign and Domestic Commerce, Special Consular Reports, No. 65 (Washington, 1914).

Dominican Customs Receivership.—*Annual Report* (Washington, 1908 to date).

Final Report of the Transactions of the Dominican Customs Receivership under the Modus Vivendi, April 1, 1905, to July 31, 1907 (Santo Domingo, 1907).

Inman, S. G.—*Through Santo Domingo and Haiti* (New York, 1919).

Knight, M. M.—*The Americans in Santo Domingo* (New York, 1928).

Malloy, W. M.—*Treaties, Conventions, International Acts, Protocols and Agreements between the United States of America and Other Powers, 1776-1909* (Washington, 1910), Vol. I.

Pan-American Union.—*The Dominican Republic* (Washington, 1924).

Schoenrich, Otto.—*Santo Domingo* (New York, 1918).

Stoddard, T. L.—*The French Revolution in San Domingo* (Boston, 1914).

Verrill, A. H.—*Porto Rico Past and Present and San Domingo of Today* (New York, 1914).

Welles, Sumner.—*Naboth's Vineyard: The Dominican Republic 1844-1924* (New York, 1928).

Periodicals

Hollander, Jacob.—"The Convention of 1907 between the United States and the Dominican Republic," *American Journal of International Law,* Vol. 1 (April, 1907), pp. 287-296.

Kelsey, C.—"The American Intervention in Haiti and the Dominican Republic," *Annals of the American Academy of Political and Social Science,* Vol. 100 (March, 1922), pp. 189-202.

Moore, J. B.—"Santo Domingo and the United States," *Review of Reviews,* Vol. 31 (March, 1905), pp. 293-298.

Rosa, Antonio de la.—"Les finances de Saint-Domingue et le controle Americain," *Rev. Gen de Droit, Int. Pub.,* Vol. 21 (1914), pp. 425-468.

DUTCH WEST INDIES

MacGowan, H. P.—*Markets of the Dutch West Indies,* U. S. Department of Commerce, Bureau of Foreign and Domestic Commerce, Trade Information Bulletin No. 405 (Washington, 1926).

GUATEMALA

Book

Winter, N. O.—*Guatemala and Her People of Today* (Boston, 1909).

Periodical

McFee, William.—"Gautemala," *American Mercury,* Vol. 9 (Sept., 1926), pp. 26-31.

HAITI

Books

Annual Reports of the American High Commissioner at Port au Prince, Haiti (Washington).

Balch, E. G.—*Occupied Haiti* (New York, 1927).

Bird, M. B.—*The Black Man; or Haytian Independence* (New York, 1869).

Buell, Raymond L.—*The American Occupation of Haiti,* Foreign Policy Association Information Service, Vol. 5, Nos. 19-20 (New York, 1929).

Dashiell, H. H., and Honaker, S. H.—*Trade Financing and Exchange in Porto Rico and Haiti,* U. S. Department of Commerce, Bureau of Foreign and Domestic Commerce, Trade Information Bulletin No. 595 (Washington, 1929).

Davis, H. P.—*Black Democracy* (New York, 1929).

Foreign Policy Association.—*The American Occupation of Haiti,* Vol. 5, Nos. 19-20 (New York, 1929).

FRANKLIN, James.—*The Present State of Haiti* (London, 1828).

Haiti: *Annual Report of the Financial Adviser-General Receiver for the Fiscal Year, October, 1928-September, 1929* (New York, 1930).

Haiti: *Blue Book* (Haiti, 1920).

HAZARD, Sam.—*Santo Domingo, Past and Present with a Glance at Hayti* (New York, 1873).

INMAN, S. G.—*Through Santo Domingo and Haiti* (New York, 1919).

KELSEY, Carl.—*Address on the Republic of Haiti Today* (Washington, 1922).

KUSER, John D.—*Haiti: Its Dawn of Progress after Years in a Night of Revolution* (Boston, 1921).

LEGER, J. N.—*Haiti, Her History and Her Detractors* (New York, 1907).

NILES, Blair.—*Black Haiti* (New York, 1926).

PRICHARD, Hesketh.—*Where Black Rules White* (New York, 1900).

Report of the President's Commission for the Study and Review of Conditions in the Republic of Haiti, U. S. Department of State, Latin American Series, No. 2 (Washington, 1930).

ST. JOHN, Sir Spenser.—Hayti or the Black Republic (New York, 1889).

SEABROOK, W. B.—*The Magic Island* (New York, 1929).

STEWARD, T. G.—*The Haitian Revolution, 1791-1804* (New York, 1914).

STODDARD, T. L.—*The French Revolution in Santo Domingo* (Boston, 1914).

TREUDLEY, Mary.—*The United States and Santo Domingo, 1789-1886* (Ph.D. Thesis, Clark University, Worcester, Mass., 1916).

U. S. Department of Commerce, Bureau of Foreign and Domestic Commerce.—*Haiti: An Economic Survey,* Trade Information Bulletin No. 264 (Washington, 1924).

VANDERCOOK, John W.—*Black Majesty* (New York, 1928).

VERRILL, A. H.—*Porto Rico Past and Present and San Domingo of Today* (New York, 1914).

PERIODICALS

ASHTON, H. D.—"Haiti Today," *Scribner's Magazine,* Vol. 67 (March, 1920), pp. 327-337.

BROWN, P. M.—"American Intervention in Haiti," *American Journal of International Law,* Vol. XVI (Oct., 1922), pp. 607-610.

DOUGLASS, Frederick.—"Haiti and the United States," *North American Review,* Vol. 153 (Sept., 1891), pp. 337-345; (Oct., 1891), pp. 450-459.

KELSEY, C.—"The American Intervention in Haiti and the Dominican Republic," *Annals of the American Academy of Political and Social Science,* Vol. 100 (March, 1922), pp. 189-202.

MACCORKLE, W. A.—"The Monroe Doctrine and Its Application to Haiti," *Annals of the American Academy of Political and Social Science,* Vol. 54 (July, 1914), pp. 28-56.

SORENSON, E. E.—"Dawn of Haiti's New Era," *Current History,* Vol. 23 (Dec., 1925), pp. 371-377.

HONDURAS

BOOKS

La République de Honduras; notice historique, géographique et statistique (Anvers, 1898).

LAZO, Hector.—*Honduras,* U. S. Department of Commerce, Bureau of Foreign and Domestic Commerce, Trade Information Bulletin No. 193 (Washington, 1924).

SQUIER, E. G.—*Honduras* (London, 1870).

PERIODICALS

MACCLINTOCK, Sam.—"Refunding the Foreign Debt of Honduras," *Journal of Political Economy,* Vol. 19 (March, 1911), pp. 216-228.

PERRY, E.—"Honduras Link of the Pan-American Railroad," *Engineering Magazine,* Vol. 46, pp. 333-340.

"Proposed Loan Conventions between the United States and Honduras and the United States and Nicaragua," *American Journal of International Law,* Vol. 5 (Oct., 1911), pp. 1044-1051.

NICARAGUA

Books

Brief History of the Relations between the United States and Nicaragua, 1909-1928 (Washington, 1928).

Cox, I. J.—*Nicaragua and the United States, 1909-1927* (Boston, 1927).

Cumberland, W. W.—*Nicaragua, an Economic and Financial Survey,* Department of State (Washington, 1928).

Nicaragua: *Report of the Collector General of Customs* (Managua, annually).

Playter, H., and McConnico, A. J.—*Nicaragua: A Commercial and Economic Survey,* U. S. Department of Commerce, Bureau of Foreign and Domestic Commerce, Trade Promotion Series, No. 54 (Washington, 1927).

Stimson, H. L.—*American Policy in Nicaragua* (New York, 1927).

Periodicals

"Costa Rica *vs.* Nicaragua," *American Journal of International Law,* Vol. 11 (Jan., 1917), pp. 181-229.

Dodds, H. W.—"American Supervision of the Nicaragua Elections," *Foreign Affairs,* Vol. 7 (April, 1929), pp. 488-496.

Hackett, C. W.—"Review of Our Policy in Nicaragua," *Current History,* Vol. 29 (Nov., 1928), pp. 285-288.

Moncada, J. M.—"Nicaragua and American Intervention," *Outlook,* Vol. 147 (Dec. 14, 1927), pp. 460-462.

PANAMA

Books

Abbot, W. J.—*Panama and the Canal* (New York, 1913).

Bakenlius, R. E., Knapp, H. S., and Johnson, E. R.—*The Panama Canal* (New York, 1915).

Bishop, Farnham.—*Panama, Past and Present* (New York, 1916).

Bunau-Varilla, P.—*Panama: Creation, Destruction, and Resurrection* (New York, 1914).

Edwards, Albert, pseud. (Ballard, Arthur).—*Panama, the Canal, the Country and the People* (New York, 1914).

FREEHOF, J. C.—*America and the Canal Title* (New York, 1916).

JOHNSON, E. R.—*The Panama Canal and Commerce* (New York, 1916).

JOHNSON, W. F.—*Four Centuries of the Panama Canal* (New York, 1909).

MILLER, Hugh G.—*The Isthmian Highway* (New York, 1929).

ROOT, Elihu.—*Panama Canal Tolls* (World Peace Foundation Boston, 1913).

SMITH, D. H.—*The Panama Canal* (Baltimore, 1927).

WHITE, T. R., and TOWER, Charlemagne.—*Our Duty Concerning the Panama Canal Tolls* (World Peace Foundation, Boston, 1913).

PERIODICALS

COLQUHOM, A. R.—"The Panama Canal Tolls," *North American Review,* Vol. 196 (Oct., 1912), pp. 513-522.

LATANÉ, J. H.—"The Panama Canal and the British Protest," *American Journal of International Law,* Vol. 7 (Jan., 1913), pp. 17-26.

PORTO RICO
BOOKS

Annual Report of the Governor of Porto Rico (Washington, 1900 to date).

CAPÓ, Claudio.—*The Island of Porto Rico* (San Juan, 1925).

CLARK, Victor S.—*Porto Rico and Its Problems* (Washington, 1930).

DASHIELL, H. H., and HONAKER, S. H.—*Trade Financing and Exchange in Porto Rico and Haiti,* U. S. Department of Commerce, Bureau of Foreign and Domestic Commerce, Trade Information Bulletin No. 595 (Washington, 1929).

DINWIDDIE, William.—*Puerto Rico: Its Conditions and Possibilities* (New York, 1899).

FLEAGLE, Fred K.—*Social Problems in Porto Rico* (New York, 1917).

MIXER, Knowlton.—*Porto Rico History and Conditions* (New York, 1926).

OBER, F. A.—*Porto Rico and Its Resources* (New York, 1898).

Rowe, L. S.—*The United States and Porto Rico* (New York, 1904).

Von Middledyck, R. A.—*The History of Puerto Rico from the Spanish Discovery to the American Occupation* (New York, 1903).

Verrill, A. H.—*Porto Rico Past and Present and San Domingo of Today* (New York, 1914).

PERIODICALS

Lopez-Dominguez, F. A.—"Original Development of the Sugar Industry in Porto Rico," *Planter and Sugar Manufacturer,* Vol. 79 (July 23, 1927), pp. 61-63; (July 30), pp. 83-85; (Aug. 6), pp. 103-105; (Aug. 13), pp. 123-124.

Soles, S. R.—"Sugar Production in Porto Rico," *International Sugar Journal,* Vol. 28 (March, 1926), p. 145.

SALVADOR

Book

Martin, P. F.—*Salvador of the Twentieth Century* (London, 1911).

VENEZUELA

Books

Bates, John, Jr., and Lindon, W.—*The Path of the Conquistadores* (London, 1912).

Beebe, William.—*The Edge of the Jungle* (New York, 1925).

———*Jungle Days* (New York, 1925).

———*Jungle Peace* (New York, 1918).

Bell, P. L.—*Venezuela, A Commercial and Industrial Handbook,* U. S. Department of Commerce, Bureau of Foreign and Domestic Commerce, Special Agents' Series, No. 212 (Washington, 1922).

Bingham, H.—*The Journal of an Expedition across Venezuela and Colombia, 1906-7* (New Haven, 1909).

Bowen, H. W.—*Recollections Diplomatic and Undiplomatic* (New York, 1926).

Cleveland, G.—*Presidential Problems* (New York, 1904).

Dalton, L. V.—*Venezuela* (London, 1912).

DEWEY, D. R.—*National Problems (1885-1897)* (New York, 1907).

DRAGO, L. M.—*La Republica Argentina y el case de Venezuela* (Buenos Aires, 1903).

EDGINGTON, T. B.—*The Monroe Doctrine* (Boston, 1904).

FRIED, A. H.—*Die Zweite Haager Konferenz, ihre Arbeiten, ihre Ergebnisse u. ihre Bedeutung* (Leipzig, 1908).

HALE, Albert.—*South Americans* (Indianapolis, 1907).

HENDERSON, J. B.—*American Diplomatic Questions* (New York, 1901).

HULL, W. I.—*The Two Hague Conferences* (Boston, 1908).

MALLARMÉ, A.—*L'Arbitrage Vénézuélien devant la Cour d'appel de La Haye (1903-1904)* (Paris, 1906).

MARTENS, F.—*Par la justice vers la paix* (Paris, 1906); annexe: Doctrine de Drago.

MOULIN, Henri A.—*La doctrine de Drago* (Paris, 1908).

MOZANS, H. J. (pseud., Zahn, J. A.).—*Up the Orinoco and Down the Magdalena* (New York, 1910).

QUESADA, Gonzalo de.—*Arbitration in Latin America* (Rotterdam, 1907).

RALSTON, J. H., and DOYLE, W. T. S.—*Venezuelan Arbitrations of 1903* (Washington, 1904).

SCOTT, J. B., Ed.—*The Texts of the Peace Conferences at The Hague, 1889 and 1907* (Boston, 1908).

SCRUGGS, W. L.—*The Colombian and Venezuelan Republics* (Boston, 1900).

SPENCE, J. M.—*The Land of Bolívar* (London, 1878).

PERIODICALS AND DOCUMENTS

CLEVELAND, Grover.—"The Venezuelan Boundary Controversy," *Century Magazine,* Vol. 62 (June, 1901), pp. 283-297; (July, 1901), pp. 405-419.

DRAGO, L. M.—"State Loans in Their Relation to International Policy," *American Journal of International Law,* Vol. 1 (July, 1907), pp. 692-726.

LATANÉ, J. H.—"The Forcible Collection of International Debts," *Atlantic Monthly,* Vol. 98 (Oct., 1906), pp. 542-550.

MOULIN, H. A.—"La Doctrine de Drago," *Rev. Gen. de Droit Int. Pub.,* May, August, 1907.

"The Venezuelan Cases," *American Journal of International Law,* Vol. 3 (Oct., 1909), pp. 985-990.

VIRGIN ISLANDS

BOOKS

BOOY, T. H. N. DE, and FARIS, J. T.—*Virgin Islands* (Philadelphia, 1918).

BROCK, H. G., SMITH, P. S., and TUCKER, W. A.—*The Danish West Indies, Their Resources and Commercial Importance,* U. S. Department of Commerce, Bureau of Foreign and Domestic Commerce, Special Agents' Series, No. 129 (Washington, 1917).

TUCKER, R. S.—*Economic Conditions in the Virgin Islands,* 69th Congress, 1st Session, Senate Documents Nos. 41 and 110 (Washington, 1926).

U. S. Census Bureau.—*Census of the Virgin Islands of the United States, 1918.*

Virgin Islands, Governor of the.—*The Virgin Islands of the United States* (Washington, 1928).

WESTERGAARD, W. C.—*Danish West Indies under Company Rule, 1671-1754* (New York, 1917).

ZABRISKIE, L. K.—*The Virgin Islands of the United States* (New York, 1918).

INDEX

Aboriginal stocks, 14, 15, 29 *et seq.*
Africanization, 34 *et seq.*
American foreign investments, 291
  Caribbean relations and, 305-7
  Caribbean, 293
    recent rapid rise of, 302-3
  Central American, 299
  Northern South American, 301
  Porto Rican, 297
  West Indian, 297-8
Ashford, Bailey K., 48
Asiento, 5

Bahamas, 4
Baker, L. D., 132
Balance of payments, Cuban sugar
  industry and, 162; extractive industry and, 157-73
Banana, commercial harvesting, 130-
  31
  culture, 129-30, 133
  exports, Caribbean, 140-2
  industry, spread of, 138-9
  introduction to America, 128
  marketing, 133-4
  markets, development of, 135-6
  production, development of, 135-8
    large companies and small oper-
    ators, 134
    large-scale operations, 134-5
  trade, development, 132 *et seq.*
    districts, 130
    European, 131
    organization, 132-3
    recent development, 131
  varieties, 129
Bananas, British trade, 141
  Canary Islands, 140
  development of European mar-
    kets, 139-40
  trade in, influence of, 141
  world trade in, 139
Barbados, settlement, 2
Barrios, Rufino, 71
Beet sugar, 18
Birth rates, 25
Bondholders protective associations,
  250
Brazil, coffee, 111
  sugar operations, 78

British West Indies, sugar, 93-4
Brussels convention, 91

Capital, American, Latin America
  and, 291-2
  foreign, 9, 157 *et seq.*
  See also Foreign investments.
Caribbean, advance, 13, 322-4
  irregular, 314
  limited, 312
  American investments in, 293, 305
  backwardness of, 201-2
  banana exports, 141-2
  climate, 316
  colonization, early, 2
  commerce, 319
  communications, 319
  conditions in 1900, 205-7
  dependence of, 312
  economic bonds with the United
    States, 210
  economic development, 308, 312
    since 1900, 210
  economic strength of, 312
  education, 318
  European colonization in, 2
  exports, 214
  foreign loans, United States and,
    285
  foreign trade, United States domi-
    nance, 227
  handicaps, 322
  imports, 212
  industry, 319
  population, 317
  resources, 314
  revival since 1900, 210
  stability, 325
  trade and United States tariff,
    230-1
  trade, character of, 226-7
    decline and slavery, 206
    increase, 214-6, 219, 228-9
    with the United States, 224-5
Caribs, 14, 15
Carter, Henry R., 45
Castro régime in Venezuela, 207
Central America, American investments and, 299
  coffee, 119

349

(1)